The Changing English Language

BRIAN FOSTER

The Changing English Language

'Slow as the rhythm of linguistic development appears to contemporary observers, hardly noticeable except to those who deliberately give their attention to it, actually it is very rapid. Since the use of writing began, a few thousand years ago, many languages have disappeared, many new ones have arisen. . . .'

JOSHUA WHATMOUGH, *Language* (1956)

M

First edition 1968
Reprinted 1969, 1970, 1972, 1974
Reprinted in Papermacs 1981

Published by
THE MACMILLAN PRESS LTD
London and Basingstoke
Companies and representatives throughout the world

ISBN 0 333 08059 9 (*hardcover*)
ISBN 0 333 31189 2 (*Papermac*)

Printed in Hong Kong

TO

PAUL, ROSALINDA

AND MICHAEL

Contents

Introduction

'... let us remember that a language is never in a state of fixation, but is always changing; we are not looking at a lantern-slide but at a moving picture.'

A. LLOYD-JAMES, *The Broadcast Word* (1935)

IN the year 1914 a young girl named Monica Baldwin entered a convent, remaining secluded there until 1941 when she was released from her vows and returned to the outer world. In the intervening twenty-eight years wars and revolutions had come and gone in Europe, her uncle, Stanley Baldwin, had guided the destinies of his country for some time, technical developments had altered the conditions of everyday life almost beyond recognition, but all these events had left virtually untouched the small religious community to which she had belonged. In 1949 Miss Baldwin published her impressions of those first bewildering years of her return to a world in which the motor-car had ousted the horse and carriage, and where respectable women showed their legs and painted their faces. Yet it was not only these odd sights that astounded her, for she was even more puzzled by what she heard. During a railway journey the term 'luggage in advance' meant nothing to her, so in desperation she implored the porter to do as he thought best. Reading the daily newspapers made her feel idiotic in the extreme, because the writers of reviews and leading articles used words and phrases such as Jazz, Gin and It, the Unknown Soldier, Lease-lend, Hollywood, Cocktail, Striptease and Isolationism. These and many others were quite incomprehensible to Miss Baldwin, who was equally bewildered when friends said 'It's your funeral' or 'Believe it or not'. Advertisements on hoardings proclaimed the virtues of mysterious products named Vim, Rinso and Brasso, while in restaurants it was difficult to make any sense of the list of dishes available.[1]

This is a rare and valuable reminder to the rest of us that the English language does not stand still any more than our other institutions. All language changes over a period of time, for reasons which are imperfectly understood. Or rather, since speech is really a form of human activity, like dancing or playing the piano – and not an entity in itself – it is more exact to say that each successive generation behaves linguistically in a slightly different manner from its predecessors. In his teens the young man is impatient of what he considers to be the unduly stilted vocabulary and pronunciation of his elders and he likes to show how up to date he is by the use of the latest slang, but as the years go by some of his slang becomes standard usage and in any case he slowly grows less receptive to linguistic novelties, so that by the time he reaches his forties he will probably be lamenting the slipshod speech of the younger generation, quite unaware that some of the expressions and pronunciations now being used in all seriousness in pulpit and law-court were frowned upon by his own parents. In this respect language is a little like fashions in men's dress. The informal clothes of one generation become the everyday wear of the next, and just as young doctors and bank-clerks nowadays go about their business in sports-jackets, so they allow into their normal vocabulary various expressions which were once confined to slang and familiar conversation.

But quite apart from additions to the language which result from the admittance into good usage of what was once slang, it is evident that numberless new words and expressions are re-quired in order to deal with the great and ever-increasing com-plexity of modern life, encompassed as it is by the rapidly changing social and technical conditions of our time. Inventions and discoveries in the scientific domain create whole vocabularies of their own, and inevitably certain expressions taken from such sources find their way into current speech. As a physician of St Bartholomew's Hospital put it some years ago, '... it is almost

[1] *I Leap Over the Wall* (Hamish Hamilton, 1949).

to confess to a lack of education if one does not know what the Oedipus complex means, and terms like *libido, inhibition, transference* and the like are, even if ill-understood, everyday verbal currency'. But although newly-minted words are especially striking, it must not be forgotten that old-established ones often take on additional shades of meaning as a result of extended technical knowledge or a changed point of view resulting from scientific or sociological causes. Still in the realm of psychiatry, it can readily be seen that such terms as 'reason', 'disease' and even 'mind' now convey ideas to the layman which are no longer identical with those intended by the experts of 1843 who framed the legal rules governing the definition of insanity, as was pointed out at a meeting of the Howard League for Penal Reform in March 1956. Language faithfully reflects the spirit of the age, so that words of long standing can readily modify their meaning in accordance with the latest outlook of a given society. It is evident that 'music' has a wider connotation today than in the eighteenth century, or even than a generation ago, for we now include within the scope of this same word a number of phenomena which would not formerly have been considered as coming into the musical sphere at all, ranging from 'concrete music' to the use of the twelve-tone scale. Similarly in 1945 the unleashing of nuclear weapons against the Japanese caused the harmless little word 'atom' to take upon itself – quite literally from one moment to the next, as far as world opinion was concerned – terrifying implications of endless destruction. From being a technical term of chemistry and physics it rapidly came to epitomize in everyday speech the alternative routes awaiting the choice of mankind: on one hand the possibility of war and annihilation, but on the other, far-reaching vistas of material improvement. As a matter of etymology it may also be observed that the original meaning of 'atom', namely 'indivisible' (Greek *atomos*) is now out of date, for scientists no longer regard the atom as being the smallest particle of matter in existence.

Such is the importance of these technical developments to modern society that we are said to be living in the Atomic Age, and in such an age it is inevitable that the scientist should gain in prestige, together with his professional jargon, or at any rate such part of it as seeps into the public consciousness. 'Scientists are inheriting, they are conquering the earth. If you do not speak their uncouth language, then you will sink to the status of the native yokels when the Normans overran England' exclaimed Dr Bronowski at a congress of the British Association in September 1955. This is no doubt a deliberately exaggerated view, but the fact remains that science is one of the most powerful influences moulding the English language into fresh shapes at the present time. Scientific writing is not highly esteemed for its elegance – one recalls the tale of the scientist who alluded to a certain domain of enquiry as 'a virgin field pregnant with possibilities' – but scientific jargon and modes of thought inevitably come to the fore in a society which equates civilization with chromium-plated bath-taps. Nor does the process date from yesterday, for we have long been talking of people being 'galvanized' into activity or going 'full steam ahead', but nowadays this tendency to prefer technical imagery is ever-increasing, so that science can truly be said to have 'sparked off a chain reaction' in the linguistic sphere.

Another result of scientific development has been the amazingly increased mobility of ideas and the language in which they are clothed, along with the mobility of human beings themselves. Cheap books and newspapers, radio, television and the cinema have shrunk distances as it were to a point where an expression coined by a journalist sitting in an office in Los Angeles may be well known all over the English-speaking world in a matter of days. It is an axiom of students of language that poor communications hinder linguistic change whereas ease of intercourse fosters it, and so at a time when words and phrases are carried all over the world on the magic carpet of science there must be a strong likelihood that a novelty of speech will more easily find a place for itself than before in the permanent fabric of English. This applies to sounds as well as to the written word, for the traditional conditions of phonetic change have been modified now that a man no longer hears only the talk of his own town or village. Here then is a force strongly working, albeit quite unconsciously, against local peculiarities of speech, though even when this has been conceded one is bound to say that it will be many a long year before the English language is one and indivisible – if indeed this ever happens at all.

Languages do not exist in a vacuum but are powerfully affected by social, political, economic, religious and technical change. If a great many more people are studying Russian today than was the case only twenty years ago this is not due solely to the intrinsic merits of that very interesting language but to the dramatic rise in status and power of the Soviet Union. The similar tremendous increase in political, military and economic strength of the United States, coupled with the relative decline of Great Britain and the Commonwealth has inevitably led to heightened prestige for the American way of doing things, and since it so happens that most of the world's films are made by Americans there exists in the cinema a perfect channel for the passage of Americanisms into the English of Great Britain, though of course industry, advertising and the press also play their part in this respect, while television is so prodigal of material that the B.B.C. is obliged to make use of a great amount of American film. This vigorous stream of Americanisms must inevitably make some impression on the language of Britain, the more so as transatlantic standards of comfort and success are on the increase there. Whether this process of imitation comes about because America is a giant big enough to impose its own outlook on the western hemisphere or whether it is simply that this young and dynamic country is leading the race along a track which others happen to be following, it is an inescapable fact that American expressions have been implanted not only in Britain but also in countries where other languages are current, so that the Germans speak of *die Teenagers* and the French of *l'automatisation*. If this is what happens to foreign languages how much more likely it is that American influence will make itself felt in British modes of expression.

Like political and religious movements, linguistic change finds its most fervent disciples among the young. In his novel *Hurry on Down*, John Wain dwells for a moment on the dissimilar modes of speech of a young man and his father. 'He talked a different language for one thing; it was demotic English of the mid-twentieth century, rapid, slurred, essentially a city dialect and, in origin, essentially American. By contrast it was a pleasure to hear his father, whose speech had been formed, along with all his other habits, before 1914' (p. 175).[1] Though the tone of this quotation is rather disapproving it does not prevent Mr Wain from using Americanisms in his own essays and articles, just like any of his colleagues, nor is there any reason why he should refrain from doing so.

Among other things, the fashion for Americanised speech fits in with the general toughening of the English language in Britain which has been proceeding apace since 1914. (To hark back to Miss Baldwin, her book more than once expresses her amazement at the vocabulary of the modern woman.) The fact that some Americans consider the English of the United States to be somewhat prudish and euphemistic as compared with the British variety does not invalidate this statement, since language is formed by the world as it appears to the speaker, and not as it really is. In the mind of many a young Briton and his girl, American speech is the hall-mark of the tough guy and the he-man. Just as the modern adolescent finds it necessary to dress as a lumberjack or cowboy in order to go to a ballroom, so he likes to ape the talk and manners of Denver and Tucson. In this he is of course no more reprehensible than a journalist or professor who uses in Britain a word he picked up during a trip to New York, and the present survey is not concerned with the allocation of praise or blame but merely records what seem to be some curious trends in the English language. Nor does it confine itself to American linguistic influence, but it must be confessed that references to America will be liberally sprinkled over many of its pages. The impact of American English is indeed far and

---

[1] Secker and Warburg, 1955.

away the greatest single influence shaping our language today.

'What is happening to the English language?' asked T. S. Eliot in some alarm when writing in 1962 about the latest translation of the New Testament now being read in many churches. The following pages are intended as a small contribution towards an answer to that very pertinent question, and deal for the most part with the period since 1930 or so. It may occasion some surprise that attention should be directed to so short a span of time, but again it must be recalled that English changes at a very rapid rate, for after all even the highly educated find the printed page of Shakespeare fairly hard going, while the Chaucerian language of the fourteenth century is the earliest he can make anything of without special study. If we are to consider the spoken word then even the conversation of some two hundred years ago would be strange to modern ears, for words whose spelling has remained unchanged have often modified their pronunciation. 'Gold' was pronounced 'goold' until well into the nineteenth century. (and the family name Gould preserves the old form alongside Gold), while 'oblige' was pronounced as 'obleege' in the eighteenth century. Bearing these considerations in mind we can appreciate that there can be noticeable change in the vocabulary, pronunciation and grammar of the English language even in the course of a single generation, and in fact it is not too much to say that if one jotted down in a notebook every new word, meaning or pronunciation met with in the course of a year the resulting list might be surprisingly long. The pages now following are indeed partly the outcome of such a haphazard method and are certainly not presented as a systematically organized survey. In these circumstances a certain subjective note is sometimes inevitable, especially in cases where memories of former usage are in question, though whenever possible chapter and verse is supplied in the form of a dated written quotation. Some of these examples afford earlier datings of the first appearances of words and expressions than those listed by the *Oxford English Dictionary* (*O.E.D.*) and works complementary to it, such as the *Shorter Oxford English Dictionary* (*S.E.D.*), though these ante-datings have not in every instance been pointed out as such.

Finally it is stressed that although for the sake of interest some references are made in the pages that follow to the earlier history of English, the main preoccupation of the work is the language of the last generation or so, and this has affected the point of view adopted in the case of certain words or other linguistic features which existed in former centuries but were extinct or not generally known in the early part of the twentieth century. So, for example, *yoghurt* is virtually a recent addition to the language, even though it first appeared in English as a borrowing from Turkish in 1625. It was totally unknown to the mass of the population as late as 1950 but is now widely sold and advertised, so it is surprising that even the most recent dictionaries, such as the 1964 edition of the *Concise Oxford*, continue to define this solid food as 'A sour fermented liquor made from milk in the Levant'. However such discrepancies often arise when a mere entry in a dictionary at last becomes a living word of everyday speech.

I

The Impact of America

THE Annual Register for 1922 records that Sinclair Lewis's *Babbitt* had a glossary appended to it in the British edition in order to explain certain Americanisms. But, commented the Annual Register, 'the cinematograph and the theatre . . . will have given the ordinary man a sufficiently large American vocabulary for his needs'. Even if this was true in the early nineteen-twenties, which seems unlikely, it was incorrect by 1935, for in that year H. W. Horwill issued the first edition of his *Dictionary of Modern American Usage*,[1] which he explained as 'primarily designed to assist English people who visit the United States, or who meet American friends, or who read American books and magazines, or who listen to American "talkies" '. On the other hand at the present day it is a fact that any English-speaking person born after about 1925 is painlessly endowed with a good knowledge of American idiom, thanks chiefly to those very films which Horwill saw as something of a linguistic problem in his own generation, and indeed it must be difficult for British adolescents of today to imagine a time before the advent of talking-films when the majority of the inhabitants were unfamiliar with American English in its spoken form except for a few remarks from an occasional American celebrity who had been brought to the microphone of the B.B.C. and when recordings by transatlantic artists were something of a rarity, for most songs were rendered in orthodox Southern English with Cockney or North-country thrown in for comic relief. Modern youngsters in Britain hear hours of transatlantic dialogue every week of their lives because of films and television programmes, so that they are much less

[1] Oxford University Press.

likely than their elders to echo the comments of Wordsworth's sister-in-law about a young American lady who had in her opinion 'the oddest manners & such a speech !'[1] And although it is likely that even at the time when this judgement was being written down some borrowings from the transatlantic vocabulary were starting to make their way to Britain, as has been shown by such an authority on the subject as Sir William Craigie, the point is that this process has lately been enormously accelerated. 'We all use your expressions now,' says one of John Galsworthy's characters in *Swan Song* (though of course poor old Soames Forsyte quite fails to understand 'to fall for') and when an Englishman casually remarks 'O.K. by me that way' he is using a sentence whose three elements each owe something to an American model (O.K. / by me / that way). With the abrupt shifting of the political and economic centre of gravity of the western hemisphere from Europe to the United States (youthful students of history are astonished to discover that neither the U.S.A. nor the Soviet Union had any part in the notorious Munich agreement of 1938) the American variety of English has forced itself, often for commercial and technical reasons, upon the attention of millions who were previously unacquainted with it, and what is even more important, it has become respectable, that is to say that it is no longer regarded as merely a quaint, barbarous or amusing appendage to the British original. Foreigners take it somewhat less for granted than before that the latter is the only true English language and it is noteworthy that the most famous of commercial linguistic institutes offers a recorded conversational course in American English. While it is true to say that most southern Englishmen regard the very phrase 'British English' as something of a pleonasm (Stephen Potter has said that in the U.S.A. it takes him about a fortnight to realize that he is 'a man with an accent'), many foreigners appear to find the American idiom in some way more accessible than British English, and in the words of one observer, 'Somehow or other

[1] Letter of 12 September 1827, *The Letters of Sara Hutchinson from 1800 to 1835*, ed. Kathleen Coburn (Routledge, 1954).

American speech seems more potent, or more easy to acquire than English speech'.[1] It is interesting to see that the International Academy of Tourism instituted by Prince Rainier of Monaco has concluded that English and American are two different languages and so require separate dictionaries for the use of travellers. Now it so happens that differences in the two vocabularies are particularly noticeable in the realm of tourism and travelling, so that from the purely practical view one approves of this decision, but while the recognition of an American language in its own right had some following amongst scholars in the United States a generation ago, and was made explicit by H. L. Mencken's book on *The American Language*, it was largely abandoned by Mencken himself in later years and is now unfashionable at a time when writers are stressing the essential unity of the English language while bearing in mind its regional variants. For, in the admirable phrase of a Spanish author, Julián Marías, 'English can be spoken in a British or American manner' (*El inglés se puede hablar britanicamente o americanamente*). Since we are at present concerned with the influence of the latter upon the former it will perhaps be convenient to speak of the standard idioms of England and the United States as British and American respectively, though the use of these terms does not for a moment imply any belief in the existence of two separate national languages.

If pressed, many Englishmen would probably admit that they think of American influence on the language as affecting only the realms of slang, and it is a strange paradox that as the flood of Americanisms in the standard language increases, so most people lose their ability to recognize them for what they are. This is doubtless a result of the fact that the process of borrowing in the linguistic sense is a largely unconscious one, especially when the words involved are not notorious Americanisms, easily picked out as such, like *sucker*, *graft* or *cinch*. In the introduction to the 1944 edition of his *Dictionary of Modern American Usage* Horwill has drawn attention to many American expressions which crept unnoticed into Harold Nicolson's biography of Dwight Morrow,

[1] Rom Landau, *Portrait of Tangier* (Hale, 1952), p. 136.

and which arose directly from Nicolson's reading of a large amount of American material. It never occurred to the biographer that such terms were until recently quite new to him and that the British reader may require an explanatory footnote. (In a similar way historians sometimes unconsciously use in their books and articles somewhat old-fashioned turns of phrase they have constantly been meeting during their reading of letters and documents of former centuries and which no longer strike them as odd.) Of course American words and idioms pass relatively unnoticed into the British vocabulary because the phonetic structure is quite familiar – in other words one easily sees that Japanese *hara-kiri* or Afrikaans *apartheid* are alien intruders in our language because of their unusual formation, whereas on the face of it there could be no reason to suppose that such American importations as *cagey* or *room-mate* have not been part of the British vocabulary for centuries, so they easily slip into everyday use and are not felt to be strangers.

As has been suggested above, pride of place must be given to films as a vehicle of American linguistic influence, always bearing in mind that American films on British television have brought transatlantic speech to the British domestic hearth itself. In the cinema and *show business* it is not surprising that much of the technical vocabulary is itself of American origin, since innovations in the entertainment world come mainly from the U.S.A. However it may be noted in passing that the cinema 'star' is simply the continuation of an old word belonging to the nine-teenth-century music-hall (cf. star turn), as is the verb 'to star', though to *co-star* is modern. Even 'stardom' is a century old and antedates the invention of the cinematograph, but when a film is said to *feature* an actor who has been *built up* by his company, then the shades of meaning attached to these expressions are American in the first place, as is the *release* of a film which is thereby put into general circulation. This word is presumably a borrowing by Hollywood from the jargon of American jour-nalists in which it means the publication in the press of a speech or document supplied to the newspapers in advance. A devotee of the cinema, or some other sport or entertainment, or indeed an admirer of a particular performer, is a *fan* – short for 'fanatic'. Indeed this label can be attached to any individual who admires someone else, so that in his *Ten Novels and Their Authors* (1954) Somerset Maugham speaks of Balzac receiving a 'fan letter'.[1] In Britain the more rabid film fans and also the film-reviewers sometimes venture to speak of *movies* but for some reason this word has never gained the favour of the great mass of the public who continue to prefer 'the pictures' or 'the flicks'.

From the jargon of film-advertising one important phrase has made its way into general British usage, i.e. *of all time*. Popularized by advertisements about 'the greatest film of all time' it was at first regarded as an amusing example of the transatlantic love of grandiloquence, but is now firmly established in the standard vocabulary, and is readily applied to subjects other than films. It is fair to say that the phrase 'all time' was itself not entirely unknown in England in the nineteenth century, but it appeared sporadically and would have remained in obscurity without the help of Hollywood. Thus in Medwin's *Life of Shelley* (1847) Byron is quoted as saying that the Italians 'consider Dante as made for all time'. Ruskin described the 'Virgin and Child' of Andrea del Verrocchio as 'exemplary for all time', having obtained this painting in 1878.

It was in connection with the cinema that Britain first heard of the *bobby-soxer*, since this expression was learned via reports about hordes of adolescent girls adulating popular actors and singers. It was well-known in this context in the late nineteen-forties even though at that date it was most exceptional for young girls to wear short socks this side of the Atlantic. Thus, speaking of a famous English actor: '. . . his air of smiling tolerance could deceive none but a bobby-soxer' (*Observer*, 8 Feb 1948). *Bobby sox* are presumably so-called because of their inordinate shortness, just as the bobcat or American lynx is distinguished by its short tail, a bobtail is a docked tail, and bobbed hair is hair cut short.

Occasionally it is possible to pinpoint a particular word or

[1] Heinemann.

expression as being due to the influence of the American cinema. *To doodle* is to sketch meaningless designs on a scrap of paper while supposedly paying attention to something else, and this verb was first heard in the film *Mr Deeds Goes to Town* (1937). It is now a respectable member of the vocabulary for the excellent reason that this verb neatly describes an action for which there was previously no name, and newspapers frequently comment nowadays on the doodling of statesmen attending meetings and conferences. Here, then, we have an addition to the vocabulary brought about by a single film, and one would like to know what genius invented such an expressive word. *Pixillated* – also launched by that same film – meaning 'slightly crazy', still survives to some slight extent and has found its way into the dictionaries. Another practical instance of the power of even a single American film to modify British usage is to be seen in the Danny Kaye picture *Hans Christian Andersen* shown in 1954. Before that date the author in question was always known in Britain as plain Hans Andersen, but nowadays he is more often than not given his full quota of names as in the United States. Until 1954 the huge majority of the inhabitants of the British Isles had not even realized that he possessed a middle name, so let us admit that this is one up to Hollywood and the educative power of the cinema. . . .

By the middle nineteen-forties the noun *natural* began to be used in Britain with the American sense of 'one who performs brilliantly without previous training' and since then it rapidly extended its meaning to include anything very suitable or successful, so that by 1953 a British advertisement for a cosmetic sold in three varieties bore the legend 'One of these is a natural for you'. However this word can hardly be classed as standard and belongs rather to the jargon of the entertainment and commercial worlds. Its most peculiar semantic feature is that the new sense virtually reverses the traditional though little-used meaning of 'idiot'.

In 1927 Logan Pearsall Smith wrote 'There are two expressive idioms from the theatre, *to put it over* and *to get it across* which are popular in America, and which will probably soon make their way into our speech in England' (*Society for Pure English*, Tract 12).[1] This prophecy has now been amply fulfilled, and indeed these two phrases have moved far beyond the theatrical world in modern usage. Also from the vocabulary of the theatre and show business is *routine*, at any rate in the sense of 'a carefully rehearsed performance' of song, dance or patter, but in America it came to mean in addition to this almost anything which is automatic or normal, and this has likewise reached Britain. Thus 'If his promotion was routine, it was bad routine' (*Daily Telegraph*, 24 Sep 1958). It will be seen that this is not quite the same as the traditional sense, which applied to a whole system of acts, e.g. R.A.F. routine, police routine, and not to a single isolated case. The corresponding adjective has also imitated American usage in this respect. Hitherto it has meant 'of a mechanical or unvaried character; performed by rule' (*O.E.D.*), and so one speaks of 'a routine task' or 'routine duties' in a slightly disparaging way. But the latest usage gives it the transatlantic meaning of 'normal, usual'. 'This has become routine critical reality', said Mr John Holloway, lecturer in English at Cambridge, in a broadcast of November 1954. Here, of course, the American model has not introduced a new word or destroyed the meaning of an old one – it has merely extended the scope of the existing word. A further point is that as a result of these developments it is in some cases difficult to see whether *routine* is intended as a noun or an adjective; for example in such a sentence as 'Danger is routine here', taken from a British newspaper. Does it mean, as a noun, that danger provides the framework for daily life, or, as an adjective, that danger is normal? The point is purely a grammatical one since the meaning remains the same in either case.

Certain Americanisms of the theatrical world have been accepted into the language of British politics. A *stooge* is properly the butt or foil of a comedian, but in a wider context the word has taken on the sense of 'figurehead' or 'puppet', so that a Member of Parliament declares that 'the strong men must have

[1] Page 31.

their stooges'.[1] From America, also, comes *double-talk*, i.e. 'meaningless talk that appears to make sense', which is frequently used in political contexts, for obvious reasons. Probably this word suggested to George Orwell the coinage *double-think* appearing in his novel *1984*, and which implies the ability to believe in two contradictory ideas at the same time.

Political commentators necessarily read a certain amount of American material and often spend part of their professional lives in the United States, so that it is not surprising if they pick up a number of new expressions which are duly carried over into their books, articles and broadcasting. Robert Waithman, who was in the United States for eleven years as chief correspondent of the *News Chronicle*, uses American syntax in his *Understanding the English* when he says of the Queen 'She can order Parliament dissolved at any time' (p. 168).[2] This handy turn of speech has not generally caught on in England, though it has actually been used in *The Times* by a special correspondent. '... the Nazis ordered his arrest and later they ordered him shot at sight ...' (13 Jan 1960). *The American way of life* has led to the discovery of a *British way of life* first heard of in the middle of the twentieth century. On 25 March 1954, when speaking in the House of Commons about a number of national sporting events, the then Home Secretary declared 'They are part of the British way of life' and in that same month the journal *Modern Languages* stated that 'Indications of what we now call our "way of life" are preserved in the words "boy-scout, fair-play" '. Our ancestors might not have understood this phrase. Actually 'way of life' was used in *Macbeth*, though evidently meaning 'course of life'.

> *I have liv'd long enough: my way of life*
> *Is fall'n into the sear, the yellow leaf.*

This was objected to as an improbable reading by Dr Samuel

---

[1] Quoted by Paul C. Berg in *A Dictionary of New Words in English* (Allen and Unwin, 1953).

[2] Methuen, 1953.

Johnson and others, who thought that 'May of life' must be meant!

Widely current, but particularly frequent in political contexts, is the use of *alibi* to denote an excuse of any kind instead of a plea of having been elsewhere at the time a crime was committed. This change of meaning of a precise legal term has been denounced on both sides of the Atlantic but is now impossible to dislodge. It gained a foothold in Britain in the 'thirties and nowadays it is probably used more frequently in the new sense than in the traditional one.

In political and economic commentary the word *breakdown* (of figures) is often substituted for 'analysis' in imitation of American usage where this habit evidently began in writings on chemistry.[1] Similarly to *break down* can now replace the verb 'analyse'. In the history of mathematical terminology the idea of 'breaking' is a familiar one, since 'fractions' are 'broken parts' etymologically speaking, while algebra itself reminds us of the opposite process of the putting together of broken parts, ultimately from the Arabic *al-jebr*, a surgical term in the first instance. To return to American English, *breakdown* is a good example of its preference for self-explanatory words, and indeed it must be granted that in this respect of immediate comprehensibility some American expressions are more sensible than their British counterparts. Thus *typesetter* is preferable to 'compositor' and *billboard* to 'hoarding', while a very welcome reform in Britain would be the substitution of the telephonic *long distance* for the bewildering 'trunk call', suggestive only of the mating cry of the elephant.

Wireless programmes use many terms of American origin. Indeed 'wireless' itself, as noun or adjective, is less and less heard among younger people in Britain, for enquiries among university students show that most never include it in their vocabulary at all, and prefer the originally somewhat academic-sounding 'radio', now a household word. Horwill sees in the American

[1] Cf. Thomas Pyles (Melrose, 1954), *Words and Ways of American English*, p. 105 of the British edition.

preference for 'radio' an example of the American dislike of words implying a negative statement (under his entry *stem*, where he discusses Am. *stem-winder* and Eng. *keyless watch*). However this may have been in America the explanation cannot be valid in Britain, where it is precisely the younger set which introduced *radio* on a large scale. Now it was the older generation which thought of a wireless as something without wires – as wireless telegraphy, in fact. So in an article of December 1923 Lord Riddell was already asking 'What effect is the Radio going to have on life? (By the way I do not like the description 'wireless'; why describe a thing as a negation?)'.[1] But to people born about the time that Lord Riddell was writing this sentence it is difficult to think of 'wireless' as a negative word, and in their linguistic consciousness 'wireless' has nothing to do with 'wire' at all. (In the same way the modern man has no conception of a link between 'holiday' and 'holy', so that he sees nothing curious in the phrase 'Bank Holiday'). It is just a word in its own right so far as they are concerned, though one can see that if 'wireless' is taken in the old literal sense then the description 'wireless orchestra' has humorous implications. Now if it has no negative connotations for those born about the same time as the B.B.C. then it has none for the generation born in the late nineteen-thirties which may be judged to be the first to have made a wide use of *radio*. In fact this is not one of those words that have suddenly come to the forefront of the general vocabulary and it made quite slow progress in Britain over the years, in spite of the official weekly magazine of scheduled B.B.C. programmes which has had the name of RADIO TIMES since the inception of the B.B.C. in 1923. As late as 1954 I was quite astonished to hear a young man ask a post office clerk for a 'radio licence', an expression I had never heard before. Such is the strength of linguistic habit that it seemed at the time almost against nature to refer thus to what had always been a wireless licence. Actually the licence is issued under the Wireless Telegraphy Act and is officially a Broadcast Receiving Licence giving permission to use 'apparatus for wireless

[1] Quoted in *The Twentieth Century*, November 1959, p. 330.

telegraphy'. The word here is always 'wireless' and never 'radio'. It is interesting to see that according to a survey conducted by the B.B.C. in 1956 about five people were still saying 'wireless' for every four saying 'radio' when alluding to their receiving set. When indicating that a programme was *not* on television more people would say 'It's on the wireless' than 'It's on the radio'. To the surprise of the investigators, very few people said 'It's on sound', which is the B.B.C. idiom. It was further discovered that some individuals considered 'radio' to be more 'U' than 'wireless', though in fact Professor A. S. C. Ross's well-known article on *U and Non-U* states the opposite while conceding that the best people may use 'radio' in a technical sense, 'as in aircraft'.[1]

One surmises that the growing use of 'radio' in Britain is not due to any idea that 'wireless' is a negative-sounding word but simply because it is the American choice and that is attraction enough for adolescents. Here, as sometimes happens, the 'Americanism' of the word is nothing more than its greater frequency in the United States as compared with Britain, and as a matter of fact its constant use was one of the surprises inflicted on British audiences by the first talking films. To anyone born before the B.B.C., 'wireless' was a firmly entrenched part of the daily vocabulary before the full blast of American linguistic influence was felt in Britain and so many members of the older generations will doubtless never adopt 'radio', but it is equally certain that 'wireless' is a doomed word in the long run because of its desertion by the rising generations. A striking fact is that in *Language*, a Ministry of Education pamphlet of 1954, 'radio' is used fourteen times in the relevant section whereas 'wireless' does not appear at all! Even more significant, 'radio' is the more vigorous form in that it is the one chosen to appear in new coinages such as 'sound radio' and indeed the single word 'radio' (meaning radio as an art form in its own right, e.g. 'It's good radio' just as one says

[1] Originally appearing in the Finnish *Neuphilologische Mitteilungen* (Helsinki, 1954), it was reprinted in *Noblesse Oblige* (Penguin Books, 1959, in conjunction with Hamish Hamilton).

'It's good theatre'). In the case of television the situation has been somewhat different because of historical reasons, and American influence has been strong almost from the first. True, it was a British invention and though the B.B.C. instituted a public service in 1936 its development was interrupted by the war, with the practical result that its large-scale growth as a mass-medium took place in the United States and not until the middle 'fifties did television really get into its full stride in Britain. Its vocabulary has therefore been much affected by American example, including the abbreviation T.V. The very pronunciation of the word 'television' has been shaped in another respect by transatlantic usage, and it is consequently often pronounced with stress on the first syllable rather than the third. In this connection it is instructive to see that the O.E.D. (of 1919) gave the latter as the stress of this word, whereas the first syllable is marked as stressed in the Supplement of 1933, as it also is in the S.E.D. third edition of 1955.[1] By the early nineteen-sixties both pronunciations, telev́ision and t́elevision, were equally common, as far as it is possible to judge of these matters by general impression, though the B.B.C. announcers used the second one, and there is every likelihood that it will eventually triumph over its predecessor. Incidentally this word is listed as first appearing in 1909, so here we have a case of language foreshadowing reality.

In 1946 Max Beerbohm published the text of a series of broadcasts under the title *Mainly on the Air*.[2] As a synonym for 'to be broadcasting' the expression *on the air* is probably American in the first place; at all events it was frequently used in the United States at a time when it was only rarely heard on the eastern side of the Atlantic, though the dating given by the S.E.D. is 1927.

A remarkable example of a facetious coinage that has become part of the British vocabulary because of the lack of any alternative term is *disk-jockey* (also *disc-jockey*), namely a radio entertainer whose business is to play records in the intervals of his own

[1] O.E.D., i.e. *The Oxford English Dictionary*, also known as *The New English Dictionary*, or *N.E.D.* The S.E.D. is *The Shorter Oxford English Dictionary*, an abridgement of the O.E.D.
[2] Heinemann.

jokes and observations. In his book *The Story of English* published in 1953 Professor Mario Pei warned that the existence of this word should not lead us to believe that the word 'disk' was ordinarily used by Americans 'for phonograph record in any other connection . . .' (p. 224).[1] British 'disc' is not infrequently used by enthusiasts in the sense of a gramophone record, however, though this habit has not gained the public in general. This is all the more surprising when it is realized that the usage goes back to the nineteenth century and that 'disc' in this meaning was, for example, part of the vocabulary of such a master of the English language as George Bernard Shaw.

To the man in the street a *quiz* is a competition designed to test the knowledge of the participants, and this is because of broadcast programmes on the American model. As noun and verb 'quiz' had long existed in the standard language, if only because it was kept alive in literary circles by the works of Jane Austen, and the sense was 'to look at someone in a curious or mocking way, make sport of', or as a noun, 'a person given to quizzing'. It is not easy to see by what semantic process the change of meaning has come about, though to hazard a guess one might imagine that part of the entertainment value of quiz competitions comes from the teasing of the unsuccessful contestants by the master of ceremonies, or *quizmaster*. In the U.S.A. this verb had certainly survived into the nineteenth century with the meaning 'fool, tease' and for the year 1839 Professor Norman E. Eliason quotes an example from a letter. 'I am not very hard to quiz, but they could not make me believe you had not written.'[2] Meanwhile the modern 'quiz' is not to be confused with another type of entertainment offered by the B.B.C., that is, the *brains trust*, where the proceedings consist of discussion pure and simple, without any obligation to supply factual information (at least, not since the memorable programme in the early days when someone asked how a fly manages to walk on the ceiling without falling down). A small linguistic point is that

[1] Allen and Unwin.
[2] *Tarheel talk* (University of North Carolina Press, 1956), p. 289.

British usage has added to the original form of the word, which was simply *brain trust*, a term invented in the 'thirties as the collective name of a group of experts, many of them from the universities, called in to advise Franklin D. Roosevelt during his first administration.

But quite apart from the various technical terms of radio and television programmes which pass into general currency, there is the broad linguistic fact that broadcasting churns out a tremendous number of American popular songs which painlessly imprint transatlantic words and idioms (or, on occasion, pronunciations) on the minds of millions of young listeners. Working in this same direction, there is also the professional liking of British song-writers for the American style of vocabulary which they consequently incorporate in their own compositions. (Though it is fair to say that no writer on the British side of the Atlantic has ever approached the striking syntax of the American song 'Is you is or is you ain't mah baby?'.)

Thus *to get by* for 'manage, make do' was made known to the British public around 1939–1940 by way of the ditty 'Run, Rabbit, Run!' and the lesson was reinforced by a later song 'I'll get by, as long as I have you'. In due course a literary critic in *The Times* wrote 'He will need . . . a private income to get by' (17 Mar 1960). By 1963 the phrase had become so much a part of the English language that it was included anachronistically in a B.B.C. television adaptation of *The Old Curiosity Shop*. This sort of misuse of twentieth-century words in nineteenth-century contexts in broadcast stories and plays is incidentally an excellent proof of the acclimatization of a new expression. It must be used with caution, however, since words which have died out in Britain sometimes survive in the U.S.A. and are finally hailed in British English as neologisms. Chaucer's use of 'I guess' is well-known.

Some years ago a song popular in this country bore the title 'Maybe', and on consulting the *O.E.D.* one finds this word described as archaic and dialectal! Yet by now it is in everyday use in Britain. It is a fact that when 'maybe' was little used in the standard speech of southern England it never wholly died out in the north (and in the literary sphere we find it for example in the *Prose Fancies* of Richard Le Gallienne, published in 1894). But in the United States it has always had a very wide popularity outshining that of the synonymous 'perhaps', and it cannot be doubted that the revival of 'maybe' in England is due to American example and not to that of native northern usage, in which by the way the pronunciation is usually 'mebbe' as also in Scotland, Ireland and certain American communities.

In 1955 a British electrical company advertised a booklet *Stage Lighting on a Shoestring*, thereby making use of an Americanism. Yet long ago 'shoestring' was a perfectly good English word and the poet Herrick spoke in the seventeenth century of

> *A careless shoestring in whose tie*
> *I see a wild civility.*

The word had survived into the twentieth century in America, but not in the standard language of Britain. A late example is found in the 1854 revised edition of *Handley Cross* by R. S. Surtees – 'I was only tying my shoestring' (p. 527). In 1857 it appeared in Trollope's *Barchester Towers*. 'You must not expect him to come to you with vows and oaths ... and kiss your shoe-strings' (chapter xlv). Even now that the word has been restored to the language it cannot be said that British English refers to shoestrings in the literal sense, for it is only the metaphorical *on a shoestring* that has caught the public fancy. The *S.E.D.* dates this phrase from 1953 but explains it as referring to 'the possibility of a breakdown or collapse' and this was certainly the first meaning, though the conscious allusion nowadays is simply to the smallness of the financial backing available for a particular scheme. Such indeed is the implication in the quotation given by the *S.E.D.*; 'I am aware ... the Minister is working on a financial shoe-string'.

John Brophy, the novelist, tells us in the periodical *Books and Bookmen* (Feb 1957) that he did not know the word *water-front* until he came across it in an eighteenth-century book about Liverpool, whereupon he used it as the title of a novel published in 1934. Mr Brophy must not have been interested in American popular songs in the early nineteen-thirties, otherwise he would have heard broadcasts of 'I cover the waterfront' which introduced the word to millions of listeners to the B.B.C. Until I read his remark my earliest British dating of 'water-front' was from Edmund Vale's *North Country* of 1937, where curiously enough the allusion is also to Liverpool. If indeed it was a British book that Mr Brophy meant then this must be another example of a word formerly current in England and revived by reintroduction from America in recent times. It is now a thriving member of the British vocabulary, especially after Marlon Brando's film *On the Waterfront*. Like a good many other borrowings from America this word incidentally shows that the hyphen is used more sparingly there than in Britain.

In standard British usage 'aisle' has traditionally been confined to descriptions of church architecture, though in the regional speech of the north it is applied to any kind of gangway, for example in schoolroom or theatre. But in the case of the theatre there has recently been a borrowing into standard British English of the American phrase 'rolling in the aisles' (i.e. overcome by uncontrollable laughter, as in 'This comedy will have you rolling in the aisles').[1] This wider application of the word is noted by Horwill in his dictionary of modern American usage, and he points out that in the United States 'aisle' can also denote gangways in trains and shops as well as in the theatre. It will now be interesting to see how far it becomes part of the vocabulary of the British theatre in the literal meaning, quite apart from the metaphorical phrase taken from America, and whether it spreads even further to take over functions now fulfilled in Britain by 'corridor' and 'gangway'. On a larger scale we are at present witnessing the spread of *main street* in this country for what is usually called 'the high street', that is, the principal thoroughfare of a particular

[1] ROLLING IN THE AISLES appeared as a heading in the *Times Literary Supplement* (26 Feb 1960).

town. *Main street* is also used in the plural to indicate the larger streets. But whether singular or plural, this expression is not listed in the *S.E.D.* though it is amusing to see that it is used at least twice in its pages to define one of the meanings of 'row', which is 'In Yarmouth, one of a number of narrow lanes connecting the main streets', and also 'In Chester, one of several raised and covered galleries running along the sides of the four main streets'. Actually this is possibly once again a case of a regional usage passing into America in the early days and then being returned to this country, because 'the high street' is not universal in Britain (as opposed to High Street as a proper name; without the article) and in Northumberland and Durham and possibly elsewhere it has long been 'the main street' (and often 'the front street', or as a proper name, Front Street. It may be significant, as a pointer to the sort of early provincial influence which helped to form the American vocabulary, that Front Street is also to be found in Nome and Dodge City). Certainly the plural form is a definite gain to the general British vocabulary as a short and useful synonym of 'the principal thoroughfares' or 'most important streets' of a town or city. To add a personal note, I remember as a student in the nineteen-forties being mildly rebuked by one of my lecturers for speaking of 'the main street', which was condemned as a provincialism for 'the high street'.

The verb *implement* is listed in the various Oxford dictionaries as 'chiefly Scottish', but nowadays it has virtually become one of the vogue-words of the language, especially in political and economic contexts. This fashion has however spread not so much from Scotland as from the U.S.A. where it has had a great success. In Britain it was certainly well established by about 1940.

In the case of 'to *quit*' there can be no doubt at all that the spectacular revival of this once obsolescent word is due to American aid. Though a good old English expression, it had come to be considered as poetic or archaic in Britain except in the case of certain set phrases such as 'notice to quit' and 'to quit the service'. Those whose memories reach back as far as the first

American talking films may possibly recall their surprise on hearing how frequently it appeared in the speech of the actors. In imitation of American usage British journalists and writers of headlines gleefully seized upon this short and expressive word, chiefly in the senses of 'abandon' (a country, area), 'terminate one's membership of an organization', or else 'surrender, give up, cease to do something'. It now looks as though the future of 'quit' is assured, although the source of its rejuvenation is obvious when one remembers that whereas the old past tense and past participle were 'quitted' we now usually have 'quit' in these functions in spite of the labelling of this short form by the *S.E.D.* as 'now dialectically and U.S. colloquial'.

A strange case is that of *transportation*. The *S.E.D.* notes that in the sense of transporting, or of conveyance of things or persons from one place to another this word was gradually replaced after 1660 by 'transport'. Yet it is possible that this old traditional sense never quite died out. A British surgeon, William Lempriere, was still using it towards the end of the eighteenth century, and in *A Tour to Morocco* he says '. . . even when that obstacle was removed there would arise one still greater from the difficulty of transportation in this country'. Nearly a century and a half later this usage was still to be found on occasion in Britain, and a reviewer in the *Times Literary Supplement* could write, during the great airship craze of the early 'thirties that 'The airship . . . will not attempt to compete with land or sea transport where time is not all-important. . . . Her role will be the transportation of passengers' (16 Oct 1930). This statement admirably contrasts 'transport' (trains, ships and so on) and 'transportation' (the act of conveying), though of course 'transport' is often used with the latter sense. Then the other meaning of 'transportation' is now historical, that is in reference to the removal of convicts to the old overseas penal settlements, and especially to those situated in Australia. The fact is that until recent years the word was rarely heard in either sense in British English. As late as 1944 Horwill was still able to say in the second edition of his *Dictionary of Modern American Usage*, under *transportation*, that in England

'. . . the word still retains its Botany Bay associations, and much merriment is apt to be caused among visitors from England when their American friends speak of making arrangements for their transportation'. The old usage had of course remained very vigorous in the United States, and has now been revived in Britain as a result. When advertising an academic post in 1955 the secretary of the Association of Universities of the British Commonwealth did not shrink from announcing that 'It is hoped that transportation to Australia . . . would be available'. As so often, it is difficult to see why this cumbersome word should be considered preferable to the shorter 'transport' but doubtless the explanation may be that its very length endears it to the official mind. (In the journalistic and broadcasting spheres, where every second counts, the longer 'quotation' is on the other hand being challenged by the short form 'quote', a nineteenth-century abbreviation that is heard very frequently nowadays. 'Here are some quotes from various countries', B.B.C. news, 9 Oct 1959).

One or two expressions hitherto regarded as being more or less confined to the vocabulary of lawyers have recently become more generally known because of their frequent occurrence in America. *Assignment* was simply the legal transference of a right, but nowadays it is well-known in the American sense of 'task, mission'. For obvious reasons it is safe to assume that its transfer to the British vocabulary in this meaning has taken place by way of the cinema. A more picturesque case, though one which is rather less well-known than 'assignment', is *mayhem* or 'the crime of inflicting bodily injury upon a person' listed by the *O.E.D.* as belonging to the vocabulary of 'Old Law', though it quotes for the year 1894 an American example alluding to 'literary mayhem'. During the last quarter of a century *mayhem* has slowly been making its way back into British use, doubtless because of American influence, since this word is relatively frequent in the U.S.A. As early as 1940 it is found in an essay by Dorothy Sayers, who in *Unpopular Opinions* speaks of an 'act of mayhem' (p. 76).[1] It might possibly be objected that this might in fact stem

[1] Gollancz, 1946.

directly from English legal terminology, in view of Miss Sayers's wide knowledge of the language, and therefore not particularly from America in the present instance, but it can be seen elsewhere that she is not averse to using transatlantic images, as when she writes 'allergic to long term planning'. Taken from an essay of 1943 included in the above-mentioned collection (p. 63), this is a fairly early case of *allergic* being used in the American sense of 'opposed, unsympathetic'. Originally a medical term meaning 'hypersensitive', it has thus come to indicate virtually the opposite, i.e. 'insensitive', thus 'I am allergic to the manner of William Saroyan' (*John O' London's Weekly*, 5 Mar 1954).

Like *mayhem*, the *merger* was once in Britain a purely legal concept, to wit 'the extinguishment of a right, estate, contract, action, etc., by absorption in another' (*O.E.D.*), while its use to describe 'the combination or consolidation of one firm or trading company with another' was considered an Americanism, but nowadays it is probably more frequent in Britain than the traditional 'amalgamation'. Frank Harris, having lived and worked in America, used it in 1931 in his book on Bernard Shaw, where the reference was to a merger of newspapers (p. 359).[1] (Nor did Shaw himself mind slipping an occasional American expression into a British context, though in fact he was not to visit the United States until 1933. A curious instance of this tendency is found in *Man and Superman* where in Act I Jack Tanner exclaims 'Double crossed!', and since the play was of 1903 it actually furnishes us with an occurrence of this expression which antedates by one year the quotation given in the *O.E.D.* from the works of the American short-story writer, O. Henry.)

Salesmanship and advertising are activities in which Americans excel, so it is not surprising that other countries often copy their styles and techniques. This field has given us such terms as *sales-talk, sales-resistance, to be sold on* (be enthusiastic about), and the new meaning of *to sell*, i.e. 'advertise or publish the merits of, cause something to be desired' (hence the startling phrase

[1] Gollancz.

attributed to the late Dr Buchman, 'I sell Christ'). But the influence of American *publicity* is general as well as particular, inasmuch as it is above all a vehicle for Americanisms as well as causing them to be invented, and British agencies eagerly copy its vocabulary which is supposed to be redolent of efficiency and up-to-date enterprise by the mere fact of being American. A curious example of this attitude was to be seen in an illustrated advertisement issued to the press some years ago by the National Coal Board. An American tourist, easily identifiable by the camera on his chest, was gazing admiringly at a coal fire and assuring his British host that 'all the big shots back home' were having coal fires installed. This half-page advertisement was evidently intended as a counterblast to the idea that coal is old-fashioned as compared with oil-fired central heating.

The vocabulary of British publishing has not been greatly affected by Americanisms, with the notable exception of the *blurb*; defined by the *C.O.D. (Concise Oxford Dictionary)* as a 'Publisher's eulogy of a book, printed on jacket or in advertisements elsewhere (orig. U.S. slang)'. Despite its comic sound, this term is now used quite solemnly as an indispensable item in the jargon of literary critics and the reading public in general. Sometimes it even appears in the blurbs themselves, and is indisputably America's greatest gift to the language of the British book-trade, since *best-seller* may not be of specifically American origin. *Blurb* was deliberately coined by Gelett Burgess, as described in some detail by Mencken in 'Supplement One' to *The American Language*.[1]

The press has doubtless done more than books to popularize Americanisms in Britain, particularly when it is remembered that the British hold the world record for newspaper reading. It must not be imagined that only the more sensational organs of the press admit the American idiom to their columns, though it is true that they often act as pioneers in the case of particular expressions. As an example of this one might cite the verb *snarl up*, to be found in the editorial of the *Sunday Times* with reference

[1] Routledge and Kegan Paul, 1948.

to 'the remediable evils that do most to snarl up the traffic' (22 Nov 1959), but the racier *Daily Mail* had already spoken of 'snarling up the traffic' five years earlier (16 Dec 1954). Like advertisers, the popular press seems to take a keen delight in using Americanisms as a proof of its enterprise and vivacity, but it is a question how far the editorial practice of the staider journals is consciously based on similar considerations. In a linguistic context familiarity may breed tolerance or even admiration rather than contempt, and British headlines may be trusted to reproduce sooner or later the exotic expressions cabled to Fleet Street from the United States. During 1954 the *Sunday Times* main headline once referred to the breaking-up of an *ice-jam*. Now this was not a comment upon improved weather conditions but was meant to convey that there had been an easing of international tension at a conference held in the U.S.A. At the time this word was totally unfamiliar to British readers, but it now appears in the London press from time to time, along with *log-jam*. As logs and ice are rarely to be seen floating down British rivers in any quantity the transatlantic origin of these images is self-evident, and their use is a splendid illustration of how some American terms can be transplanted into a British context in spite of the exotic nature of the imagery involved. Since British dailies and weeklies receive a great deal of material from American news agencies or from British correspondents long resident in America it is not surprising that transatlantic shades of meaning quietly slip into words used in the British press. In this way the *Daily Express* reported that 'The people of Bombay threw rose petals instead of rocks today when Marshal Bulganin and Comrade Kruschev drove in state through the hastily tidied streets' (24 Nov 1955). The spelling of the name in the form Kruschev, preferred in America to the British transliteration Krushchev (or Khrushchev), gives one indication of the origin of this cable, while a moment's reflection shows that 'rocks' must mean 'stones', for in correct British usage rocks are heavy masses of stones whereas in the United States the word 'rock' is regularly substituted for 'stone', for reasons explained by

Thomas Pyles in the first chapter of his *Words and Ways of American English*. It is evident that the sentence used by the *Daily Express* was American in essence, having passed through some American intermediary on the way from Bombay to Fleet Street. Presumably some vigilant sub-editor ought to have translated it into British idiom, and indeed the usual expression is found on the same page, lower down the column, where we can read the heading MOB THROWS STONES IN PARLIAMENT.

This type of influence is accidental and unconscious, but at the same time it cannot be doubted that some British journalists deliberately ape American style and vocabulary. Thus in 1953 an article appeared in the American *Reader's Digest* which consistently alluded to old age as 'the vintage years'. There was nothing for it but to wait for its emergence in the British press, which duly took place in the pages of the *Daily Express* (12 Feb 1954). Similarly for *this day and age*, which likewise reached the London newspapers in early 1954. Two years later it was incorporated in a parliamentary speech about Premium Bonds (British for *Loterie nationale*) made by Mr Harold Wilson, and by the end of the decade had been honoured by inclusion in the remarks of the Master of the Rolls in the Court of Appeal, according to *The Times* (29 Jan 1960). Another fashionable synonym for 'now' is *at this stage*, though this is perhaps not of American provenance. First heard by me from a British army officer in 1943, this phrase would seem on the face of it to suggest that what is being done at present is one stage in a process, but in fact it is often used to camouflage the fact that nothing is really being done at all, and is thus an excellent bureaucratic smokescreen. 'It is not proposed, at this stage, etc. . . .'

A modern device that has been borrowed by the press and even the B.B.C. news bulletins consists of placing the name of a town in the genitive in the manner of *Time* magazine. Thus, from the *Daily Mail*, 'Wreckage . . . near Newcastle's Central Station was cleared yesterday', though it is hard to see how this improves the traditional 'Newcastle Central Station'. Even the staider newspapers use this trick. 'More than 10,000 travellers had left London's Victoria coach station by 9 a.m.' (*Observer*, 9 Jun 1957). But so far this remains a journalistic or news-reader's habit and it is not to be heard in conversation.

In his presidential address to the Bradford English Society in 1956 the editor of the *Yorkshire Post*, Sir Linton Andrews, had something to say about certain Americanisms that have become too popular with young reporters, instancing *balding* and *gangling*. 'Do not "going bald" and "lanky" meet our needs?' he asked. On the whole they probably do, but there is no doubt that these two words are spreading in at any rate written usage. In an article on prices charged by hairdressers the Newcastle *Evening Chronicle* reported a belief in some quarters that *balding* men should pay less (22 Apr 1954), and as for *gangling*, this was used by John Wain in *Hurry On Down* in 1955 but he was beaten to it by the Tyneside novelist Jack Common in the previous year, for in *The Ampersand* we read of 'a big gangling man in a smart little tweed jacket . . .' (p. 26).[1] To attempt a reply to the question asked – perhaps rhetorically – by Sir Linton Andrews, one can only say that whenever a new word is used it is because the neologism seems somehow preferable to the speaker or writer, and that consequently it meets his needs better than the traditional expression. This is not to claim that 'gangling' is in itself superior to 'lanky', but the person making it part of his vocabulary may do so because of non-linguistic motives; to show that he is up to date, or simply to have a change. In the same way this year's car does not meet our mechanical needs any better than the same model that appeared last year, but plenty of people will make the exchange because of a superficial alteration that proclaims its modernity.

In 1936 Horwill quoted from American journalistic style such verbs as *ban* (prohibit), *crash* (collide), *cut* (reduce), *probe* and *quiz* (investigate), *sue* (prosecute) and *wed*, together with their corresponding nouns except in the case of the last two words.[2] *Sue*, *ban* and *wed* were to be regarded as Americanisms only in the

[1] Turnstile Press.
[2] *Society for Pure English* tract No. 12, p. 190.

sense that they were subjected to incessant use, though in fact *wed* had come to be rather archaic or dialectal in Britain. So far as *cut* is concerned Horwill correctly noted in the preamble to his dictionary that in the sense of 'reduction' it was adopted almost overnight in Britain during the financial crisis of 1931, and indeed many people will remember the notorious 'ten per cent cut' inflicted by the government of the day upon the salaries of schoolteachers and others, thereby reducing public purchasing power and further increasing unemployment. It seems incredible that *crash* was not yet used in the Britain of 1936 to denote a collision between vehicles and one is tempted to think that Horwill is a little late in his dating. However the *S.E.D.* shows that the word was used in the Great War of aeroplanes, etc., coming down violently out of control, but does not define it as applying to a collision. In that same publication of 1936 Horwill pointed out the American habit of alluding to the head of each department in the offices of a newspaper or magazine as an editor; *sports editor, fashion editor,* and so on. These are now taken quite for granted in Fleet Street, together with other formations such as *industrial editor, science editor, financial editor, foreign news editor* and even *beauty editor.* (*Editorial* – which appeared first about a century ago, but throve chiefly in the U.S.A. until recently – is now a strong rival of 'leading article' and 'leader', and it is probable that it will oust them in due course, being much more self-explanatory.) Meanwhile in *A Word in Edgeways* (p. 8) Ivor Brown has drawn attention to the use of 'fiction executive' as the title assumed by the editor of a large magazine-producing firm.[1] *Executive* is an Americanism now firmly implanted in the British vocabulary, having triumphed there in the course of the nineteen-fifties. By 1954 there was a Chief Executive in British European Airways and in the course of 1958 the Beecham Group officially changed the post of managing director to 'chief executive'. *Executive* sounds an impressive word, the more so as the average Briton is not quite sure what exactly it means.

Stock phrases of a conversational type are often of American

[1] Cape, 1953.

provenance. As an avowal of ignorance, British English has long used 'I couldn't say', but this is often replaced now by the *I wouldn't know*. (This is incidentally not regarded as a particularly elegant formula by all Americans. It may be borrowed in the United States from a similar German form, via the usage of immigrants.) In Britain it started making headway in the 'thirties, and in a British serial film (*Pimpernel Smith*) of 1940 the late Leslie Howard remarked 'In the deplorable argot of the modern generation, "I wouldn't know"'. Yet this phrase is nowadays very widely used in the British Isles, and has called forth from the pen of Monsignor Ronald Knox a trenchant paragraph on the arrogance often implicit in it.

Let's face it has a brisk transatlantic ring about it and may well be American in the first instance, but it had found its way into the vocabulary of Somerset Maugham by the time he wrote *The Breadwinner*, first staged in 1930. This early attestation is somewhat surprising since Maugham's English is relatively timeless, and one would not expect such a phrase to be used by him at a time when it was not even generally current. More typical of Maugham was his complaint some years ago that he couldn't read modern novels without a dictionary since the authors used so much slang. 'What, for instance, is dig?' But it is to be feared that even armed with the 1964 *Concise Oxford Dictionary* Mr Maugham would not find this word defined in the modern sense of 'enthusiastically to approve', or as an imperative, 'examine, investigate' ('Dig him!'). Here indeed we are in the realm of slang coming ultimately from the vocabulary of American musicians-cum-drug-addicts which also gave *hip* (earlier *hep*), *cool*, *square*, etc.

As simple as that is another catch-phrase that may well be American so far as its starting-point is concerned, but again we find it at an early date in an unexpected quarter, namely in Hilaire Belloc's *The Path to Rome* (1935), during the incident of the bi-lingual mayor.[1] Of course, since no new word is involved it may be that in these cases both Maugham and Belloc simply

[1] Nelson.

happened to use a phrase quite independently of any later vogue for it, and in such an eventuality it would be merely a coincidence that they happened to put together the words which made up an expression coming to the fore many years later by other means. There is no means of throwing further light on the matter until we have yet earlier datings of the phrases involved.

As late as 1958 some viewers were still objecting vigorously to the use of *by and large* in television discussion programmes, yet they must be reconciled to it by now if only because of its appearance in *The Times*, e.g. 'By and large, Malinowski's views have stood the test of time since he propounded them' (23 May 1963). In its present sense of 'on the whole, all things considered' this has come from the United States, for Horwill notes it in his own day as 'rare in English but common in American'. In fact, Mark Twain gives a good example of the metaphorical use of the phrase at the beginning of the sixteenth chapter of his *Autobiography*, at a point written on 30 July 1906. '. . . and by and large he looked like a gasometer.'[1] As a nautical expression meaning 'to the wind and off it', as the *S.E.D.* has it, this idiom is attested as early as the second half of the seventeenth century. But what is the connection with the modern metaphor? In reply to an enquiry in the pages of the *Radio Times* a master mariner claimed that 'By means "by the wind" and *large* is a very old term meaning "off the wind". To a seaman of the very early nineteenth century the phrase would mean "on all points of sailing" ' (4 Mar 1960). From this technical sense it would obviously be easy for the secondary implication of 'in the main' to evolve.

Finally, it is perhaps noteworthy that in spite of Horwill's justifiable assertion – as late as his 1944 edition – that the metaphorical use of *by and large* was rare in England the fact remains that the phrase is included in Logan Pearsall Smith's well-known volume on *Words and Idioms* as an idiom of nautical origin.[2]

Another cliché from America is intended to cast sudden doubt on the statement the speaker himself has just made, and it is very

---

[1] Chatto and Windus, 1960.   [2] 4th ed., Constable, 1933.

effective in that it wakens up the listener who has been comfortably nodding agreement all the while. Thus, 'That is the end of the story. *Or is it?*' A curious feature of this construction is that it is always in the positive and not the negative, though logically one might have expected to find, in the imaginary example just given, a form '*Or isn't it?*' In Britain it did not become really popular until the nineteen-forties, though examples can be found in the 'twenties, as in 1927 when Sir Arthur Quiller-Couch, as King Edward VII Professor of English literature at Cambridge, followed the new fashion in *A Lecture on Lectures* when he said '. . . and Balzac was not a "worker" – or was he?' (p. 18).[1] How far this usage stretches back in the English of the United States would be difficult to say at the moment.

Another of the conversational gambits in the early American talkies which were surprising to British audiences was the frequent 'Tell me . . .', followed by a pause for breath, followed by a question. Now although this was not a general feature of British conversational technique around 1930 it had existed in Shakespearean times.

> *Tell me, where is fancy bred,*
> *Or in the heart or in the head?*
> (*Merchant of Venice*, III. ii)

But since Elizabethan times this usage had evidently suffered an eclipse, at all events in Britain, and even in the nineteen-sixties it had not been entirely accepted there, since at the beginning of that decade the *Radio Times* published a letter from an indignant reader protesting against its constant use (5 Jan 1961). Whether it had entirely died out in the eighteenth century is not clear at the moment, but it is certainly found in the closing years of the nineteenth century, in Oscar Wilde's *An Ideal Husband*. 'But tell me, Robert,' says Lord Goring in act 2, 'did you never suffer any regret for what you had done?'. Yet even this is possibly due to transatlantic example, for Wilde had spent several months in

[1] The Hogarth Press.

the States in 1882 and again in 1883. In the earlier twentieth century the same gambit appeared once in Kenneth Grahame's *The Wind in the Willows*, and was a favourite phrase in the vocabulary of Max Beerbohm. Nor must we forget that it has been set to music.

> *Now tell me, pretty maiden,*
> *Are there any more at home like you?*

But it was only towards the middle of the century, when American influence was in full blast, that the phrase really came into its own.

To return to Oscar Wilde, it would be pleasant to think that the *Oscar* of the cinema industry had some distant connection with the Oscar lode in the American silver mine opened by Wilde with a silver drill and named after him by the miners who later presented him with the drill as a memento of the ceremony, instead of – as he complained – offering him shares in the lode. But unfortunately for such conjectures it turns out that the Oscar statuette is not even made of silver, but is gold-plated. From 1927 to 1931 it was officially the Motion Picture Academy Award. One account of its present name does in fact link it with Wilde, claiming that when he arrived in America he was asked whether he had won the Newdigate Prize at Oxford. Faced with this rather improbable question he is supposed to have replied 'Yes, but while many people have won the Newdigate, it is seldom that the Newdigate gets an Oscar'. A likelier version says that Mrs Margaret Herrick, a member of the awarding academy, once looked at the statuette and exclaimed, 'It's just like my uncle Oscar'.

Another possible Americanism in Wilde's *An Ideal Husband* foreshadows the widespread British adoption of the American habit of making *philosophy* mean 'outlook, point of view'. In the first act Mrs Cheveley says that women are usually punished for being charming, whereupon Sir Robert Chilton comments 'What an appalling philosophy that sounds!' It took another half-century for this weakening of a noble word to affect British usage on a large scale, but this has now happened. 'It is our fundamental philosophy that teaching boys is a man's job', exclaimed the secretary of the National Association of Schoolmasters in March 1955, and in the *Sunday Times* Sir Miles Thomas set down his reflections on the subject of A NEW PHILOSOPHY FOR THE ROADS (19 Mar 1957). This is a far cry from the definition of philosophy as 'love of wisdom, a system of conduct for life', but this narrowing of meaning is perhaps symptomatic of modern specialization of interests and attitudes. The ultimate semantic shift is seen in 'the philosophy of the nuclear deterrent', mentioned in a University of London petition to the then Prime Minister (29 Mar 1958).

Expressions relating to time and place have not always developed along the same lines on both sides of the Atlantic, and the story is told that when Charles Dickens was in the United States he was asked whether he would have his meal *right away*, but that after a moment's careful consideration of the question he replied that he would like to have it just where he was.[1] This mistake would be impossible today in Britain, where this synonym of 'immediately' has enjoyed so great a success over the last twenty years that it is to be thought of as belonging to the standard language. *Right now* is perhaps not quite so well established, but even so there must be many people who do not remember – or have never known – that it is an original Americanism. In a British film of the nineteen-fifties, *The Man Who Loved Redheads*, it was used anachronistically in a scene set in 1917. In reality *right now* (like *right away*) was one of the phrases in the first American talkies which were quite novel to British audiences.

The various American compounds of 'just' have also met with great popularity – *just when, just where, just what, just how*, and so forth. These tend to supplant the native 'when exactly, what precisely' and similar expressions. 'Many who value the name

---

[1] For the British usage, cf. Surtees in *Plain or Ringlets?* (1860) '. . . the hounds had found their fox immediately and gone right away, nobody knew where'.

of Christian still find it reasonable to believe that he did just that,'
said Monsignor Knox in a sermon preached on 13 June 1943.[1]
But this is quite an early example for Britain.

At one time 'that way' was used in British when indicating a
direction in space; 'You go that way to London', or in descriptions of processes; 'You catch the ball that way'. It could also
apply to the recipe for a particular manner of doing something,
and thus in *Kipps* (1905) H. G. Wells wrote that 'Some people
like it that way' when referring to whisky and soda. American
habits of speech caused the phrase to be used in wider contexts,
and particularly with abstract verbs, in sentences where British
idiom would normally have chosen to say 'like that'. Naturalization of this phenomenon was especially helped round about 1930
by a very successful song heard in an early American musical
film, for in it were the lines

> *When I pretend I'm gay*
> *I never feel that way . . .*

The phrase reappeared in 1934 in the autobiography of a
Scottish working-class writer, *I, James Whittaker*. 'The War
upset the whole world, and it did the ordinary social movements
no good – at least, I feel that way' (p. 23).[2] Of course, when a
phrase already exists in a certain speech-community it can easily
take on an extension of usage without anyone being very conscious of what is happening. By 1955 an advertisement for a
make of shoes was able to portray two feet, along with the
legend

GOOD NOW

KEEP THEM THAT WAY

So far as actual British usage is concerned – as opposed to passive
understanding of the Americanism – *that way* in the new sense
started becoming popular towards 1948 or so, and is now simply
regarded as part of the language by most people.

[1] *The Occasional Sermons of Ronald A. Knox* (Burns and Oates, 1960), p. 227.
[2] Rich and Cowan.

American English frequently produces such compounds as *way over*, *way down* or *way back* in which the first element adds emphasis and some vague idea of motion or distance. 'Now Scottish, Northern and U.S.' says the *S.E.D.* 'Way down upon the Swanee River' must have been most Englishmen's sole acquaintance with this type of idiom until the nineteen-thirties when some younger speakers began to copy it. In the 'fifties it started appearing in print. 'Way over on the other side of Paris ...' wrote the author of an article in the *Daily Telegraph* (8 Apr 1954). Some people appeared at that same time to find 'way' too colloquial and so replaced it by 'away' in this type of phrase. Thus 'away back' was used by a Fellow of Magdalen College, Oxford, in a Third Programme talk (11 Jul 1954). However it is difficult to know how to classify this fuller form, for it may be (*a*) a direct adoption of the American full form, (*b*) a British remodelling of 'way' into 'away', or (*c*) an extension of an older British – but probably provincial usage. So far as this last is concerned, we find in a book published in 1895, *The Maister, A Century of Tyneside Life*, that 'the "Keelers" of Tynemouth were a recognised class away back in the days of the early charters' (p. 35).[1] At all events Horwill did not know it as British in 1944, when he explained in his dictionary that 'Am. *away back*=Eng. *as long ago as*'.

In the phrase *to go back on* (one's word, etc.) the Americanism really lies not in 'back' but 'on', since in Victorian English the expression was 'to go back from one's word', though this was not very frequently used.[2] The new phrase can be employed with a variety of nouns. In *Old Men Forget* Duff Cooper quotes from his diary of June 1944 '. . . only I could persuade him to go back on his decision' (p. 332).[3]

A well-known feature of American idiom is the liking for the construction 'verb plus preposition(s)', e.g. *to meet up with*, and a

[1] Geo. H. Haswell (W. Scott Ltd.).
[2] '. . . for some reason of her own, she wants to go back from her word' writes Trollope in *Barchester Towers* (1857), chapter xxv.
[3] Hart-Davis, 1953.

great many expressions of this type have percolated into standard British: *to slip up, to stand for,* 'tolerate' (hence Groucho Marx's statement that in his day a co-ed stood for something – and some of them stood for plenty), *to stand up to, to get away with* (cf. a *getaway,* and *make a getaway*), *to get by with, to fall for, to beat up, to shoot up,* etc. *To check up on,* for 'check', shows that American is not always more concise than British, though in fact the two expressions are not quite the same in American usage, for one. checks the battery of a car but checks up on a statement (a more abstract process than that involved in a mechanical or chemical test). However both are now equally current in Britain, though it is still possible to use the verb 'test' of batteries and other devices.

In spite of the American love of prepositions there is at least one expression which is now losing its preposition as a consequence of American example. A well-established British synonym of 'male adult' was 'a grown-up man', as when G. K. Chesterton wrote in his essay on *Fear,* 'I know a grown-up man who is still frightened of the dark'. But the American phrase *grown man* leaves out the preposition and this neologism is now taking hold in Britain.[1] (Possibly the American preference for this form without any preposition is based on the corresponding German *Erwachsener* by way of the speech of immigrants, as described in the following chapter.)

To *cash in on* is now standard usage, as in Duff Cooper's *Old Men Forget,* in which he wrote in 1953 that '. . . it would be as well to precipitate a General Election so as to cash in on our triumph' (p. 251). It will be seen from this example that the allusion is figurative and indeed the idiom does not necessarily imply any financial gain, so that the advantage involved is often one of a rather abstract kind. To *make out* in the American sense of 'succeed, manage, get on' as opposed to the traditional British meaning of 'to claim' ('He makes out he knows the answer') is steadily gaining ground east of the Atlantic but is perhaps not quite standard just yet, whereas to *make* in the new sense of

[1] e.g. 'The Russian did not approve of giving grown men time off from work to study general subjects' in the *New Statesman* (13 Sep 1963).

'attain, succeed in reaching' – hitherto used only of ships making port so far as Britain is concerned – is now generally acceptable. 'It is sometimes said that officers have very little chance of getting on in the Army if they fail to make the Staff College' says *The Times* (3 Sep 1955). 'Making the grade' is even more firmly entrenched, being dated by the *S.E.D.* as appearing in Britain in 1930.

To *break even*, cited by Paul C. Berg's dictionary as being an Americanism, is now very widespread. In *The Life and Times of Baron Haussmann* (1957) we find '... thereafter it gradually recouped its losses by means of the tax and broke even in 1863' (p. 126).[1] This is certainly a useful addition to the vocabulary as a short way of expressing 'to make neither gain nor loss', and in essence is presumably a development of the American phrase 'an even break', in the sense explained by Horwill's dictionary as equivalent to 'quits' (and not quite the same as in the well-known piece of advice 'Never give a sucker an even break').

Get around to means roughly 'to summon up enough energy, or have the time, to do something'. So, from the *Spectator*, 'The fact is that Whitehall had been contemplating changing the regulations for years, but never got around to it' (19 Nov 1954). And, in the sense of existing or being extant, *to be around* is probably more frequent by now than the traditional form 'to be about'. A relatively early case is seen in an article on Arnold Bennett in *John O'London's Weekly* which speaks of someone who 'rebukes the enemies of Bennett who are still around' (11 Jun 1954). With regard to the single word 'around' – a latecomer to the language which is not attested in Shakespeare or the Authorized Version – Horwill points out (1944) that in the U.S.A. it is used in some cases where an Englishman would say 'round', and his dictionary instances 'The Little Church Around the Corner'. Yet this is now quite familiar to Englishmen, who in 1963 were informed in an advertisement issued by the National Savings Committee that THE WAY TO SAVE IS ONLY AROUND THE CORNER. Some years ago John Wain also made a similar statement to the effect that

[1] J. M. and Brian Chapman (Weidenfeld and Nicolson).

this use of 'around' for 'round' was an Americanism, but that it was becoming frequent in the works of Robert Graves. True as that all is, one cannot avoid the impression that phrases of the type 'around the corner' have been current in provincial English for some considerable time now, and certainly during the last generation at least. Was it a British or an American author who wrote the words for Gracie Fields' song, current in the early 'thirties, *Around the Corner and Under the Tree*?

In accordance with the modern love of piled-up prepositions one no longer merely 'faces' a difficult situation but *faces up to it*. Sir Walter Raleigh, the Oxford professor, used this expression in a letter of 4 September 1920 when mentioning someone who 'faced up to the paradox of man'.[1] It is highly significant in view of his inclusion of this Americanism that he had been to the United States, and this early British example is a splendid illustration of the way in which personal visits to the other side of the Atlantic can play a part in bringing American expressions back to England.

Horwill's dictionary pointed out that 'win' in its intransitive sense was often intensified in the States by the addition of 'out', and gave the example 'The wild extremists always win out', adding that an Englishman would say 'pull through' or 'carry the day'. (He did not mention the American *lose out* though this is now constantly heard in Britain along with *win out*).[2] 'Already there are some signs,' wrote the editor of *Encounter*, 'that the spoken word . . . may finally win out over the recorded image' (Jul 1955). Horwill likewise drew attention to an American usage whereby *stop off* or *stop over* meant 'to break one's journey', but by 1955 Mrs Nicholas was able to tell us in one of her accounts of holiday travel in the *Sunday Times* that 'you cannot expect to be able to stop off at Paris, Bordeaux and Madrid on the way and pay no more' (24 Jul), and three years later the same newspaper

[1] *The Letters of Sir Walter Raleigh* (Methuen, 1928), vol. 2.

[2] 'Nearly one in every two, 47 per cent, think that Labour gains from this difference in ages. Only eight per cent think that Labour loses out because of it' (*Daily Telegraph* 9 Mar 1963).

produced the heading PREMIER STOPS OFF IN SINGAPORE (19 Jan 1958), although in that same week a writer in the *Times Literary Supplement* had sternly reproved an author for using this type of expression in a non-American context. Along with *stop off* goes *take time off* which is now quite at home in British writing and talking. A *Spectator* article talks about 'theorists who indulge the undemocratic vice of taking time off to think' (10 Dec 1954). This idiom is curiously typical of a certain American attitude which suggests that there is something faintly improper about having any leisure time at all – an outlook which is unfortunately becoming very common on the British side of the Atlantic also.

The American verb with the extra preposition does not invariably take rapid root in Britain, however, witness the expression *start in*, for 'start'. As early as 1922 C. E. Montague was making use of this in his *Disenchantment*. 'The new company commander who started in as a captain . . .' (chapter 2). Yet it had made but little headway here, quite unlike *start out*, pointed to by Horwill as an Americanism, though this is probably a revelation to most people. Occasionally the Americanism consists of the substitution of one preposition for another, as in *catch up on* for 'catch up with', and in this way Mr Henry Brooke, as financial secretary to the Treasury, was able to say that '. . . the Inland Revenue is constantly seeking new means to catch up on tax evaders' (28 Oct 1954). More famous than this is the well-known replacement of 'aim at' by the American *aim to*. So, in *The Times*, 'Professor E. J. Richards aims to develop the study of missile and space technology' (9 Jan 1958). Actually, this Americanism would seem to be merely the survival in the United States of a former English usage widely current in the eighteenth century, and to be found, for example, in Samuel Johnson's *Prologue Spoken by Mr. Garrick at the Opening of the Theatre in Drury-Lane, 1747.*

> *Vice always found a sympathetic friend;*
> *They pleas'd their Age, and did not aim to mend.*

Less well-known is an old rhyme quoted by Thomas Cooper on p. 20 of his *Life* and evidently inscribed above a picture he saw during his boyhood at his uncle's house, about 1814.

> *Gamesters and puss alike doe watch,*
> *And plaie with those they aim to catch.*[1]

The modern advantage of this construction is that it requires the infinitive instead of the gerund and is therefore shorter and more convenient for newspaper headlines, as in the *Sunday Times* where we read that POLAND AIMS TO SELL MORE BACON (1 Nov 1959). In the general structure of the English language it is possibly felt to be parallel with the similar construction of the near-synonymous 'to hope to' and 'to mean to' which cannot of course be followed by 'at'.

To *consult with* is not quite the same as 'consult', since the latter is liable to imply that there is a willingness to accept any advice received from the consultant, whereas the longer expression simply conjures up a picture of people putting their heads together in the hope of finding a solution. The present vogue for *consult with* seems to have been inspired by American practice, though in fact it was not unknown in Britain even in the nineteenth century, for it is used not only by Dickens, but also by Meredith in *The Egoist* (1879), by Trollope in *Barchester Towers* (1857) and by R. S. Surtees in *Plain or Ringlets?* (1860) where a lady went to 'consult with the cook'. An early example – though strictly this is not perhaps British English – is from evidence given by a constable and recorded by the Clerk of the Court at Sydney in 1811 at the trial of James Hardy Vaux. 'Prisoner told him, that he had been consulting with Mr Colles . . .' (p. xlv of preface to *The Memoirs of James Hardy Vaux*).[2]

The recent *arrive back* is also of American origin. An early British example is to be found in the year 1938 in vol. II of D. B. Quinn's *The Port Books of Southampton for the Reign of*

[1] 5th edition (Hodder and Stoughton, 1873).
[2] Heinemann, 1964.

Edward IV where in the introduction it is stated that a medieval galley 'arrived back in Southampton from Flanders'.

Another American curiosity pointed out by Horwill was the expression *let up* which he explained as 'to slacken'. Yet it was used by General Montgomery in his order of 20 March 1943. 'We will not stop, or let up, till Tunis has been captured.' Indeed even this is not the earliest British dating since the *O.E.D.* points out that Galsworthy made use of it.

Changed social habits facilitate – and necessitate – the introduction into Britain of certain Americanisms. Young married couples going out for an evening's entertainment engage the services of a *baby-sitter* to look after the children (not always babies) and she is often a *teenager*, formerly described as 'a girl in her teens'. *Teenager* was well established by the late nineteen-forties, and is a monument to the process whereby adolescents have become a coherent and demanding group in their own right rather than incomplete adults. Conversely there has been a blurring of the sharp lines of pre-war courting customs and the modern tentative camaraderie which may or may not end in a more formal engagement required a new terminology, hence the adoption of *boy friend* and *girl friend* from America. True, G. K. Chesterton wrote of Swift's correspondence with 'his girl friend, or rather, his girl friends' in his essay *Contradicting Thackeray*, published well before the first world war, and earlier still in Oscar Wilde's *An Ideal Husband* Mrs Cheveley said 'I am afraid I am not fond of girl friends', but in these cases the reference is merely to female friends and is different from the present usage. In *A History of Courting*[1] the historian of the subject, E. S. Turner, states that 'from some unknown source the expressions 'boy friend' and 'girl friend' had come into use' (p. 216), not realizing that the source was America, although *boy friend* is attested as a written form for the year 1925 in the *Dictionary of Americanisms* compiled by Mitford M. Mathews.

Because of differences in the physical conditions of the two countries it often happens that British speakers and writers use

[1] Michael Joseph, 1954.

American figures of speech which, if interpreted literally, form no part of their own experience. This is the case for a number of metaphors taken from the life of farm, field and wood, since Britain is much more urban in character than the United States. The result is that British people have little or no knowledge of the customs and practices behind certain expressions which they are quite prepared to use metaphorically. Thus *to have a chip on one's shoulder* is to behave in an aggressive manner, because of the American custom of placing a chip of wood on one's shoulder and defying someone to invite a fight by knocking it off. The traditional British expression was 'to trail one's coat', now somewhat old-fashioned. *To scrape the bottom of the barrel* is something that probably very few Englishmen have done in a literal sense, but they like to use this American phrase nowadays with the meaning of using up the last of one's resources. And to be *out on a limb*, that is, in a precarious position, is an idiom borrowed into Britain from a nation that has in its time had great experience of felling timber. As a matter of fact the use of 'limb' for 'branch' is something of an Americanism in itself and a confirmation of the origin of the phrase. But the most curious borrowing of this type is *backlog*, a word that has had a sad fate in British usage. The literal meaning in the United States is 'a large log at the back of the fireplace to keep the fire going', and so quite logically the American metaphorical sense is 'something to be relied on in emergency, something to fall back on', witness the following sentence from the *Atlantic Monthly*, written by a lady who found herself suddenly widowed and in financial need. 'What backlog there was we had saved together' (Oct 1954). Similarly when an American manufacturer speaks of having a backlog of orders he means to imply that his firm is fortunately situated, since there is plenty of work to be done. But in Britain this borrowing has taken on an unpleasant note, implying arrears of work due to strikes, shortages and difficulties in general. So deep-rooted is this interpretation of it in the British mind that sometimes the very form of the word has been known to be altered into 'backlag', on the analogy of 'lag'. Thus in the *Daily Telegraph* of 2 April

1954, although *backlog* appeared in an article, 'backlag' occurred twice in a reader's letter. At all events it can definitely be laid down that *backlog* as used by an Englishman invariably denotes an unpleasant problem to be dealt with, rather than a comfortable margin of safety. This semantic change can be regarded as a classic example of how language is affected by national psychology and local material conditions, but the misunderstanding was made possible only by the rarity of log-fires in Britain and the consequent lack of familiarity of the literal sense and implications of the word. So we shall continue to hear about 'serious backlogs' and 'formidable backlogs' in the British economy.

On 12 September 1954 the *Sunday Times* published an article by its music critic under the heading HINDSIGHT IN CRITICISM. *Hindsight* is a most useful addition to the British vocabulary, for hitherto we have had no single word to denote 'wisdom after the event'. In the United States it appears to have originated as something of a pun on 'foresight', since the hindsight of a rifle is the opposite of the foresight. However this play on words does not survive the crossing of the Atlantic, because in Britain the soldier speaks of the backsight of his rifle and not the hindsight, though in fact the latter term occurs in the S.E.D. for both literal and metaphorical uses in the nineteenth century. In spite of the dictionary there is no doubt that this word had died out in Britain by the first half of the twentieth century and that its present use there is due to its revival by American influence. It is also possible that the American preference for speaking of the hindsight of a rifle is due to the fortuitous resemblance of 'backsight' to 'backside', thus causing its avoidance in polite society.

Gimmick, a device for the purpose of attracting publicity, is an Americanism which made its way into Britain during the 'fifties, though it was certainly current in the United States in the nineteen-twenties. The origin is unknown, though 'gimcrack' has been somewhat implausibly suggested, and all that can be said is that the present meaning is really metaphorical, since in

American usage the first recorded sense applies to 'a mechanical device whereby a gambling apparatus (as a roulette wheel) can be secretly and dishonestly controlled' as the 1961 edition of Webster has it. From this rather specialized application it seems to have come to denote any new and ingenious device, and then a novel or unconventional technique or angle of approach. The adjective *gimmicky* has also passed into British English, though not much has yet been heard of the corresponding verb *to gimmick* which, as shown by Webster, is extant in the United States with the meaning 'alter or influence by means of a gimmick'. *Gimmickry* implies a systematic use of gimmicks and an undue reliance on them. All told, this is certainly a useful family of words at a time when highly competitive commercial methods rely more and more upon the unorthodox and the unexpected in order to achieve high sales.

American is sometimes more pompous and long-winded than British, as in the cumbersome *in the event that* for 'if', a ponderous phrase which is gaining ground in Britain though only very slowly. (Yet as early as Chaucer's time there was a similar construction 'in case that'.) A police report about the probable effect of a proposed change in the law said that 'it would preclude them taking proceedings in the event that they were required to investigate suspected illegal ownership . . .' (*Daily Express*, 3 Mar 1954). The relative pomposity of some American nomenclature was commented on by Vera Brittain, recounting her experience in the United States, when she said that questions put by members of the audience were elevated to the dignity of a *forum* (*Atlantic Monthly*, Jun 1935). Yet nowadays this word is very frequently met with in Britain and is used in radio and TV programmes, newspapers and magazines to denote the section devoted to general comment and discussion. At one time the B.B.C. had a weekly 'Domestic Forum' where speakers debated the merits of a particular shade of green for the kitchen curtains, and so on. Indeed twenty years after Miss Brittain's comment on this word, the organisers of the National Corset Week (a fine example in itself of the American-inspired habit of consecrating particular weeks to worthy causes) held a 'Forum on Form' in a well-known London hotel in March 1955. It is perhaps by now necessary to tell ourselves that not so long ago 'forum' was a reminder of the glories of ancient Rome.

It is not surprising that such inveterate travellers as the Americans have added new expressions to the vocabulary of the booking office and tourist agency. The *round trip* neatly expresses a concept which had borne in Britain the dangerously ambiguous label of 'return journey'. (Though our 'return ticket' shows no signs of becoming a round-trip ticket.) As an early official example of this expression we may instance its use by Mr Petei Masefield, Chief Executive (itself an Americanism that has spread very rapidly) of B.E.A. in the *Sunday Times* (4 Jul 1954). And one wonders whether the headline in the *Daily Telegraph*, SATELLITE HAS MADE 249 ROUND TRIPS (21 Oct 1957) is a case of conscious or unconscious humour! *Commutei* has taken some time to establish itself in Britain. (In the United States a season ticket is a *commuted fare ticket*, so the holder was known as a *commuter*.) The word began to appear in the London press in 1954, usually as the pseudonym of correspondents complaining about overcrowded trains, and put into inverted commas. In March of that year the *Daily Express* thought it necessary to explain the meaning of *commute* to its readers when discussing the travelling arrangements of an American boxer, though the *Southern Daily Echo* took the word in its stride a couple of months later. 'He spends the winter in the West Indies and summer in England, commuting back and forth like the migrating swallows' (25 May 1954). This somewhat metaphorical use is rather surprising at such an early date. By 1960 *commute* showed signs of being used for driving a car to and from work every day, an idea which cuts adrift from the original 'commuted fare ticket', which in any case was never known to most British speakers. There has been some unmistakable opposition to this verb and its noun, possibly because to the thoughtful speaker it seems totally 'unmotivated', i.e. to have no connection with the normal sense of 'commute'. At the back of the British mind there is also the consciousness of the legal sense 'of commuting' a death sentence to one of life imprisonment, and it may seem almost improper to use the word in any other way. Yet the new usage seems well established by now, at least in journalistic and official circles, in spite of the ordinary speaker's relative lack of enthusiasm for it. As late as 1962 there was still a certain amount of active opposition to this 'vile and canting term', and the commuter was described as 'somehow only half a man, defined by the way he buys his railway ticket'.

To remain in the sphere of railway transport, we may note that it has recently become fashionable to speak of a goods train as a *freight train* in the American fashion that had caught the attention of earlier commentators. Referring to American usage in *Our Language*, Simeon Potter wrote in 1950 that 'A goods train is called a freight train' (p. 160), and rather earlier Horwill had said 'In England this term [freight] is applied to goods transported by water only. In America it includes land transport also' (p. 141). As a matter of fact 'freight' is nowadays also used of merchandise carried by air, but a point to notice is that in some of the expressions usual in the terminology of the American railroad there can be detected a nautical influence, as though the early pioneers of transport had considered railway travel to be an extension of navigation (and probably the navigation of rivers rather than of the sea). Hence, the application of *crew* to the men operating a locomotive. In Britain this borrowing has attached itself particularly to bus transport, e.g. '... according to one trade-unionist, London bus crews have a worse rating than grave-diggers' (*Observer*, 3 Nov 1963).

It so happens that the terminology of rail travel is strikingly different in British and American English, for the obvious reason that the invention of the passenger railway took place well after American independence. So the British 'sleeper' is the American 'tie' (in full, 'cross-tie'), the 'line' is the 'track' and so on. (Though 'track' has made great progress in Britain in late years.) *Railroad* is often thought of as being characteristically American. During the first half of the present century this was virtually the case, though it is now appearing more frequently in purely British contexts. But the interesting fact is that this is really a resuscitation, by way of American influence, of an originally British word! It is too often forgotten that while passenger railways using the steam locomotive on iron rails did not appear until the early nineteenth century, the invention of iron rails belongs to the eighteenth century, while the use of wooden rails for the transport of coal from colliery to river or sea was common in Northumberland and Durham by the seventeenth century. (The concept of rail transport of a primitive sort can actually be found in the first century B.C. when the Roman architect Vitruvius reported that certain engineers had the idea of moving a whole monument by hoisting it on to *regulae* i.e. wooden rails which would 'regulate' the movement.) So it was that 'railroad' was being used in England in the eighteenth century, though 'railway' seems to have preceded it by a generation or so, and the newer use continued until about the middle of the next century, after which it died out for no obvious reason, except in America.[1] The result was that for about a century the word was thought of as an Americanism, and indeed even at the present day it has only limited currency in Britain as a result of American influence. Here again we see an example of an obsolete term being reimplanted from America, however.

Real estate is also a surprisingly old expression and dates back to the seventeenth century, but whereas in the British Isles it remained mostly within the strictly technical domain it soon became in America the everyday way of referring to immovable property, or what an Englishman simply calls 'property'. It has made only slow headway in Britain so far as general usage is concerned and this is curious when it is reflected that a man dealing in property has long been known as an estate agent. Perhaps the truth of the matter is that to the British mind the word 'estate' is somehow linked with the spacious lands of the aristocracy; indeed another meaning of 'estate agent' is that of the

[1] Thackeray tells us 'There were no railroads made when Arthur Pendennis went to the famous University of Oxbridge' (1850).

overseer of a nobleman's estate. Furthermore *real estate* seems an incomprehensible and slightly comic word to the average man on the British side of the Atlantic, who wonders on hearing it whether there is any such thing as 'unreal estate'.

By the way it must not be implied that Americanisms infiltrating into the British scene do not meet with opposition. Indeed the well-known B.B.C. announcer Alvar Lidell denounces 'the tendency not to be so resistant to Americanisms. I am very much aware of them and dislike them' (*Time and Tide*, 28 May 1960). Sir Compton Mackenzie describes *the British way of life* as 'that ridiculous phrase' (*Spectator*, 7 Nov 1954) and a contributor to the *Daily Mail* voiced the opinion of many when he wrote that 'our daughter is what is hideously termed a teen-ager' (25 Mar 1954). Sometimes repugnance is mingled with grudging admiration as when in 1951 a member of Parliament said in the House, 'I hate some of these American expressions, but in this case manufacturing 'know-how' explains best what I mean'.[1] In America *know-how* is over a century old, but it crossed the Atlantic on a large scale only in the late nineteen-forties. Curiously enough it was brought to the attention of the British public by a South African, the late Field-Marshal Smuts, during a famous speech in which he said 'You have the know-how'. The same speech contrasted the relative decline of the military and economic power of Britain as contrasted with those of the U.S.A. and the Soviet Union. This was a novel idea at the time, and could not have been acceptable to the correspondent who wrote to the *Radio Times* asking 'Why has the B.B.C. succumbed to the use of the word 'Britisher'? . . . Britons never shall be slaves, not even to American forms of diction' (17 June 1955). In the following year a reader of the *Daily Mail* was still holding out (to use an Americanism) on *know-how* and protesting against 'this two-syllable word' and asking 'What is wrong with "knowledge"?' (14 Mar 1956), to which the answer can only be 'Nothing except the fact that it has two syllables!'

In the middle 'fifties a British judge vehemently rebuked the

[1] Quoted by Paul C. Berg in *A Dictionary of New Words in English*.

American defendant's use in 'his' court of the expression *witness-stand* and insisted with some heat on having 'witness-box'. (Yet on 6 December 1957 the B.B.C. news mentioned 'witness-stand' in connection with the so-called Bank Rate tribunal. Perhaps the Americanism was regarded as slightly more suitable for proceedings of this exceptional type where no-one was actually being accused.) Strong emotion also must have been experienced by the *Daily Telegraph* reader who denounced *transportation* in the sense of 'transport' as 'this vile word', though he was prepared to allow an exception in the case of ships calling at Sydney, 'which may well have Botany Bay within its civic bounds' (7 May 1956).[1] The same newspaper once published a letter from a reader with a hyphenated name who expressed indignation about the statement of a Cabinet minister that 'We are not suckers'. Was this 'proof of our solidarity with our American cousins?' asked the writer (17 Oct 1958). The editor of *Time and Tide* was likewise taken to task by a sorrowing reader who complained that in the space of three months that periodical had used 'the Americanisms freighter, pollster, radio, back-log, sidewalks, stag-line, phoney and movie. I do not see that any of these improves in precision or euphony on the English cargo-ship, voter, wireless, pavements, false and film. Back-log and stag-line are mere guess-work to me' (15 Oct 1955). There are one or two points calling for comment here. First, a *pollster* is not a voter but someone conducting an opinion poll. Then it is interesting to see that in 1955 *radio* could still meet with opposition on the score of being an Americanism, and that in the same year *back-log* could be totally unknown to a literate Englishman.

The fact is that in some quarters the denunciation of Americanisms is a major hobby, and the correspondence columns of newspapers can always be relied on to provide criticism of the B.B.C. along these lines. Indeed the B.B.C. itself must be a linguistic battleground on occasions, if one is to judge by variants of vocabulary in successive readings of the news bulletins of a

[1] The creation of a Chair of Transportation in the University of Birmingham called forth (unavailing) protests in January 1964.

given day. For example on the occasion of Mr R. A. Butler's wedding in 1959 the 6 p.m. television news bulletin announced that 'The village grapevine spread the news', but by the time of the 7.25 version this had been amended to 'Village rumour had spread the news'. Authority must have expressed its displeasure in the meantime. In this meaning *grapevine* is equivalent to the British 'bush telegraph', but in its literal use it alludes in the U.S.A. to the vine. Of course in Britain this would usually be regarded as a pleonasm, but the point is that in American English 'vine' is used of any type of creeping plant; rose vines, pea vines and so on. But *grapevine* is certainly a useful word for that mysterious system – no doubt as convoluted and inextricably intertwined as the plant itself – which spreads rumour so rapidly.[1] It is a pity not to have any written evidence of its early appearance in Britain, though in 1955 I was fortunate enough to hear from an anonymous informant that it had for some time been current in Brixton prison. It is also pleasant to reflect that *The Grapevine* is the title of a periodical published by the Institute of Education of Durham University.

In their absorption with individual words many linguistic historians tend to overlook phrases, so it may be as well to stress the importance of this aspect of borrowing from American idiom. Phrases are usually spread by the B.B.C. and journalese, though occasionally they come to us as technical terms, as *in the red* meaning 'insolvent, in debt', which is a reference to the useful banking custom of entering the details of an account in red ink when the point of insolvency has been reached by the customer. This phrase, together with its opposite *in the black*, is commented on by Horwill as coming from American accountants, and gives a quotation including them both which is taken from a speech of Franklin D. Roosevelt delivered in 1933. Colloquially, *in the red* was to be heard in Britain from the middle nineteen-forties, but

[1] It is incorrectly glossed by the 1950 and 1964 editions of the *Concise Oxford Dictionary* as 'rumour, false report'. A good example, by the way, of the American use of 'vine' is found in the 'tomato vines' mentioned in the opening paragraphs of Mark Twain's *Tom Sawyer* (1876). It is surprising that Compton Mackenzie used *grape-vines* in the literal sense in *Sinister Street* (1913).

it took another ten years for it to pass into serious contexts. 'Already some companies are operating in the red . . .' wrote the *Manchester Guardian* (27 Nov 1956) while in the following year a *Times* heading declared RUSSIA IS IN THE RED (14 May 1957) and the report of the Arts Council in October 1957 was starkly entitled ART IN THE RED.

In the United States a *bandwagon* heads a circus procession and so *to be on the bandwagon* is simply to be on the winning side, particularly in politics. As an institution this homely vehicle is unknown in England, but language is never hampered by concrete realities and its name now appears in British idiom as in the United States. A *Sunday Times* article said '. . . if Britain is not ready to jump on the bandwagon of Brazilian development, there are plenty of competing nations who are only too ready to do so' (13 Feb 1955) and only a few days later the *Times Educational Supplement* stated in the editorial 'Civil servants and university teachers jumped on the band-wagon moved by a mixture of opportunism and fear'. As early as the final months of the inter-war period the B.B.C. used the word as the title of a weekly entertainment headed by Arthur Askey, though it is likely that at that time very few listeners realized that this was an Americanism and they mostly imagined that it had been thought up by some inventive scriptwriter.

A phrase which is no longer thought of as particularly colloquial is *in a big way*, an expression which can boast of having been used by Mr Justice Pilcher at the Kent Assizes held at Maidstone towards the end of 1954, though it is perhaps relevant to say that it was to an American airman that the learned judge put the question 'She was going for the beer in a big way?' (*News of the World*, 5 Dec 1954). In the next year this phrase was in the annual statement of the chairman of the Amalgamated Press Ltd. who alluded to 'a large receptive readership having money to lay out regularly in a big way' (*Sunday Times*, 10 Jul 1955). A curious fact is that 'in a small way' has existed from the eighteenth century, but the opposite of this was supposedly 'in a great way'. But as will be seen later there is reason to believe that *in a big way* is ultimately due to German example.

To hold down is often used of the retention of a post or situation and the correct performance of the duties attached to it. '. . . our self-respect and our sense of being of use in the world are closely bound up with the ability to hold down a job'.[1] Yet when Horwill was compiling his dictionary of American usage he felt obliged to point out this expression as an Americanism, and here as so often his dictionary is now out of date because of British acceptance of a transatlantic idiom. *To hold up* 'rob', and *hold-up* 'armed robbery' are now part of the British vocabulary, but it is not easy to trace the origin of these usages. Both Horwill and the *S.E.D.* take it that the starting point is the fact that the victims were made to hold up their hands at the point of the revolver, but this explanation does not seem quite satisfactory. After all, it is the criminals who 'hold up' their victims and it would be strange if the term should be derived from an action carried out by the latter, as Horwill appears to have realized. Surely the truth of the matter is that *hold-up* for an armed robbery arose from the 'holding up' of vehicles, which is quite an old idiom in the United States, attested as early as 1837 and defined by M. M. Mathews's *Dictionary of Americanisms* as 'Holdup. A check or stoppage in the progress of a vehicle, a delay or obstruction'. In order to rob travellers it was necessary for bandits first to bring their vehicle to a halt, and so presumably *holdup* took in this way the additional sense of 'armed robbery of the contents of a vehicle', being applied later to armed robbery in general. This modern general meaning dates back to 1878 in the United States according to Mathews.

Wait on, meaning 'await, expect with desire or anxiety' is marked as obsolete by the *O.E.D.* but it now appears in the press as a result of American influence, never having become archaic in the U.S.A. However an early non-journalistic example dates from 1951, when Simone Weil's *L'attente de Dieu* was translated as *Waiting on God*, unlike Beckett's *En attendant Godot*, rendered by the more usual construction *Waiting for Godot*. Also in 1951,

[1] *The Economics of Everyday Life*, Gertrude Williams (Penguin Books, 1950).

in a letter written on Michaelmas Day, Rose Macaulay said 'It [a book] is very good on waiting on each moment and meeting God in it'.[1] But only by 1961 did the expression become more widespread. 'The nation waits on the railwaymen, to see if there will be a strike or not, and the railwaymen wait on Claude William Guillebaud' wrote the *Observer* (7 Feb 1960) and three weeks later a contributor to *Time and Tide* kept the stylistic repetition when saying 'There seems to be an increasing danger in all this that the Government may wait on the TUC for action while the TUC wait on the Government'. An advertisement for a camera in the *Daily Mail* during the following year claimed that 'This Swiss-built masterpiece doesn't have to wait on the sun' (10 May 1961) showing that the idiom had descended into the market-place by then.

Thomas Pyles cites the use of *begin to* (with a negative) as an Americanism.[2] An early British example is to be found in a letter from Sir Walter Raleigh, significantly written from Rhode Island during a tour of the United States. 'I can't begin to tell about America' (30 Mar 1915).[3] This type of construction is now very widely used in British speech and writing, having become popular during the second war, as when Sir Alan Brooke's war diary for 22 February 1944 says 'It is quite clear to me . . . that he does not begin to understand the Italian campaign'. So far as American is concerned this idiom is at least a century old, judging from a letter of 1858 written in North Carolina. Speaking of the local young ladies, the writer stated 'they can't begin to compare to our amiable, generous, high minded, open hearted mountain gals'.[4] Perhaps the only surprising feature of this particular borrowing is that it has taken so long to establish itself on the British side of the Atlantic.

It is impossible to omit from this short review some mention of the art of *passing the buck*, that is, the evasion of some difficulty

---

[1] *Letters for a Friend.* The book she means is surely Simone Weil's.

[2] *Op. cit.* p. 163.

[3] *The Letters of Sir Walter Raleigh* (1879-1922).

[4] *Tarheel talk*, ed. Norman E. Eliason (Univ. of North Carolina Press, 1956), p. 96.

or responsibility by pushing it on to someone else. The phrase is now at home in Britain where it has evidently filled a semantic gap. 'It was the breakdown of civil authority that allowed the soldiers to pass the buck,' said an article in the *Spectator* (10 Dec 1954). This 'buck' is not of course the American dollar but evidently comes from the game of poker. In his admirable *Phrase and Word Origins* Alfred H. Holt suggests that it may in this connection be linked with the old scape-goat idea or with 'bucking the tiger', an old phrase for gambling.[1] In British English, at any rate, the buck is metaphorically passed without the slightest awareness of any link with gambling.

An article in *The Times* about Thackeray made a reference to 'magazines that folded up then as now in untimely fashion' (23 Dec 1963). *Fold up* or *fold* in this sense of failing or going bankrupt is of pure American origin but has gained a strong foothold in the British vocabulary. Curiously, Horwill's dictionary makes no mention of this at all, perhaps because it had very nearly died out of use in the U.S.A. round about the time that Horwill was first writing, in 1935. Since then this figure of speech has become quite vigorous on both sides of the Atlantic.

It is not often that writers are so obliging as to furnish us with passing comments on the Americanisms put into the mouths of their characters, but in Monsignor Ronald Knox's detective story *The Three Taps*, first published in 1927,[2] we find what is by now a necessary reminder of the origin of *home town*.

'*Chilthorpe was his home town.*'
'*Indeed,*' *said the old gentleman, wincing slightly at the Americanism.*

Like some other American expressions, this one was reinforced in the 'thirties by a popular song which took it as a title and theme, and the truth is that it is a useful addition to the British vocabulary, since 'native town' is slightly stilted in conversation, and also because the very concept of the home town is becoming more generally important in British life. It is a well-known fact that loyalty to the town of one's birth and upbringing

[1] Dover Publications, 1961.   [2] Methuen; p. 39 in the Penguin edition.

tends to vary in proportion to its distance, so that it is not surprising that this feeling has always been very strong in the United States where distances are enormous and movement is frequent. But in Britain – or at any rate, in England – there has been a more settled population, particularly at the lower social levels, as can be seen from the relatively strong localization of many surnames, and most easily in those of geographical origin. The more mobile upper classes have, it may be suspected, always divided their territorial loyalties among London ('Town' *par excellence*), one of the ancient universities, and some isolated country seat, in addition of course to one of the public schools, and so have never felt the need for such a phrase as *home town*. But in the second half of the twentieth century there has come about an increased geographical mobility of the population at large, together with a corresponding growth of nostalgia for the old places left behind, and so *home town* usefully fills a gap in the vocabulary.

Speaking of a governmental appointment – nothing less in fact than the post of Prime Minister in succession to Harold Macmillan – *The Economist* wrote 'Lord Hailsham seems to be raring for the job' (26 Oct 1963). The original expression is 'rarin(g) to go', an Americanism which has in its time been heard on B.B.C. television news (often a shade more colloquial than the Home Service bulletin, since a daring expression can be carried off by a smile or gesture from the announcer). The dictionaries do not give much help with this mysterious idiom. Is it the same as the 'rearing' of an animal straining to dash away? This hypothesis would seem to be borne out by the variant forms of another American expression, the adjective *rare* meaning 'underdone' as in 'a rare steak'. (This in fact is once again a case of a seventeenth-century English usage that has become more or less obsolete in England while continuing to thrive on the far side of the Atlantic.) But the interesting point at the moment is that there exists, at all events in the pages of the *S.E.D.*, a variant form 'rear' for 'rare' in this sense. So it seems that conversely *raring* may well be merely a phonetic variant of 'rearing', i.e. the action of an animal impatiently rising on its hind legs.

Similar considerations may apply to the expression *root for*, that is, encourage a team by shouts and cheers. This has shown signs of infiltrating British English in recent years, and the *S.E.D.* lists it as 'U.S. slang' under the same rubric as the British uses alluding to the rummaging of a swine with its snout and so forth. But supporters who are enthusiastically rooting for a team are not rummaging about for food so much as shouting and cheering, which leads us to examine more closely another verb in the *S.E.D.* which has, or had, the sense of 'to roar, make a loud noise, behave riotously'. This is 'rout', which could evidently be pronounced to rhyme either with 'lout' or 'loot'. When it is further realized that there exists a verb 'rout' as a variant of 'root' even in the sense of rummaging then it is clear that in recent centuries there has been a great deal of fluctuation and variation in this type of verb, with the practical result that the modern *root* of sporting use must surely go back to the 'rout' indicating noisy behaviour.

Some years ago a writer in the *New Statesman* asked whether people had been 'rooting for a phony'. Here we have two Americanisms in a single phrase. *Phon(e)y* is listed as such by the *S.E.D.* with the laconic comment 'Perhaps variant of *fawney* (worthless) ring, from Irish *fáinne* ring. Counterfeit, sham'. It is hailed by Thomas Pyles in his chapter on adoptions into the American vocabulary from foreign tongues as 'certainly the noblest contribution of Irish to American English', and is explained by him, on the strength of Grose's *Classical Dictionary of the Vulgar Tongue* (2nd ed., 1788), as stemming from a confidence trick in which a rogue sells a cheap ring for a high price.

A practical difficulty in studies of this kind arises when a British writer uses an American word in an American context, for here it is hard to know whether he intends it as an aid to the creation of local atmosphere or as a part of his own normal vocabulary. So when an Englishman writes 'The American simply regards a car as a means of transportation', it is not easy to see into which category the final noun should be placed. Is the writer using it in his own right or speaking from the point of view of the American whose thought he is explaining? Of course, there is no real answer to this question, the truth being that this very ambiguity is a channel for American additions to the British vocabulary. Words and phrases first learned in descriptions of the American scene are later transferred to a purely British context, perhaps semi-humorously in the first place, and finally are accepted by imitators who never realize that such expressions have ever been anything else but standard British. The whole process may take several years. As long as the trans-atlantic origin of such a word is remembered it appears in inverted commas, which are dropped when it is accepted as a fully-fledged member of the British vocabulary. An example is *set-up* meaning 'the structure or arrangement of an organization'. In the 'thirties of the present century it was an American intruder into the spoken language of Britain. In the 'forties it appeared in writing in inverted commas, but these have now disappeared and it is virtually a British word. 'The main body of the book is taken up with a study of the set-up of society' says a reviewer in the *Durham University Journal* in 1955. The final stage in this type of evolution is reached when heated Englishmen indignantly deny that the word could ever be considered as anything but a native term. Hence, in the journal *Modern Languages* a protest is regis-tered to the effect that 'It is nonsense to describe *hitch-hike* as American' (March 1954). This, of course, is partly a subjective matter, for it is doubtless felt to be vaguely American by those who remember its introduction, together with the practice it denotes, into the Britain of the middle 'thirties. I can still recall my bewilderment at seeing a character in an American film of those days making the curious jerking gesture with his thumb. The point is that the age of the commentator is all-important in such matters. In this connection it is odd nowadays to read what Horwill wrote in 1936: 'Everyone recognizes, of course, that such terms as *blizzard, bogus, bunkum* came to us from across the Atlantic' (S.P.E. Tract No. 45). Equally surprising nowadays is the realization that he was able to quote *disgruntled* as an Ameri-canism from a British newspaper of 1934.

Needless to say, the examples of borrowing from American quoted in the preceding pages are a mere fraction of what might be adduced. Yet the most striking lesson to be drawn from an investigation of this type is not even the multiplicity of Americanisms in good British use, but rather the fact that these borrowings take place largely on the unconscious plane. Only the possessor of a good linguistic memory, or better still, a thick notebook, can fully realize the truth of this statement. It is confirmed by the experience of Horwill, who, speaking of some expressions taken into British, says that if he had trusted to his memory alone he would scarcely think of them as coming in the first place from America. 'But when I find examples of them set down in black and white, with dates, in my notes, I know for a certainty that, in the early years of the century, they struck my attention as not being then in use at home' (preface to the 1935 edition of his *Dictionary of Modern American Usage*).

The average person accepts a useful neologism without worrying overmuch as to how and where he first came across it, and indeed the very nature of the American idiom makes it striking, forceful and irresistibly practical, with the result that the naturalization of Americanisms in British usage tends to be rapid and painless so far as the mass of people are concerned. Speculation as to the desirability of this process is an unprofitable pastime. What is certain is that the interaction between American and British is largely from west to east nowadays (with some exceptions, like 'gremlin' and – surprisingly! – 'gadget'). As the outcome of this, the forebodings of those who once prophesied a radical split between the two linguistic forms are now seen to be wide of the mark, while the contrary opinion of Otto Jespersen, expressed some thirty years ago, that everything pointed to increased intercourse between the two English-speaking nations, has been justified. Meanwhile there seems to be no reason to assume that American and British usage will ever become identical, for there is still a wide field of differences distinguishing the two greatest representatives of the English language.

2

Foreign Influence

THROUGHOUT its history the English language has always been hospitable to words from other tongues and while it is doubtless true to say that all forms of human speech have to some extent borrowed from outside models there are grounds for thinking that English is more than usually open to foreign influence as compared with other great languages. The French, indeed, have set up an organization whereby they hope to stem or at all events regulate the influx of foreign words into their vocabulary, but this would probably seem a strange idea to most English speakers, who seem to believe in a species of linguistic free trade and argue that if a term of foreign origin is useful it should be put to work forthwith regardless of its parentage. In this we are helped by the nature of the language itself which very conveniently allows us to use a word as verb, noun or adjective without any change of form, unlike the other major European languages. In this way the B.B.C. has borrowed the French noun *compère* as both noun and verb, and has even been known to apply this masculine word to a woman, thereby unconsciously illustrating another reason why foreign expressions soon make themselves at home in English, namely the Anglo-Saxon dislike of analysis. A word used by an English speaker is considered by him as more or less incapable of further sub-division, and as long as it serves his purpose he has little desire to know the why and wherefore of its inner structure. This may be somewhat annoying to the purist but the practical result is that English is able to adopt the most nondescript expressions from foreign languages and set them to work with a minimum of fuss. This process was in full swing a millennium ago, when the Anglo-Saxons were busily taking over words from the Scandinavians settled in the northern parts of the country ('take, get, sky' and many others), while after the Norman Conquest so many words and idioms were incorporated into English from French that some scholars have even come to doubt whether the resulting vocabulary can properly be regarded as typical of a Germanic language.

What is of interest in this connection is that we still borrow from other tongues in the same uninhibited way as our fore-fathers. In the artistic sphere French continues to provide us with new terms. With *avant-garde* we meet an old friend in a new guise, for our 'vanguard', taken from across the Channel in the fifteenth century, shows what the English tongue did to *avant-garde* when it was borrowed at that time as an addition to the vocabulary of war. In France itself the word did not acquire artistic associations until the nineteenth century, when French journalists wrote of the '*artistes de l'avant-garde*'. In the closing years of that century it achieved independence as part of the literary and artistic vocabulary, indicating those men who were precursors of new movements. In English the word is more often than not employed as an adjective, as in a letter by Rose Macaulay, written on 20 October 1957 about a priest to whom she was suggesting a 'jazz Mass'. 'I said he ought to be avant-garde from time to time . . .' (*Letters to a Sister*). But in fact the word is not easy to define in its modern use, and it is significant that the *Times Literary Supplement* devoted two special numbers in 1964 to the concept of the *avant-garde*, while in 1962 Leonard C. Pronko wrote a whole book on the theme, defining it summarily on the first page as being 'what the beat generation would call "way out"'.[1] On the third page he quotes the opinion of another writer to the effect that it involves 'a refusal of accepted discipline and behaviour'. This is a reminder that the term no longer denotes a mere band of precursors leading to a future stage of development, but indicates a movement in its own right. Incidentally, it is striking that from a semantic point of view

[1] *Avant-Garde*, Cambridge University Press.

'avant-garde' and 'way out' both suggest the same image of separation from the main body.

'Avant-garde' reminds us that artistic and cultural innovations frequently have their origins in France, and in spite of the English wording it would seem that the so-called 'New Look' in women's fashions is also of French manufacture, since it was introduced by Christian Dior in the Paris collection of 1946 and is to this day known to the French by this name (or else *niou louque* in the gallicized spelling invented by Raymond Queneau, but this is merely a matter of orthography). More recently we have been submerged by the *New Wave* in the cinema, and this is simply a translation of the *Nouvelle Vague*, appearing in English in 1960. In France it has been claimed by the left-wing weekly *L'Express* that it invented the expression at the end of 1957 as the title of an investigation into the outlook of young people aged between 18 and 30 and that only later was it applied to the work of revolutionary young film-makers.

In the world of films and television it is quite usual to come across the word *photogenic*. Meaning 'worthy of being photo-graphed' this has existed as a dictionary-word for a long time but only in recent years has it come into real use, obviously in imitation of the much more commonly used *photogénique* which is quite a household word in France. In both languages the original meaning was 'producing light' in accordance with the Greek etymology. Here it is the French meaning, rather than the form, which has had an influence on English. The same has occurred in the case of another item of cinema vocabulary, i.e. *sub-title*, as applied to the translation of dialogue appearing at the bottom of the screen when a foreign film is being screened. The traditional meaning of the word was simply 'the alternative title of a book' (*Eric* or *Little by Little*) but it so happened that this literary con-vention went out of fashion in the early part of the twentieth century, with the result that 'sub-title' was left unemployed and so became available to translate the French *sous-titre*. Foreign-language films were somewhat late in reaching the English-speaking world and that is why French influenced this sphere of cinema jargon. For the benefit of those who do not remember the days of silent films it may be mentioned that the explanatory flashes of written dialogue or description appearing on the screen ('Came the dawn') were known as captions. It is difficult to see why the same word has not been applied to what we now call sub-titles, apart from a sort of sloth which makes us clutch at a foreign solution for our linguistic problems.

When sub-titles are not used with foreign films then an English-language sound-track is substituted for the foreign dialogue, and this process is known as *dubbing*. It is not easy to find any dictionary explanation of the origin of this verb 'dub' but maybe it is perhaps an abbreviation of 'double', the literal translation of the French verb *doubler* which is applied to this technique. When this hypothesis first presented itself to my mind I felt that its weak point was that there seemed to be no proof that 'double' had ever been used in this way by English-speaking technicians, but since then Simone de Beauvoir has spoken in her autobiographical volume *La force de l'âge*[1] of *le dubling* [sic] in this connection, which goes to show that there used to be an English word 'doubling' (now 'dubbing'). At all events it is quite unlikely that our verb 'dub' should be an off-shoot of the old-established word referring to the dubbing of knights, and on the other hand it is quite probable that it should be of French provenience since so many French terms are found in the vocabulary of the cinema.

Sympathetic and *unsympathetic* have latterly taken on an extra meaning in imitation of French idiom (or possibly also Spanish), where *sympathique* means 'likable'. So the Annual Register for 1945 says that 'Dreiser was a most unsympathetic personality' (p. 438). At first sight one might imagine this to mean simply that Dreiser was lacking in sympathy for his fellow-men, but the context shows that what is implied is in fact his disagreeable character. 'Unsympathetic' has the continental sense, in other words.

Sometimes the foreign influence amounts to a turn of phrase rather than the use of a particular word, and in this way we must probably see a French idiom behind the increasingly common

[1] Gallimard, 1960.

expression of time which includes 'already', in such phrases as 'Already in the twelfth century . . .' (=as early as the twelfth century . . .) which would appear to be a literal adaptation of a well-known French manner of expressing this concept, though it is true to say that it is also found in German.[1] It must not be forgotten that translation often plays a part in this type of inter-national linguistic influence and that a literal rendering of this type will end by imposing itself if repeated frequently enough. In this way a foreign idiom slips into the language almost un-noticed.

Black Africa is an expression frequently to be met with nowa-days in political articles, and here is a very obvious borrowing from French, where *l'Afrique noire* has long been used for an excellent reason, namely that for the average Frenchman Africa is likely to mean in the first place the North Africa of the Arabs rather than a continent inhabited by negroes. On the other hand 'Black Africa' sounds vaguely pleonastic to the Englishman who unconsciously takes it for granted that Africa means Kenya and other such territories chiefly peopled by men of black race. At first, indeed, the English version of this French phrase was applied in the press only to contexts involving French relation-ships with Africa, and it was not until 1958 that it appeared in connection with Anglo-African affairs. 'But the key to Black Africa lies in the vast territory of Nigeria . . .' (*Observer*, 2 Nov 1958).[2]

The *atomic club* (or *nuclear club*) is also an originally French expression, arising precisely because the French leadership was resentful of France's alleged exclusion from the 'club' of countries possessing nuclear weapons. It will be interesting to see whether the phrase continues to thrive in France now that she is a member

[1] 'Already in the twelfth century the Catholic Church had lost its power to absorb Outsiders', wrote Raymond Mortimer in the *Sunday Times* (20 Oct 1957).

[2] But in the most recent usage the contrast seems to be with white rule in Africa, past or present. Incidentally, *the third world* – i.e. all the politically uncom-mitted nations – is a copy of French, *le tiers monde*, itself modelled on *le tiers état*, the 'Third Estate' of eighteenth-century France.

of the club, for human beings are perhaps most conscious of those groupings from which they are excluded.

On a happier note, there is the use of *boutique* for a particular kind of shop. In France this word merely indicates a small shop of almost any type. For a definition of its British connotation one cannot do better than to quote the *Observer*. 'More and more the word is coming to mean not just a small shop but one that offers something individual in design or service: one that will provide near-exclusive designs and make dresses – not cheap – that are constructed or altered to fit the customers' requirement. Many also sell cheaper ready-to-wear clothes, and they can be a godsend to those who want something out of season or in an odd shape, or who simply hate crowds and big shops' (30 Dec 1962). But in spite of this final point the truth is that the *boutique* may well be found actually inside a large shop.

At the other pole from the *boutique* is the *flea-market*, an obvious borrowing from the French *marché aux puces* whose prototype is the immense junk market at Clignancourt in the north of Paris. This loan-translation made its way into English in 1964 by way of the quality newspapers, its way into the language being made easier by the existence of such a slang word as 'flea-pit', a low-class cinema or theatre.

In the sphere of syntax an idiosyncratic use of 'but' which has been slowly spreading over the years would seem to be an imitation of an ordinary French construction; so 'But of course!' on the analogy of '*Mais naturellement!*'. It is true to say that the type is largely confined to artistic and intellectual circles and may be regarded as too affected in tone to be capable of extension to general use. As it is, it chiefly appears as a form of emphasis, with repetition of the word being stressed. 'But I do wish readers would realize that nobody (*but nobody*) knows the future course of markets' (*Observer*, 24 Jan 1965). There is some reason to believe that this particular gallicism is more frequently found in the feminine vocabulary than in that of men.

A more successful construction, from the point of view of rapid diffusion, is that which is in process of adding an indefinite article to 'nonsense' where there was none before. Enoch Powell makes use of this device to magnificent effect in *A Nation Not Afraid* (1965). 'In short, an incomes policy is a nonsense, a silly nonsense, a transparent nonsense. What is more and worse, it is a dangerous nonsense . . .' (p. 102).[1] By that same year this indefinite article was already inside the House of Lords, where it was declared that cuts in University building 'had created a nonsense' (*The Times*, 2 Dec 1965). Clearly – though the statement is difficult of proof – it is a gallicism imitating the construction 'C'est un non-sens'.

Brouhaha retains in English a very exotic and somewhat amusing form which rather suits its meaning of 'hubbub, uproar'.[2] Unknown to the 1950 edition of the *Concise Oxford Dictionary*, it finds its due place in the fifth edition, of 1964. This reflects the period of its entry into English, i.e. the nineteen-fifties, but the word is by no means a newcomer in its native land. In a fifteenth-century French farce a priest disguised as a devil cries '*Brou, brou, brou, ha, ha, brou, ha, ha*'. According to the Bloch-Wartburg etymological dictionary of the French language this may either be an onomatopoetic phrase or more likely an imitation of the Hebrew formula *baruk habba*, 'Blessed is he that cometh' (in the name of the Lord), which is frequently repeated in the synagogue. Other imitations of this type are to be found in Italian vocabulary. Another Hebrew word in French itself, not so far removed in sense from *brouhaha* is *tohu-bohu*, originally describing the chaos existing before the creation of the world as set forth in Genesis (1, 2) and now indicating any disorder. Unfortunately this expressive word has not yet made its way across the channel.

On a more everyday plane of existence we have the *au pair* girl, who is of course not necessarily French. It is reliably stated, by the way, that a large number of people imagine the spelling to be *au père*, as though she were a sort of patriarch's perquisite. To be quite fair, the phrase is by no means self-explanatory. The

[1] Batsford.
[2] 'Her comment on all the brouhaha her bikini poster aroused: "I'm just a plain little housewife" ' (*Daily Express*, 20 Nov 1964).

etymology has nothing to do with 'father' or 'couple' but ultimately leads us back to the Latin *par* 'equal', and is also therefore a relative of English 'peer' (a man who is more equal than others, as the author of *Animal Farm* would have it), with the curious result that in the unlikely sentence 'The peer's *au pair* girl is feeling below par' we have three words going back to the same Latin ancestor, *par*. In French itself, to be *au pair* in a house has long meant that one is unpaid but has 'all found', as the saying is. This was first applied in England to an arrangement whereby 'mutual services are rendered without consideration of payment'. So says the *S.E.D.* and gives 1928 as the dating. It seems to me that there was a short period when the phrase *au pair*, in the context which interests us, referred to what is now known as an 'exchange', i.e. two young people of different countries exchange more or less protracted visits to each other's homes without any cash payment. At all events it was not long after the second world war that the present meaning of the '*au pair* girl' began to be heard, at first as the off-shoot of the earlier friendly sense. Let us quote the delightful Miss Katharine Whitehorn in this connection. 'The original idea of the *au pair* girl was German: a 'house-daughter' she was to be, living as one of the family, morally protected and not asked to do much more than arrange the flowers and take the children to the park. With the decline of domestic service, however, the *au pair* girl, like her employer, had had a distinctly grittier time' (*Observer* supplement, 22 Nov 1964). Perhaps it can be left at that, but not before noting the ingenious creation of a verb 'to *au pair* it' by Rayner Heppenstall.

Reportage has taken on an extra dimension as a result of recent French influence. Glossed as 'report, gossip' in the *S.E.D.* it is explained in a more up-to-date manner by the 1950 and 1964 editions of the *Concise Oxford Dictionary* as '(typical style) of reporting events for the press', which is one of the French meanings. The word is not of course strictly confined to allusions to press writing, and so it is perfectly possible to speak of a novel as being a piece of reportage, i.e. an unemotional recording of events, devoid of rhetoric or philosophizing.

On a homelier plane is *aubergine*, the French name of the egg-plant, now known to some extent in Britain by its purple fruit about the size of a small fist. It is listed in the *C.O.D.* of 1950. How it is supposed to be pronounced in English is another matter.

Discotheque became part of the English vocabulary towards 1965. In French this word was in existence in the nineteen-forties, and though it is glossed as 'record library' by the 1954 supplement to Harrap's French and English Dictionary it meant rather more than that, being a shop in France where records could be bought after being listened to by means of an unhygienic system of earpieces rather like those attached to a doctor's stetho-scope. As a French word *discothèque* is formed by an analogy with the term for 'library', that is, *bibliothèque*. In English the meaning has undergone a change, since it now implies a place of enter-tainment where young people dance to recorded music.

Son et lumière is something of a mouthful for the average Briton, which explains why this tends to be mostly a written form. It is also a recent creation in French, invented to describe a type of cultural entertainment whereby a building such as a castle or cathedral is floodlit at night while a dramatized com-mentary on its history is broadcast by loud-speakers. A sentence from the *Daily Telegraph* illustrates this phrase in an adjectival use . . . 'Christopher Ede's remarkable *son et lumière* spectacle at Hampton Court Palace, which was to have been finished tonight, has been extended until Oct. 15' (24 Sep 1966).

In French *cinéaste* is a somewhat elastic term but certainly it can in that language be applied only to someone engaged in the production side of the cinema. In British journalistic usage on the other hand there is a strong tendency for it to be understood as simply a connoisseur of films. A *Radio Times* article on the Swedish film director Ingmar Bergman implies this sense when saying '. . . woe betide any crass outsider in a gathering of *cinéastes* who confused Ingmar with Ingrid' (20 Apr 1967). Though a barbarous usage from the French point of view this is admittedly a useful acquisition in English for 'discriminating cinema fan'.

The American provenance of a word does not necessarily rule out an ultimate French source. Such is the case for *picayune*, listed by the 1964 *Concise Oxford Dictionary* as 'mean, contemptible' and derived by way of Louisiana French from the Provençal *picaioun*. As a noun it is a small coin, or else a thing or person of no great consequence. 'His action was unwarranted, picayune, and vindictive,' stated an American judge, as reported in the *Daily Express* (2 Dec 1964). The Louisiana Purchase of 1803, involving a much larger area of the United States than the present state of Louisiana, brought many French speakers into the American union and thereby introduced a number of French words into the vocabulary—'butte, chute, praline, shivaree' (noisy screnading of a newly-wed couple, from *charivari*) and others. 'Prairie', now regarded as one of the most typical of American words, had existed as a borrowing from French settlers since the eighteenth century. Indeed it would be surprising if we did not find a few words of French ancestry in a continent containing such places as Baton Rouge, Des Moines, Pierre, Sault Ste Marie, St Louis, New Orleans, Montpelier, Boisé and Detroit. With a little imagination one might even derive *corny* (passed on to British speakers by 1942 at the latest) from the French *corné* (dog-eared, hackneyed, out of date) but this theory is knocked on the head by the unanimous explanation of American scholars that it comes from 'cornfed', a word going back to Washington Irving at least, and meaning 'countrified, plump'. *Corny* itself has been traced as far back as 1890, in Western Nebraska, in an article by Marie Sandoz in *American Speech* of October 1946.

Although we have seen something of America's contribution to the changes operating in the English language, the story has not been fully outlined. Writers on the subject of Americanisms have usually made little of the fact that in the past millions of Americans have had a foreign language as their mother-tongue, though in fact it is incredible that the language of the country should not have been affected thereby. Horwill says that immigrants 'have been content to take the language of their adopted country as they found it' (p. xi), while Professor Norman E. Eliason's conclusion on the subject as put forward in an article on American English appearing in *English Studies* (Aug 1958) was that 'Foreign influence on American English has been very slight'. S. Robertson shares this judgment in *The Development of Modern English* where it is claimed that 'In general, American English has been surprisingly little affected by the speech of immigrants' (p. 338).[1] Sturtevant and Hockett, both American professors, see respectively only a few traces of such influence such as '*smear-case* and *kosher*' or '*delicatessen, hamburger, wiener* and *zwieback*'. And indeed a whole doctoral dissertation on the subject presented by Ruth M. Stone to a German university in 1934 lists German contributions chiefly of the type '*frankfurter, schnitzel, schneider, spiel*' and so forth. In other words there has been a natural tendency to see foreign influence as consisting solely in straightforward loan-words from German, Yiddish, Spanish, Italian or whatever the language of the immigrants may have been.

Fortunately there have been some signs in recent years that scholars are becoming rather more aware that foreign borrowing into American speech has been taking place on a larger scale than had been thought. So Mitford M. Mathews in the preface to his *Dictionary of Americanisms* acknowledges that 'American borrowings from foreign languages are much more numerous and significant than has hitherto been suspected. The student of American English has always to keep in mind the important fact that many people of many tongues took part in shaping the language of the United States. There are many phenomena in American English that cannot be intelligently explained within the limits of the English language' (p. vii). This is not surprising, and might well have been expected on theoretical grounds, for only an observer who has missed all the lessons of linguistic development could fail to foresee foreign influences in American English. After all, such trends are easily observable in spheres other than language. Negroes gave to America jazz and a taste for gaudy

[1] 3rd printing (New York, 1938).

clothes, while Indians contributed smoking and the crew-cut. What is important, moreover, is that such influences did not stay confined within the American continent, but have spread throughout the white man's world, and we shall see that in a similar way some words and phrases have used America as a launching-site from which to bombard British English and indeed other European tongues for that matter.

American table-manners are European rather than English, and of course a taste for various exotic foods has been implanted in the United States by foreign immigrants. The iced birthday cake, to revert to something now quite at home in Britain, appears to have spread to America from Northern Germany in the middle of the nineteenth century, and was brought back across the Atlantic to England in the closing years of that century. And so the iced birthday cake is in a way symbolical of the process whereby German and other foreign words and expressions have modified linguistic usage in the United States as a result of immigration, often thereby influencing the English of the British Isles, as we shall see in due course. But let us first examine more closely the question of German infiltration into American English.

Since the end of the eighteenth century, the Germans have always been the most numerous foreign immigrants entering America, with the movement reaching its peak in the decade 1880-1890 when well over a million and a half Germans settled in the United States.[1] They were notoriously fond of retaining their own language and customs and even ensured that at one time the State laws in Indiana were published in German. The German-American press was extraordinarily vigorous. In the eighteen-nineties there were more than 800 German publications in the U.S.A. and it was a proud boast that there were more speakers of German in New York than in any city in the world except Berlin and Vienna. Before the first war, according to an

---

[1] Some very comprehensive statistics on the subject are given by Karl-Heinz Schönfelder in his *Deutsches Lehngut im amerikanischen Englisch* (Max Niemeyer Verlag, 1957).

article by Taylor Starck,[1] Baltimore had four elementary schools in which all teaching was carried out in German, and indeed at that time German was the first foreign language to be learned by American students. Even less than forty years ago it could be said that in central Pennsylvania the majority of the population could speak German, while some 30 per cent of the inhabitants of that district used it constantly. It is true to say that this spoken German often underwent a marked process of anglicization so far as vocabulary was concerned, being interlarded with English words or changing the meaning of German expressions in accordance with English idiom. This was indeed inevitable in all the foreign languages spoken in the United States, and the classic example is taken from the Portuguese of North America, where *grosseria* means 'grocery store', though properly it meant 'a rude remark'.

We are not directly concerned here with the effect of English on foreign languages spoken in the U.S.A. but the point is that the reverse process is frequently found, and an immigrant carries into English an idiom from his mother tongue. Thus, 'to touch wood' in order to ward off bad luck is *auf Holz klopfen* in German literally 'to knock on wood'. And so it comes about that 'knock on wood' is the phrase used in American English. Occasionally it .is to be seen in British written usage, and the *New Statesman*, whose contributors appear to make a point of honour of using Americanisms even when denouncing America, uses this idiom. 'The wise man who enters a formal jazz contest crosses himself, knocks on wood, or, if a rationalist, merely hopes that this time it will come off' (14 Feb 1959). Can it be doubted that this Americanism was ultimately due to a mistake of idiom made quite unconsciously by German immigrants—a mistake made so frequently and widely that at last it was taken over by the community in general?

Sometimes the correspondence is not so clear-cut, particularly in cases where it may be that an old usage which has died out or become obsolescent in Britain is retained in the United States

[1] Publications of the Modern Language Association of America, December 1957.

because of what might be termed the preservative influence of a similar German idiom. In Britain the ejaculation 'For God's sake' has traditionally been followed by an imperative, e.g. 'For God's sake shut up!' This type is old-established.

> For God's sake, let us sit upon the ground,
> And tell sad stories of the death of kings.
>
> (*Richard II*, Act III, ii.)

Formerly there was also another construction in which the accompanying sentence was not imperative. 'For Godsake [*sic*] what do you call want of Indulgence then?' asked John Dennis in 1704. Rare in Britain nowadays, except as an imitation of American English, this type is common in the U.S.A. though it is difficult to say whether:

(*a*) it simply is a survival of the eighteenth century use,

(*b*) it reflects the similar way in which German speakers use *um Gotteswillen*,

(*c*) or whether it stems from a combination of both these factors.

Similarly for the adjective 'lonesome', which seems to be used almost invariably in the United States in the place of [feeling] 'lonely'. Though the word is well attested in British English, going back to at least the seventeenth century, it may owe its tremendous popularity in America to reinforcement by the German *einsam*, for given a choice between 'lonely' and 'lonesome' a German-American would tend to prefer the latter since its second syllable reminded him of the suffix *-sam* of his own word. It is curious that in spite of the present strength of American influence 'lonesome' has not regained much currency in Britain, notwithstanding a boost around 1930 from Paul Robeson's recording of the song 'Lonesome Road'.

It would be quite feasible to prolong the list of Americanisms due to the influence of the German language, but in the present context we are interested chiefly in those German-Americanisms

which have made their way into British usage. Such an idiom is
'*to iron out*' (differences, disagreements, etc.) and this may be
compared with the corresponding German use of the parallel
ausbügeln. The standard dictionaries of Americanisms do not
appear to have noticed this special idiom, though the *O.E.D.*
supplement mentions a British example from 1929. This was
certainly an early appearance of the phrase in Britain, where it
did not become really current until the nineteen-fifties.

In the nineteen-thirties Horwill had been surprised to observe
'the American use of *in, with* and *among* after *belong*, which in
England is invariably followed by *to.* . . .' This was written in
1936 but was even then no longer quite correct for in 1932 A. H.
Gardiner had written in *The Theory of Speech and Language*[1] that
'The ultimate thing-meant belongs outside both speech and
language'. This was just possibly an Americanism on Gardiner's
part, though it could more probably be a Germanism in the most
direct sense since the German language has this same use with the
corresponding verb *gehören*, 'belong', and Gardiner's book shows
by frequent and lengthy quotation that he had a good knowledge
of that tongue. Indeed it is noticeable that students of language
have long used Germanic constructions with the verb 'belong',
so that for example we find on p. 1534 of Weekley's *Etymological
Dictionary* the sentence 'It is uncertain whether *traps* . . . belongs
here'. Similarly in the case of an editorial comment in the *O.E.D.*,
viz. 'It is not certain that these belong here' (under *rooter*).
(Strictly speaking a similar though by no means identical usage is
to be found in the regional speech of north-east England. 'He
doesn't belong here; he belongs Newcastle'. But this idiom is of
purely geographical application and has nothing at all to do
with our present point at issue). Now the editor of that part of
the *O.E.D.* was Sir William Craigie, who happened to live for
many years in the U.S.A. and was the author of *A Dictionary
of American English*, so it is likely that his use of 'belong' without
a preposition was directly due to an unconscious imitation of
American idiom, though of course as a philologist he had a

[1] Clarendon Press.

knowledge of German. At all events the ultimate origin is Germanic since this type of idiom is clearly of German proveni-ence in American itself. It is curious that Horwill did not suggest as much, because he was well aware of a Germanic influence in American English though he ascribed it to the great prestige of German scholarship in the universities of the United States. This explanation has at one time and another been shared by a number of commentators and is quite possibly true in the present instance affecting the construction used with 'belong'. But this theory of the academic origin of American Germanisms must be true of only a small number of them. Obviously, when an off-print (i.e. a separately printed copy of an article appearing in a periodical) is known in America as a 'separate' this is a scholarly borrowing from the equivalent *Separatabdruck* in German. But when on the other hand we read in Norman Mailer's *The Naked and the Dead* that 'In the brothel the girls wear halters and trim panties' it is clear that while this use of 'halter' is connected with the near-synonymous German noun *Büsten halter* the process of borrowing has been colloquial rather than academic.

An unexpected parallel to the American use of *belong in* is to be found in the regional French of the district around Metz, where the verb *appartenir* 'belong' can likewise be followed by various prepositions in the sense of 'being in the proper place'. A literally translated example reads 'They (the boundary marks of the former frontier) belong in the museum, but not on our roads and in our fields'.[1] This sentence is taken from a Metz newspaper and the reason for this Germanism is not far to seek, since Metz is in Lorraine and was occupied by the Prussians as part of the German Empire after the French defeat of 1871. So this curious coincidence of American idiom and a French provincialism can be ascribed quite simply to a common origin; their German model.

Needless to say this type of construction has greatly prospered in recent British usage. 'They are found where they belong, side

[1] 'Elles appartiennent au musée mais pas sur nos routes et dans nos champs'. (Quoted by *Le français moderne*, vol. 4, 1936.)

by side' (*Times Literary Supp.*, 29 Oct. 1954) and 'There is little doubt that Michael Tippett belongs in the second category' (*Observer*, 23 Jan 1955). Nor must we omit a special shade of meaning which can be attached to the use of 'belong' without any preposition and which appears to have been evolved in America without any help from German. The meaning is 'to be completely at home in a particular environment', and the idiom is quite at home in Britain now, as shown by the following quotation from an obituary notice in the *Spectator*. 'Westminster gave him . . . the chance to mix, the feeling of belonging' (14 Jan 1955). A slightly earlier example comes from 1947 and is found on the first page of Graham Greene's *Brighton Rock*. '. . . anybody could tell that he didn't belong.' Here we may surmise that the American inspiration giving rise to this rather neat idiom is in part due to the importance accorded in the United States to the idea of joining one's rightful group, and that if there is a progressive breakdown in Britain of the traditional notion of individual non-conformity we may hear this use of 'belong' rather more frequently.

In British English the verb 'to warn' has hitherto been transitive, so that some following object had to be expressed, but in German this is not the case; thus, *vor Anarchie warnen* is rendered in a recent translation of Thomas Mann's *Doktor Faustus* as 'to warn against anarchy'. The sentence reads 'Thus bourgeois imperialism . . . could not do enough to warn against anarchy'. Now this would have sounded odd in English some time ago, for it would have been felt by the reader that some object of the verb ought to be expressed ('people, the world, Germany' or some such word). The new usage has come from America, where it was surely introduced as a Germanism, and is now found in British contexts. It may incidentally be observed that the task of the translator from German into English is sometimes eased nowadays precisely because of the existence of German idioms which have found their way into the language by way of the linguistic habits of German-Americans, and the quotation from the translation of *Doktor Faustus* is a case in point. Another example of this is to be found in the same work in the rendering of *ich wüsste nicht* by 'I would not know' on the first page of the sixth chapter. '. . . and I would not know whether its architectural profile . . .', etc., for it is likely, indeed, that this type of German construction is at the root of the new 'I wouldn't know' idiom in English.

'To get to' do something is found in the best linguistic circles nowadays. 'How are we to get to see an important source?' asked the speaker on a Third Programme talk on Purcell manuscripts. This expression was originally an Americanism, presumably of German provenance, since the word *kriegen*, equivalent to 'get', is used in the same way. 'To get wise to' would also seem to be German-American in the first instance, for there is a German idiom which is identical except for the preposition following the verb. It is also true to say that this type of expression is found in Scandinavian, and in view of Scandinavian immigration into the United States we must not neglect the possibility of Scandinavian speech-habits reinforcing German influence.

A Third Programme discussion (9 Jun 1963) on changes in the English language included a suggestion that the expression 'You've never had it so good' had found its way to America after being invented by the then prime minister, Mr Harold Macmillan.[1] But this is certainly not the case, although there is no doubt that his use of this phrase as a political slogan served to popularize it in Great Britain, and one thinks with pleasure of a caricature drawn at the time of his election as chancellor of Oxford University in which he was pictured as rendering the slogan in Latin – *Nunquam id habuistis tam bonum*. The fact is that Americans were using this idiom by the end of the Second World War, and possibly long before that. In German it is old-established, being used by no less a person than Goethe himself, while in modern German it is heard a dozen times a day. This seems to imply that once again we are dealing with an idiom

[1] Strictly speaking, the prime minister's speech said that 'our people' had never had it so good.

carried over into American English by the speech-habits of German immigrants.

Another American colloquialism copied widely in Britain consists of emphasizing a statement by inverting the word-order which therefore becomes identical with that of a question, though the intonation is not at all interrogative. "Am I tired !' 'Could I use a beer !' This type is very widespread in German, which has doubtless passed it on to spoken American by word of mouth. The exclamation mark is virtually inescapable when this sort of sentence is shown in the written form, though the same is not always true of German, e.g. *War das ein Tag* (Was that a day !), from a novel by Heinrich Böll. Borrowings of this kind, which actually give to the language a new formula, as it were, are obviously more important even than borrowings from foreign vocabulary. They are also much rarer.

Still in the sphere of colloquialisms, it may be seen that the slangy 'D'you know something?', copied in Britain from American speech, may well be a Germanism, in which case it would be derived from *Weisst du 'was?* The point is that in conversational German *was* is used as a shortened form of *etwas*, meaning 'something', though its true meaning, as a word in its own right, is 'what'. One assumes that German immigrants did not realize the existence of the traditional 'D'you know what?', and quite unconsciously evolved 'D'you know something' on the strength of their native expression.

On the other hand, the slang verb 'to neck' *i.e.* 'kiss', which is sometimes connected with the German *necken* 'tease' is possibly not from German at all, as it would appear to have been extant in the sense of 'to hug and kiss' in north-eastern England in the year 1842, according to a diary written that year by a paper manufacturer of High Wycombe who heard it at Sunderland (*Notes and Queries*, Jan 1959). Yet the word is not listed in Brockett's *Glossary of North Country Words* of 1824, and its exact origin must for the present remain a mystery. All that is certain is that as a piece of American slang it became known in Britain in the late nineteen-thirties.

A *Times* review of 30 January 1958 speaks of 'an account of motoring in a Land-Rover along the Barbary Coast from Tangier to Tripoli, taking in a little history on the way'. This use of 'take in' is also to be found a little earlier in a letter to the *Spectator*, speaking of 'the only two items which 90 per cent of B.B.C. customers of any intelligence wish to take in . . .' (4 Oct 1957), while in the *Universities Quarterly* of May, 1958, it is a question of a student who 'can take in American history . . .'. These uses are in fact quite different from an older use of 'take in' meaning 'grasp, comprehend', though in the last quotation only the context allows us to be sure of this. But the new sense of 'take in' has come to Britain from America, though it is similar to an idiom in German, so that the expression *Amerikanische Filme in sich aufnehmen* might be translated fairly closely by 'to take in American films'. Once again the likelihood is that this latest shade of meaning of 'take in' is of German-American origin, the sequence being (1) German (2) German-American (3) American (4) British. It is with something of a sense of wonder that one grasps the general drift of this process whereby the style and vocabulary of writers for *The Times* and academic periodicals in Britain are enriched by the errors and misapprehensions of immigrants landing on the shores of the New World.

'All in all' meaning 'of paramount or exclusive importance' is old-established. 'Must eyes be all in all, the tongue and ear nothing?' asked Wordsworth in 1846, just as Byron said 'They were all in all to each other'. Shakespeare had earlier used 'all in all' in a rather different way, seemingly in the sense 'of all things considered'.

> *He was a man, take him for all in all,*
> *I shall not look upon his like again.*
>
> (*Hamlet*, Act I. ii).

But in British usage this evidently died out. In American writing, however, the idiom lived on, as in Chapter LVI of Melville's *Moby Dick* (1851) where we read 'But, taken for all in all, by far the finest ... presentations of whales and whaling scenes to be anywhere found; are two large French engravings ...' Possibly the expression was reinforced in the United States by conscious-ness of the corresponding German idiom *alles in allem genommen*. At all events, by the twentieth century the usual American version was simply 'all in all'. The American scholar Sapir used this shorter phrase, for example, in his famous *Language*, published in 1921. 'All in all, we may conclude that our English case system is weaker than it looks'. In 1925 we find in a British context the older and fuller phrase in the *Modern Languages Review* (p. 106). 'Taken all in all these four volumes constitute a rich harvest'. But it is significant that the author of this sentence is W. E. Collinson, a specialist in the German language and consequently familiar with the parallel German idiom. (It may incidentally be men-tioned that in Norwegian we find the shorter form, *alt in alt*, corresponding to 'all in all.') In this individual case it is possible and indeed probable that the idiom was an unconscious borrowing from German, and if so its use illustrates admirably this type of transference which has so often been operative in the case of the English of the United States, though usually in a context where German was a native language and not one used for academic purposes. On the other hand, of course, Collinson may simply have himself borrowed the phrase from American usage.

In British usage, *all in all* was current in a small way by the early thirties. So, in the autobiography *I, James Whittaker* (1934) we find 'The company was good, and the men, all in all, were a decent lot' (p. 206). Whittaker was a Scottish working–class writer, but after an interval of ten years the same expression is used by Lieutenant Raleigh Trevelyan, a Wykehamist. 'All in all, I'm building up a clique of first-class fellows in this platoon ...' (entry for 19 May 1944, in *The Fortress*). After yet another decade or so it receives the accolade of use in the *Times Literary Supplement*, admittedly in a reference to American literature. 'All in all, surveying American fiction of the past few years, one would have said that the atmosphere was one of great promise and vitality' (5 Aug 1955). By 1963 even *The Times* leader had been invaded. 'All in all, not the first of ten days to shake the world . . .' (19 Dec 1963).

The verb 'to stem' has gained a new meaning as a result of an American usage going back to German idiom. For centuries this English verb has been used in such expressions as 'stem the tide', but nowadays it can also be given quite a different sense, i.e. 'spring from, originate in'. 'My proposition is that there are more great plays for radio stemming from the theatre than great plays for radio derived from novels', wrote a correspondent of the *Listener* (6 Jun 1957). The new meaning is listed in the *S.E.D.* as originally coming to us from the United States. However it appears to be relatively recent even there, as it is dated for the year 1932 in Mathews's dictionary. It seems self-evident that the new sense has been carried over from the German *stammen*, and the transition has been all the easier in that 'stem' – like its horticultural relative 'root' – can without difficulty be imagined to have something to do with origins or causes. Here, as so often, we see that similar-sounding words in two different languages are readily supposed to be equivalent. In German *stammen* actually means 'to be descended', as in the compound word *Stammbaum* meaning 'genealogical tree'. The only connection of *stammen* with the English verb 'stem' was originally a vague similarity of form, but that has not prevented the German meaning from filtering into English. In linguistic matters it often happens that misapprehensions become correct usage.

Humbler examples of this process whereby the errors of German-Americans have enlarged the scope of the English dictionary are seen in the cases of 'dumb' and 'fresh'. In German the equivalent word for 'fresh' as in 'fresh air' is *frisch*, but there is another word *frech*, 'cheeky', impudent', which is vaguely similar in sound to the English 'fresh'. It appears that German immigrants in the U.S.A. must have taken 'fresh' to be equivalent not only to *frisch* but also to *frech*. Hence 'to get fresh' equals 'to make amorous advances'. Here we are of course in the realm of slang, as in the instance of 'dumb' meaning 'stupid'. The point is that German *dumm* means 'stupid' and not 'unable to speak', which would be *stumm*. Ill-educated settlers from Germany must have assumed that 'dumb' had the same meaning as their *dumm*, with the result that we now speak of 'dumb blondes', who more often that not have an unending flow of chatter! A secondary consequence of this development is that there is a movement away from the old phrase 'deaf and dumb' and a person so afflicted is increasingly described as 'a deaf mute'.

During his series of television appearances towards the end of 1958 Field-Marshal Lord Montgomery used the expression *moneywise*, meaning financially. 'No nation can have the ability, moneywise, to do this'. Here we have the potentially fruitful American development whereby it is possible to make an adverb of this type by adding the termination *-wise* to almost any noun. Lord Montgomery might equally well have said *cashwise*, and in fact we find this term in a statement made by the managing director of a television series earlier in that same year. 'Cashwise the Independent Television Authority has been unable to help us' (*Daily Telegraph*, 18 Jan 1958). One wonders whether the victor of El Alamein learned this type of word in his television studio at the B.B.C. or from the pages of the *Times Literary Supplement* where it was said, for example, that Saint Patrick was 'silkily shaven Romanwise' (21 March 1958). *The Times* itself is not averse to this type of compound, for on the last day of 1959 we find *armchairwise* in its pages, while a recent book on meteorology was entitled 'Weatherwise: The techniques of weather study'.

Now this type of word is not new in itself, witness such old expressions as 'likewise, contrariwise, clockwise' and so on. For the present language it is illuminating to read the comments of the *S.E.D.* under *wise* sb.[1] 'Old English *wise* was used in various kinds of adverbial expressions meaning 'in such-and-such a manner, way, or respect', in which it was qualified by an adjective or a substantive with or without a governing preposition. Several of these, with similarly-formed later ones, have survived as simple words, e.g. *crosswise, likewise, nowise, otherwise*. The free use of wise in such expressions, apart from the established simple words, is now only archaic'. The situation has changed somewhat since the writing of this paragraph for the *S.E.D.* It cannot be denied that such expressions as 'engineeringwise' are very readily coined in modern English and that this habit comes from America where in turn the astonishingly free use of the ending '-wise' owes something to the equally free application in German of the parallel *-weise* (as in *beispielsweise* 'for example', *gastweise* 'as a guest', and others). The usage is evidently quite standard in the United States, and in his book entitled *A Course in Modern Linguistics* Professor Charles F. Hockett uses such words as 'fashionwise' and 'community-wise'.[1] In Great Britain the vogue for *-wise* had attained such proportions by the end of the nineteen-fifties that in December 1959 the columnist Pendennis recorded in the *Observer* his resolution not to make use of this suffix in the New Year (along with 'egghead, beatnik, Establishment, status symbol, high octane, brand image' and so forth). At all events we see here an astonishing reversal of fate whereby an 'archaism' suddenly becomes the latest fad. It may well be that the old usage had lingered on in the United States to a greater extent than in the English of Britain, but it can scarcely be doubted that its blossoming forth in the twentieth century was due to a more or less unconscious transference of a German habit, whether on the part of scholars or – more likely – of immigrants.

Amongst phrases very much in vogue there is none which has risen to prominence more quickly than *the turn of the century*. It is in fact somewhat difficult to understand the reason for the rapid naturalization in British English of this expression which on the face of it seems to add nothing to its synonym 'the beginning of the century'. Perhaps it is somehow felt to be more precise or on the other hand the attraction may merely be that of novelty. It came into anything like general use in Britain only in the nineteen-fifties, and was first heard by me – with total lack of comprehension – in 1954, but had in reality been used much earlier by British authors. In 1937 Michael Roberts had written

[1] New York, 1958.

in *The Modern Mind* 'Since the turn of the century the quarrel has died down' (p. 207).[1] Earlier still, John Cowper Powys indirectly defined a variant of the expression in his *Autobiography* of 1934. 'How well I remember watching out the turn of the centuries – the nineteenth becoming the twentieth – in the little dining-room at Court House . . .' (p. 300, 1949 reprint).[2] Powys had lived for many years in the U.S.A. and perhaps felt that the British reader needed some guidance as to the sense of an unfamiliar expression, though it will be seen that he himself gave it an idiosyncratic twist. Actually the more usual expression had appeared in the previous year in Owen Barfield's *History in English Words* (p. 195).[3] As a matter of fact it had not settled down to an invariable form even by 1955, so that in a *Time and Tide* article of November 19th of that year Ivor Brown wrote of 'the tunes of the century's turn'. More significant than this is the frequent ignorance of the true meaning shown at that date, for in the previous October an unsigned article in the *Spectator* inadvertently betrayed a faulty understanding of this phrase coming to be very fashionable just then. 'One way and another, we may now see emerging, at the turn of the century, a new position for the professional author in Britain' (14 Oct). That anonymous writer not unreasonably thought that what is meant is the middle of the century – when the first half turns into the second half. But in the following year a reader sending a letter to the *Manchester Guardian* thought that the meaning had to do with the end of a century when he wrote 'Music had a golden age in the days of Mozart and Beethoven at the turn of the eighteenth century' (17 Sep 1956), for it will be recalled that Mozart died in 1791. This was still the case for a literary critic speaking on a television programme in November 1959 and saying 'It starts at the turn of the century – about 1890'. After such false starts as these the expression was thoroughly at home in Britain by about 1960, though it must be remembered that there was already in British English an old expression 'the turn of the year' which had never quite died out of the vocabulary, or, at any rate, the memory,

---

[1] Faber.   [2] Bodley Head.   [3] Methuen.

of many elderly speakers. The earliest *O.E.D.* dating of this is 1859 in Meredith's *The Ordeal of Richard Feverel* where the allusion is clearly to the first stirrings of Spring. But in reality this dating can be bettered since R. S. Surtees gives us an earlier one in 1853 in *Mr Sponge's Sporting Tour*. 'Who doesn't know the chilling feel of an English spring, or rather of a day at the turn of the year before there is any spring?' (chap. 68).[1] But this cannot be the origin of 'the turn of the century', not at any rate in Britain where the boot is on the other foot since it is now the 'turn of the year' which is being either reinvented or given a new lease of life by analogy with it, as when the *Sunday Times* speaks of 'the turn of the year with its sharp reminder of tax dues' (20 Dec 1959).

British dictionaries give no help with 'turn of the century', which passes unrecorded even in the 1964 edition of the *Concise Oxford Dictionary*, where we find however an explanation of such an expression as 'a turn of Fortune's wheel'! It is to America that we must direct our attention. M. M. Mathews's *Dictionary of Americanisms* (1951) makes no mention of our phrase, nor does the 1934 edition of Webster, but in the 1961 edition, *Webster's Third New International Dictionary*, there is at last some recognition of its existence, listed under *turn*. Three undated examples of use are recorded, including – from the pen of W. A. White – 'years at the turn of the century are vintage years'. So it would seem that it is a comparatively modern phrase even in the United States. What is also noteworthy is the existence of parallel expressions in other languages, particularly in German, where *die Jahrhundertwende* is quite frequent. There is no direct listing of this in Grimm's *Deutsches Wörterbuch* but this is scarcely surprising, since the relevant volume (no. 4) is of 1877. In volume 14 (1955), however, there is an incidental mention of the word under *wende* (turn). In Dutch there is a similar word, *eeuwwisseling*, a compound made up of elements meaning 'century' and 'turn'.[2] Spanish has *a vuelta de siglo* 'at the turn of the century'. In French

[1] p. 484 in the O.U.P. reprint of 1958.
[2] This information about *eeuwwisseling* has kindly been supplied by Mr Noel Osselton of Southampton University's English Department.

one very rarely finds any evidence of *au tournant du siècle*, and when it does appear it invariably seems to be an anglicism coming from the pen of some writer who has either lived in the United States or at any rate has a good knowledge of English. More off the beaten track, Norwegian has *århundreskifte*, listed by the 1954 edition of *Gyldendal's* dictionary and glossed as 'turn of the century'. Clearly all these stem from a common source, but there is some difficulty at the moment in saying what that source is, though German and American English are presumably the most likely candidates. The problem must rest there until we have reliable early datings in the various languages.

It often happens that there are gaps in the resources of a given language, so far as families of words are concerned. So at one time, there was the verb 'choose', the noun 'choice', but no adjective to denote the quality of exercising very careful choice. American English provides the missing adjective, namely *choosey*, and this has had some success in Britain. 'We get more choosey and want more different kinds of satisfaction,' writes Gertrude Williams on page 21 of *The Economics of Everyday Life* (1950). But it is striking that a corresponding adjective exists in German, where there is the verb *wählen*, the noun *Wahl* and the adjective *wählerisch*, usually glossed as 'dainty', but equivalent in effect to 'choosey', and is it not likely that German Americans themselves created – probably unconsciously – the neologism 'choosey' as a parallel to the usage of their native tongue?

This type of process is all the more feasible because the average speaker fully imagines that the vocabulary of one language is merely the translation of the vocabulary of any other; that is he tends to disregard questions of idiom. In this way the Frenchman, who is used to wishing people *Bon appétit!* when he happens to see them seated at a meal, wonders why he is met with uncomprehending stares if he exclaims *Good appetite!* for the benefit of English diners. The phrase could in theory exist – it just so happens that it does not occur in this way in English – and in fact it has caught on in some European languages as a result of French example.

Similarly, then, the American phrase 'in a big way' is presumably due to Germans settled in the United States who felt the need for some English equivalent of their word *grossartig* in its adverbial use, which might be glossed, in fact, as 'in a big way', because of the components *gross* (big) and the root noun *Art* (way). If this supposition is correct, the new phrase would be all the more readily accepted in general American – and later British – usage because it forms a useful pendant to the old-established phrase of opposite meaning, 'in a small way'.

While the Briton has hitherto 'filled in' official forms, there are now some signs of his filling them 'out' in imitation of American idiom, which in turn might well be due to the similar German verb *ausfüllen*, whose prefix would naturally cause a German-American to use 'out' in his attempt to remember the English expression. And to *leaf through* a book, which is very recent in England, is probably of similar origin. In seventeenth-century English there was a verb 'to leaf', meaning to turn or turn over the leaves of a book, and the *O.E.D.* gives an example coming from the year 1613 in which the full expression is 'to leaf over'. The use of the verb 'to leaf' is marked in the dictionary as 'Now U.S.'. But in fact the modern American expression has a different preposition, since it is 'to leaf through', and it is significant that in German there is the verb *durchblättern*, of the same meaning. Again we find that the prepositional prefix *durch* is equivalent to the preposition used in American, namely 'through'. By now it is perhaps necessary to remind oneself that in England the traditional expression for this action was 'to thumb' the pages of a book.

The Americanism 'up and coming' is well established in Britain. Listed in the *S.E.D.* as 'U.S. 1889' it is defined in that dictionary as 'Active, alert, wide-awake', though one would have thought that its implications were rather those of a promising future. At all events, the origin seems to be the German adjective *aufkommend*, from *aufkommen* 'to come up, prosper, come into fashion'. But the last few years have seen the emergence of the synonymous 'upcoming', as when an article speaks of 'an upcoming tourist centre' (*Observer*, 7 Feb 1960). What is odd about this pair of adjectives is the chronology of their creation, since it might reasonably have been expected that 'upcoming' would appear first. Logically it is hard to see why 'up and coming' was formed at all, though perhaps its genesis was as fanciful as that of the slang American phrase 'out of sight' which is said to be a phonetic adaptation of German *ausgezeichnet* 'excellent'.

Expressions of time such as 'the first time for twenty years' are challenged by a newer form with a different preposition, namely, 'the first time *in* twenty years'. John Galsworthy commented on this usage as an Americanism in his *Castles in Spain*,[1] but saw it as an older English habit 'which time has murdered for us', and quoted the early Jacobean diary of Lady Anne Clifford in which he found the phrase 'I determined not to play again in three months'. Perhaps this is so, but what is even more striking is that in some parts of Germany the preposition '*in*' is used in the same way instead of the normal '*seit*', when speaking of past time. What strengthens the suspicion that the American idiom is due to German influence is the realization that English 'for' in such cases would sound rather like German *vor*, and since this means 'ago' the Teutonic immigrant would feel it to be confusing and would tend to substitute 'in'. What is curious is the rapidity with which the new phrase has spread in England, and it is not too much to say that it threatens in time to oust the traditional formula.

An unmistakable instance of an American expression coming from dialectal German rather than the standard language is the verb 'to dunk'. This first became known in England in the sense of dipping a biscuit or doughnut into some liquid such as coffee or milk, but evidently it can now denote any kind of rinsing. 'Do look at this pretty little blouse here . . . so simple to dunk' (*The Times*, 26 Oct 1959). This useful word is ultimately an off-shoot of the Pennsylvania German *dunken* (to dip) and not the standard *tunken*. Also in the domestic sphere, the cookery-book

[1] Heinemann, 1928, p. 54. The address 'On expression' in which the comment occurs was delivered in 1924.

is now often spoken of as a *cook-book*, in imitation of an American usage inspired by the corresponding German *Kochbuch*. A fashion of this type spreads extremely rapidly by way of women's magazines and entertainment programmes specially meant for women, and so it was that an early example of the word appeared, in a *Radio Times* announcement about the 'Woman's Hour' for 27 June 1955.

Round trip, which has been mentioned above as an Americanism successfully transplanted into British usage, is itself an obvious Germanic formation, based upon German *Rundfahrt*. An equally obvious borrowing from German-American is the use of 'mammoth' as an adjective indicating huge size, for the word *Mammut* is found in German compounds expressing vastness, and this even from the pen of such a writer as Thomas Mann. In Britain it has become something of a vogue-word, particularly in discussion of public affairs. 'The coal industry today is having to undertake this mammoth reorganization because of the failure of honourable Members opposite' as was said in the House of Commons (10 May 1956).

It is not often possible to quote a particular individual as having introduced a word to the country, but this is the case for 'slap-happy', which was popularized in a wartime broadcast by the American commentator Quentin Reynolds when he alluded to Reichsmarschall Goering as 'slap-happy Hermann'. One surmises that such compounds of -happy are echoes of a similar German use of the adjective *freudig*; for example a German scholar writing of the great upsurge of literary activity occurring at the Renaissance denoted this period as '*eine papierfreudige Zeit*', which might now be translated as 'a paper-happy time'. It might be thought, incidentally, that 'slap-happy' would be too colloquial a word ever to find its way into the austere pages of a learned periodical, but this is not so. The following sentence is taken from the weighty judgment of a scholarly reviewer. 'Apart from being slap-happy about facts and making astonishing inferences from them, he has left out the most important one' (*Modern Language Review*, Oct 1956). The basic feature of words such as this one, together with the wartime *bomb-happy*, *sun-happy* and *sand-happy* is that they originally refer to a species of lightheadedness induced by physical or emotional strain. *Trigger-happy* sprang from this same psychological origin, since nervous troops are likely to fire at anything which suddenly alarms them. 'Slap-happy' presumably refers to the mental state of a boxer who is 'punch-drunk' though in the extract cited above it has come to mean mere negligence. At any rate, this type of formation is of the utmost interest, for here we have not merely a new word or two but the means of forming an unlimited number of neologisms of the same pattern.[1]

A journalistic habit which comes from German by way of America is the prefacing of a politician's rank to his name; thus Prime Minister Harold Wilson, and so on. This ponderous usage is mostly avoided by the more thoughtful press but is evidently considered fashionable elsewhere. Indeed the popular newspapers extend the process to cover almost any conceivable human activity, and will readily refer to 'Champion weight-lifter John Smith' or 'Marathon peanut-eater Billie Robinson'. Fortunately this method of identification has not yet invaded conversational English, though it can be heard from the lips of B.B.C. announcers.

In 1944 Horwill explained 'the next man' as meaning 'anyone else, the first comer' in the United States, though this is no longer regarded as specifically American and furthermore this pattern can be applied to any noun at all. So 'He can appreciate the "excruciatingly bad taste" of a Lancashire living-room as well as the next designer' in the *Sunday Times* (5 Mar 1961) and 'The Bishop of Münster was as stout a nationalist and anti-Bolshevik as the next prelate' in the *Observer* (15 Nov 1964). It is possible that in the United States this type of phrase was originally of Irish paternity. Thus in O'Casey's *Juno and the Paycock* (1925) a character exclaims towards the end of the play 'We have to live as well as the nex' man'. This suggestion is very tentative indeed,

[1] Cf. FIGURE-HAPPY CONSERVATIVES, a heading in the Roman Catholic weekly, *The Tablet* (9 Nov 1963).

but if it is correct it can be added that the idiom would particularly commend itself to those Americans whose first language was
German, because English-speaking Germans often in any case
mistreat the word 'next', making it mean 'nearest' like their own
similarly pronounced *nächst*. A German enquiring in a London
street for the 'next' Underground station may cause some
consternation, though the question seems quite logical to him,
and would indeed be quite normal when travelling below ground,
but he tends not to realize that in English the adjectival 'next'
implies order in a series rather than proximity.[1] Similarly in
Arthur Koestler's first book in English, *The Scum of the Earth*, 'He
asked him where the next military barracks were' (p. 130),
where he really means 'nearest'. (Mr Koestler is of Hungarian
origin, but has a good knowledge of German.) The point is that
in German *nächst* can on different occasions fulfil both functions
('next' and 'nearest'), so that the German who is speaking English
naturally imagines that the same is true in his adopted language,
hence 'the next drugstore, the next cinema' and so forth. 'The
next man' may bring the same process into play.

    If 'the next man' is indeed of Irish origin in the first place it is
not the only phrase to have reached the United States from Erin.
The birthplace of a curious idiom involving the use of the
preposition 'on' may be guessed from the first few lines of act 2
of *The Tinker's Wedding* by the Irish writer J. M. Synge.

    'There she is washing up on us, and I thinking we'd have the
job done before she'd know of it at all.'

    Similarly Synge writes on p. 53 of *The Aran Islands* (1912) 'A
farmer was in great distress, as his crops had failed, and his cow
had died on him'.[2] This sort of idiom became widely current in
the U.S.A. and is now frequent in Britain and is very graphic
inasmuch as it would be extremely difficult to express by any
other words the exact shade of meaning that it conveys. Nor does
it seem to be regarded as particularly colloquial. Graham Hough,

[1] Though proximity is implied in certain stock expressions: *next door, my next
neighbour*, etc.
[2] London and Dublin, 1912.

Fellow of Christ's College, Cambridge, said in the course of a Third Programme talk 'The woman who has been unsexed before you suddenly turns woman on you after all' (2 Dec 1956), while the final accolade of approval was conferred on this grammatical construction by a *Times* leader on 2 July 1960. 'Ever since the Castro revolution began to turn sour on it, the United States government has leaned over backwards to avoid provocation.' Whatever its exact starting-point – whether Ireland or not – there is no doubt that in the short run this type of expression found its way into Britain from America. The sentence just quoted from *The Times* also contains another Americanism, the ever-popular 'leaning over backwards', which presumably started life as a metaphor derived from some specific literal usage, as did 'scraping the bottom of the barrel'.

In addition to Germanisms imported via the United States there have been a number of borrowings from German as a result of the second world war, either from military vocabulary or from Nazi jargon. Hitler's constant denunciation of the Versailles Treaty as a *Diktat* has led to the entry of this word into the English language, complete with the original spelling, and it is used not only in the political sphere, as for example by Mr Macmillan – then Foreign Secretary – at Geneva in 1955, but also on any plane at all, however prosaic. Thus a *News Chronicle* article of 22 November 1955 was critical of the Potato Marketing Board and stated that 'To ensure that its diktat is obeyed, the board's inspectors may enter and inspect a grower's land'. A similar fate has overtaken the haughty concept of *Lebensraum*, once envisaged as the vital living space of the Aryan master-race, for in *The Times* of 13 January 1960 it was actually used in an article on rabbits. On the same page, by the way, was to be found a reference to 'American belief in Fortress America', which is obviously modelled on the phrase summing up the German strategy of defending their European conquests, i.e. *Festung Europa*. Most famous of all is 'blitz' to denote a massive aerial attack on a town, and this useful word filled the semantic gap caused by the inadequacy of the existing 'air-raid' to render the idea of prolonged, large-scale bombing of a type rarely experienced in the First World War. Linguistically this is of course a misnomer, the original *Blitzkrieg* being applied to the 'lightning war' which would crush an enemy before effective resistance could be brought to bear. Probably due to the inventiveness of some unknown journalist, the English abbreviation rapidly established itself in our vocabulary, together with the accompanying coinage of the verb 'to *blitz*' which made it possible to speak of blitzed towns and so on. Also from German is *flak* for anti-aircraft fire, being the abbreviation of the compound *Fliegerabwehrkanone*, 'anti-aircraft gun'. But here we have merely a case of a word dating back to the context of the war itself, like the similar 'archies' of the First World War.

In addition to the more obvious wartime borrowings from German it is tempting to see that language as the origin of the phrase 'to put someone into the picture'. Much favoured by British officers briefing their subordinates it corresponds exactly to the idiom *ins Bild setzen*, so it may be that it was by way of translations of enemy documents that this useful bit of jargon passed into British military terminology in the first place and thence into general currency. The general idea of 'the picture' as a term for a particular situation had been brought to the fore just after the first war in the expression 'to come into the picture', dated 1919 by the supplement to the *O.E.D.*

The subject of wartime English is a vast one in itself and cannot even be summarized here. Many creations of that time were in the nature of things quite ephemeral and have passed into history. How many now remember Medloc, or Paiforce or a B release? But some coinages have been more durable and a good treatment of the topic will be found in *Wartime English*, by Professor Zandvoort and his assistants.[1]

All borrowings from German are not the product of hostilities, however. A vogue-word nowadays is *angst*, literally 'fear', but used to denote a species of anguish (a historically related word, by the way, since like *angst* it ultimately derives from Latin *angustia*).

[1] Groningen, 1957.

A general disgust and dissatisfaction with the state of the world, in fact. Phonetically, *angst* has perhaps been all the more readily accepted since it begins with the same syllable as the synonymous 'anguish', just as such related words as 'blast', 'blight' and 'blow up' paved the phonetic way for 'blitz' by their initial consonantal group. 'It is only here in the West that one experiences *angst*. *Angst* is not known in Finland,' says the *Sunday Times* (6 Mar 1955). The term has come into English via literary and philosophical jargon. In a more mundane sphere the Germans have been among the pioneers of road-making in the twentieth century, so that their word *Autobahn* has been taken into Italy as *autostrada*, into France as *autoroute* and now into English in the form 'motorway', which of course is constructed as a word-form on the model of the European terms. It may also be the case that another recent vogue-word *built-in* is ultimately from the German *eingebaut*, alluding to such things as the built-in radio set of a car, built-in cupboards of a house and other installations. In a catalogue issued in 1957 by the world's most famous motorcar manufacturers the claim was made that 'Space is provided for in-built heater and radio' and what is interesting here is the structure of the variant 'in-built' which exactly recalls that of *eingebaut*, with the preposition in first place. In view of German technical proficiency and activity it is certainly likely that 'in-built' and 'built-in' are loan translations of that word. Round about 1960 these expressions, and especially the latter, began to be worked to death by public speakers and writers, with the abstract sense of 'inherent' or 'inborn'. 'We have an in-built resistance to advertising,' stated a speaker in a B.B.C. programme of 1 December 1959. It should be noted that the metaphor does not imply any deliberate intention, in spite of the allusion to building. 'It looks as if this long-term, built-in shortage of teachers is here to stay . . .' (*Time and Tide*, 24 May 1964). The least that can be said is that this usage is very revealing of the importance of the technological type of thinking prevalent in our society.

Scandinavia has handed on one or two words in the last few

years. The *anorak* – that is, a jacket with attached hood for use in cold climates – originally took its name from the Eskimos, and was used in Danish. Thence it was borrowed into French, where it was extant by 1934, somewhat earlier than in English, which did not use it to any great extent until the nineteen-fifties. An amusing article which appeared in the *Sunday Times* of 19 January 1958 mentioned this garment in connection with a man's duties during a ski-ing holiday. '... he can wax your skis, carry extra gloves, hood, glasses, purse, lipstick and powder, which would otherwise, in bulging pockets, spoil the line of your anorak.' Whether the word came into English direct from the Scandinavian languages or whether it was borrowed by way of the Swiss Alps would be difficult to say. 'Ombudsman' certainly was taken direct from Scandinavia, and was first heard of in 1959 as the name of an official whose function is to investigate citizens' complaints against officialdom, though in fact the Norwegian *ombudsman* would appear simply to mean 'official' or 'commissioner' in the first place. By January 1960 it was already possible to come across the English form of the plural, i.e. *ombudsmen*, though here as in the singular there is evidently some uncertainty as to whether the stress falls on the first or second syllable. Then in 1966 an ombudsman (though that was not his official title) was appointed by the British government, and styled a Parliamentary Commissioner.

Though names of foods such as *scampi* and *risotto* are becoming better known in Britain than at one time, the greatest contributions of the Italian language to our vocabulary are undoubtedly the names of the Espresso coffee-bar and the Vespa motor-scooter. *Motor-scooter* is in itself a new compound dating from wartime days when parachutists used a somewhat smaller version than the type now ridden by housewives on shopping expeditions and clerks on their way to the office. There seemed at one time a distinct possibility that the Vespa trade-name might become a generic description used indiscriminately of all makes of motor-scooter. (This type of development delights manufacturers initially, as a sign of commercial success, but they are rightly alarmed when they ultimately realize that they have thereby lost their distinctive identity.) Vespa is in origin simply the Italian word for 'wasp', and it is a pity in some ways that it has not in the event become adopted as a proper noun in English, leaving 'motor-scooter' (or 'scooter', as it often is) to denote the 'motor-assisted pedal cycle' that has been called a *moped* after a lengthy period without any fixed name.[1]

If the Espresso bar is of recent appearance, the expression 'coffee-bar' is old-established, figuring in the Supplement to the *O.E.D.* as 'a bar or barrow at which coffee is sold. . . .' This is not of course the coffee-bar beloved of present-day youth, so that this word has in reality undergone a modification of its sense. T. E. Lawrence uses it with its old meaning in *The Mint*, alluding to an incident during his R.A.F. service in 1922. 'Snaggletooth went to the coffee-bar (which a humane custom permitted till midnight just inside the gate, to refresh those coming off late pass) and brought back a mess-tin of hot tea' (p. 75).[2]

The most noteworthy contribution of the Spanish language to the contemporary English vocabulary is to be found in the fashionable phrase *the moment of truth*, meaning a moment of crisis in which someone is facing a danger or difficulty that will test him to the full, stripping bare any bluff or inadequacy. It is a translation of the Spanish expression *el momento de la verdad* (there is also *la hora de la verdad*) which has a number of senses, including that one just mentioned, but in particular the supreme instant of the bullfight when the matador is about to deliver the final thrust of his sword while exposing himself to danger. It is this application of the phrase which explains its passage into English, probably by way of a specific piece of writing in Ernest Hemingway's book on bullfighting, *Death in the Afternoon* (1932). 'The whole end of the bullfight was the final sword thrust, the actual encounter between the man and the animal, what the Spanish call the moment of truth . . .' (p. 68). The popularity of this work

---

[1] *Moped* is itself an ultimate Swedish loan-word, according to Charles Barber, p. 100 of *Linguistic Change in Present-day English*, Oliver and Boyd, 1964.
[2] Cape, 1955.

and the growing interest taken in bullfighting by the English-speaking peoples would be sufficient to cause the spread and adoption of this graphic term, but in an interesting note on the subject published in *Word Study* (1964, vol. XL, p. 7) Paul O. Williams of Duke University points out that 'truth' here means something rather different from the usual meanings of the word, and that even the obvious sense of 'the real state of affairs' is not quite apposite in this case where 'truth' '. . . narrows this meaning by implying something about the real state of affairs, namely, that a man is being shown to embody frailty or inadequacy. Hence it is an expression well suited to the uses of the plentiful ironists of our time.' In particular *the moment of truth* is a welcome addition to the vocabulary of writers on political and economic themes. R. W. Thompson, writing on the military subject of *The Battle for the Rhineland* (Hutchinson, 1958) used the phrase as a chapter heading, and also wrote 'It is possible to fix the moment of truth with some precision' (p. 114), meaning that January 1945 was the final decisive clash in the western assault on Germany.

Spanish has likewise contributed *aficionado* by way of the United States, where it was applied first of all to a devotee of bull-fighting and then to a 'fan' of any sport or activity. In Spanish this noun derives from a verb *aficionar* 'to inspire affection'. The spelling of *aficionada* is sometimes a little shaky in British hands, and the form 'afficionadoes' has even been detected in one of the more scholarly newspapers. Some words of Spanish origin which have long been familiar in American English have become generally known in the British Isles only in recent times, as in the case of *rodeo* and, later still, *bonanza*, which in the original language meant 'fair weather at sea, prosperity' and has now come to indicate any 'boom' or time of quick profits. *Barbecue*, going back by way of Spanish to a Haitian word, has long appeared in the English dictionaries, and is attested in the late seventeenth century in the sense of a framework used in the New World for smoking or drying meat over a fire, but only in the last few years has it become fashionable because of the American meaning of an open-air social gathering at which animals are roasted whole. It will be seen that these borrowings are from the Spanish of the American continents, but with the greatly increased numbers of British visitors to Spain it is likely that words may now come directly into English from that country, if only as the names of delicacies such as *paella* and *gazpacho*.

With the tremendous upsurge in power and prestige of the Soviet Union it is to be expected that the Russian language will now become a rich source of neologisms. The successful launching by the Russians of the first space satellite in October 1957 posed many problems for the western nations, the least weighty of them being the actual naming in the various national languages of that epoch-making device. At first the British press expressed itself in lunar metaphors for a few days with allusions to 'the artificial moon' and 'the Red moon', but very soon the Russian word *sputnik* arrived on the scene and is by now a well-established member of the English vocabulary, though only in reference to Soviet space-ships. The importance of this borrowing is that it has given a new lease of life to the suffix *-nik* which had already made its appearance, at any rate in the U.S.A., as a loan from Yiddish. So far new creations in *-nik* have usually been of a humorous nature; thus, a device which failed to go into orbit was derided in December 1957 as a Kaputnik (*Daily Express*), a Flopnik (*Daily Herald*), a Puffnik (*Daily Mail*) and a Stayputnik (*News Chronicle*), the latter being faintly reminiscent of *sputnik*. An exception to the general rule that new words in *-nik* are ephemeral and not to be taken too seriously is *beatnik*, since from about 1962 it had to be reckoned that this was going to be a permanent member of the vocabulary. Curiously enough, a certain amount of confusion surrounds the origins of this neologism, so much so that it is not even definitely known whether its final syllable is to be ascribed to a copying of the Yiddish or the Russian *-nik*, and to make matters worse its root syllable is also variously explained, though it seems likely that it is connected with the idea of the Beat Generation, whose original spokesman was the writer Jack Kerouac. In fact Kerouac claims to have invented the name of the movement in 1948. The *Britannica Book of the Year* recorded its appearance in 1958. According to William and Mary Morris's *Dictionary of Word and Phrase Origins*[1] this use of 'beat' came from the slang of jazz musicians and means 'worn out, exhausted'. They further explain that Kerouac claimed that the origin was to be found in '*beatified*', but rightly refuse to accept this. With regard to the most likely source, the allusion to exhaustion, one might recall *dead beat*, British soldiers' slang of 1914–1918, and glossed as 'Utterly fatigued, worn out and past caring' in *The Long Trail* by John Brophy and Eric Partridge.[2] Or to put it at its simplest, 'beat' has for a long time been a variant of 'beaten' in many parts of the English-speaking world. The beat generation 'couldn't care less' what happens.

To return to Russian, Trotsky apparently used to be in the habit of using a relative of *sputnik* when speaking of non-Communist writers who sympathized with Soviet aims, and that was *poputchik*, literally 'fellow traveller'. Like *sputnik*, this has as its root the word *put'*, i.e. 'way' or 'path'. A *poputchik* is one who takes the same path. It is unknown in English in that form, but is widely used in the translated version *fellow-traveller*, 'Communist sympathizer'. This sense is dated 1942 by the *Shorter Oxford English Dictionary*. A characteristic feature of the Soviet power-system is the *apparatchik*, a firmly entrenched bureaucrat who is the equivalent, more or less, of the western 'organization man'. The Russian term is not very well known in Britain, but is occasionally used by journalists and others, who will write, for example, about the 'apparatchiks' (with English plural form) of the B.B.C. Possibly it will be used more frequently in future, with the proliferation of state activity in Britain.

That is less likely to be true of *troika*, a Russian term indicating a group of three, a 'threesome' as it were (and in particular, three horses running abreast in a team). Meaning 'triumvirate' it became known to some extent in the British press as a result of the Soviet political events following the downfall of Khrushchev, and lingers on to some extent, as in Anthony Sampson's *Anatomy*

[1] Harper and Row, 1962.   [2] Deutsch, 1965.

of Britain Today (1965) where on p. 113 he speaks of 'James Callaghan . . . the third in the troika'.[1] It will indeed be interesting to see whether *troika* survives in the English vocabulary. Because of the initial group *tr-* it is easily associated with such words as 'three, triple, trio, triad' but possibly the average Englishman will wrongly imagine that *troika* is the name of a Russian musical instrument on account of the ending *-ka* which seems to put it into the same category as 'balalaika'.

At intervals in the course of its history the English language tends to feel the need to borrow from a foreign tongue a term describing small bands of fighting men operating more or less independently of one another and striking deep into enemy-held country, e.g. guerrillas and commandos. During the Second World War the Russian language gave *partisans* (or *partizans*) and though this word is rarely heard at present it will no doubt always be used by historians of that war in connection with the Russian war effort. Though it is indisputable that it achieved fame because of that war it is possible to trace its appearance in English back to the Spanish Civil War, in fact to its inclusion in Hemingway's *For Whom the Bell Tolls*, where in the first chapter a Russian asks the hero, Robert Jordan, 'How do you like *partizan* work?' In the following sentence Hemingway defines the word by saying 'It was the Russian term for guerilla work behind the lines'. So evidently it had gained a certain currency in the jargon of soldiers on the Spanish republican side as a consequence of unofficial Soviet participation in the civil war. Since the date of publication of Hemingway's novel was March 1941 it antedates the direct borrowing of *partisan* from fighting in the Soviet Union, which did not suffer German invasion until April of that year.

Also from the Slavonic family of languages comes *robot*, a Czech word in origin. It comes from a work of imagination, Karel Čapek's play *R.U.R.* (Rossum's Universal Robots), where it indicates an automaton with apparently human powers and intelligence. Though the play was successfully produced in London in 1923 it was not until the eve of the 'thirties that this word

[1] Hodder and Stoughton.

(based, by the way, on the root meaning 'work') became really fashionable. As this period coincided with the introduction of automatic traffic signals in Britain it so happened that 'robot' was initially applied to them, though in fact it has never really caught on in popular usage in that sense, and though the 1964 *Concise Oxford Dictionary* still retains this as one of the definitions of the word they are universally known as 'traffic lights'. Because of the suffix '-ot' it sometimes came about that 'robot' was taken for a French word and accordingly pronounced 'roh-boh'. Around 1930 the belief that a word is made more intelligible by pronouncing fully-fledged vowels in unstressed syllables was not as strong as it is now, so that the other usual pronunciation was simply 'Robert'. It was interesting to see that in the 1964 B.B.C. television serial 'Dr Who' there was still an echo of the Frenchified pronunciation in the name of the Robomen, humans deprived of normal reactions and initiative and responding only to instructions. During the war the so-called *Doodlebugs* or *flying bombs* were officially known as the *Robot bomb*, presumably since they were pilotless and hit their target once the power supply was automatically cut off. In a technological society there is every likelihood that 'robot' has a long career ahead of it, in application to either people or machines.

Just as American Negroes have imposed upon the Western world their love of gaudy colours and raucous music, so they have provided their countrymen with a number of words of ultimately African origin, one or two of which have made some impression on British English. The *juke box* takes its root word from the Gullah dialect of Negroes living in South Carolina and Georgia. These Gullahs have hitherto lived in great isolation, with the result that their speech retains a good many African features. 'Juke' has been shown to be of African origin in Professor Turner's *Africanisms in the Gullah Dialect* (Chicago, 1949), its meaning in Gullah being 'disorderly', particularly in the expression 'juke house'. One imagines that the connection between 'juke' in its latter sense and 'juke box' is the same as that explaining the link between the name of 'jazz music' and the original verb 'jazz' denoting the human male's most important generic activity (itself probably an African word), for as has been pointed out by the blues singer Billie Holiday in her autobiography, there used to be a time when white Americans only heard such music in brothels. The verb 'tote' meaning 'carry' is perhaps only slightly known in Britain, but it is probably another example of a Gullah retention of a word brought to America by African slaves, for Turner has shown the existence of *tota* 'to pick up' in certain West African languages. On those occasions when the word is used in British English it is probably always in an ultimately American context (to tote a gun, and so forth) so that it is far from being completely naturalized. Its most noteworthy occurrence was in the song *Ole Man River*, imported from the United States some four decades ago.

The *calypso* is defined by the *S.E.D.* as 'A song, characteristic of the West Indies, composed spontaneously on some topic of present interest, to the accompaniment of a band' and is listed as being of unknown origin. According to Mr Michael Hinkson in a letter to the *Observer* (24 Nov 1957) it was first a joyous song of the Caribs, the original inhabitants of Trinidad, but when African slaves were brought there they introduced their own type of instruments and made the 'carieto' of the Caribs into the calypso of the eighteen-nineties. Then as now the calypso was essentially a commentary on some person or event making an impression on the singer. A well-known B.B.C. programme had until 1960 what it called a 'Topical calypso', recounting items of the day's news with humorous comment, but this title was something of a pleonasm since a calypso is topical by definition. It might almost be said that in the English-speaking world the calypso is the nearest equivalent to the witty songs of the French *chansonnier*.

Before leaving the topic of exotic music we may make passing mention of the *didgeridoo*, a primitive instrument played by Australian aborigines. This curiously named instrument was duly listed in the Addenda of the *S.E.D.* but not dated.

In the past Dutch has passed on a number of words into British

English by way of transatlantic uses coming from Dutch settlements in America, and one thinks in this connection of such examples as 'boss, dope, poppycock, waffle, Santa Claus'. This source of neologisms has not been very prolific of late, however. It is just possible, though, that Dutch is at the root of the Americanism 'how come?' that has been struggling to get a firm foothold in colloquial British usage since before 1939. The point is that in Afrikaans, the Dutch of South Africa, there exists the interrogative *hoekom* meaning 'why?', whose function is normally performed in the Dutch of Holland by *waarom*. It is not suggested that Afrikaans has had any influence on American colloquial speech but (and this is very tentative) it seems possible that *hoekom* was part of the dialectal vocabulary of Dutch settlers in America and therefore it was adopted as 'how come' by those who apprehended the word as such. The expression has a precarious existence in Britain, at any rate in the spoken language, and was first heard by me in this context about 1937. But written examples are hard to find from that period.

The Dutch of South Africa (*spoor, trek* and *veld*), has given the word *apartheid* to the English language as a result of the South African policy of racial segregation. Curiously enough, not all English speakers recognize the root idea *apart* in this expression, and so they may pronounce the *th* with the same value as in either 'the' or 'think', whereas in fact the *t* and the *h* belong to different syllables. The *S.E.D.* lists *apartheid* with the dating 1949, and this was of course with the original specific meaning proper to its South African context. Later it came to imply segregation of any kind, and so in discussing the concept of 'the working-class writer' a writer to the *London Magazine* said 'Labels which unconsciously proclaim a brand of apartheid strike me not only as self-conscious but also as seriously inhibiting' (Mar 1956). So far has the process gone that this word can now be applied to countries other than South Africa and Britain, in a manner which might at one time have seemed somewhat incongruous. 'Apartheid in India was, and often remains, extreme,' states Raymond Mortimer in the *Sunday Times* (8 Feb

1959). Perhaps it is fair to say that terms descriptive of a rigid caste system will·always find a ready home in British English.

Recent Chinese derivatives are not common in contemporary English, though some political slogans have become widely known, such as 'a great leap forward', an expression launched by Mao. *Brainwashing* dates from about 1951. Consisting of the application of psychological pressures whereby a human personality is broken down and reshaped in the interests of a particular ideology, it is nothing new in human history, but this name is an imitation of a Chinese expression for the technique widely practised by the Chinese authorities in the handling of political prisoners and prisoners of war. The metaphor is a striking and unusual one which seems to arouse strong feelings of horror in many people, though it is difficult to prove why it should be improper to brainwash a Jack the Ripper or Adolf Hitler into being at any rate innocuous members of society.

On a happier note, let us record the entry into the British vocabulary of the *cheongsam*, Hong Kong's greatest contribution to the happiness of mankind, being the attractive slit skirt worn by the young girls of that town and occasionally seen in the West.

Passing to Japanese, we have *origami* which is the art of folding paper into intricate designs. This began to be widely known in Britain by 1964 and at least two books had been written in English on the subject. *Tycoon*, a high-powered business magnate (or 'big bug' as the *S.E.D.* has it), is correctly thought of as coming into Britain from the United States, but in origin it is the Japanese *taikun* 'great prince', the title applied by westerners to the Shogun of Japan in the middle of the nineteenth century. In Britain 'tycoon' has been well-known and used since at least 1950 and is no longer thought of as an Americanism. *Karate*, 'empty handed', the art of fighting with the bare hands, is Japanese, as is *kamikaze*, the name of the Japanese 'suicide pilots' who crashed their bomb-laden planes on enemy ships during the war.

3

The New Society

SOCIAL, technical and economic conditions in Britain have changed at a tremendous rate since the ending of the first world war and indeed it is evident by now that science transforms man's environment at a pace which is not merely rapid but swiftly accelerating. Throughout all the ages the elderly have lectured their juniors on the happiness of the old days and the decadence of present manners, but nowadays change is so rapid that anyone out of the first flush of youth tends to feel slightly out of date. The tramcar belongs to a former age and the steam locomotive is already a living museum piece, while there are those who speak of ripping up the railway lines altogether and replacing them by motorways. After the proud triumphs of the earphones and loud-speaker even wireless has taken on an old-fashioned air alongside the television set and is patronisingly alluded to as *steam-radio* – steam being a symbol of antiquity, one supposes. Technical changes have inevitably had their repercussions in the social and moral spheres, and it has been claimed with much reason that sexual morality has been greatly influenced by the invention of the internal combustion engine. Certainly it is true that in effect the world has shrunk because of easier means of travel and communication, so that in the realms of politics the average man is perhaps more conscious of events in the Far East or darkest Africa than his grandfather was of happenings in the neighbouring county. Yet paradoxically the individual is possibly at the same time more cut off from the other members of the community in which he lives and is faced by moral dilemmas his ancestors never dreamed of. Even the very vocabulary of such moral problems would have been incomprehensible not so long ago. 'Why, by the way, should it be thought *anti-social* for people to buy durable *household equipment* (say a wardrobe) on *hire-purchase* but not to buy their house (with perhaps a *fitted* wardrobe included) on the *instalment plan*?' (The third Fawley Foundation lecture, 1956.) *Anti-social* is not in itself a new word, but its meaning has changed twice since first it was coined in the late eighteenth century. It then meant 'opposed to society or com-panionship', but by the middle of the following century it had come to mean 'opposed to the principles on which society is constituted'. The present sense of 'contrary to the interest or welfare of one's fellow-men' is first attested in 1934 according to the *S.E.D.* One occasionally comes across *anti-sociability* in this sense, though this is too reminiscent of 'sociable' ever to serve as the obvious substantival form of the new 'anti-social'. It is found however in *The Modern Mind* by Michael Roberts (p. 61).[1]

The old personal criterion of right versus wrong has to some ex-tent gone by the board, so that one does not merely speak of a man as devoid of conscience but as lacking a 'social conscience', while it is not enough to say that he is brutal and domineering – he is 'fascist-minded'. The great movements of the twentieth century, themselves partly the product of technical change, have powerfully affected men's thinking in these matters. Meanwhile modern psychological doctrine has so impressed itself on the popular outlook that even an account of a football match calls forth Freudian imagery. 'But Blanchflower in essence conducts a love-hate relationship with the game,' states the football critic of the *Observer* (22 Nov 1959).

In such circumstances it is hardly surprising that the English language has had to admit new words descriptive of the new scene, for an age is characterized by its vocabulary and imagery and it would not be difficult for the linguistic historian to come to the correct conclusion that our own time has been shaped by scientific technique above all else. Even writers on educational affairs speak of 'stepping up' the 'output' of graduates who are the 'end-product' of university training and who have presumably

[1] Faber, 1937.

been suitably 'processed'. *Processing* is 'any alteration in properties intentionally induced [in food] by physical, chemical or biological means', i.e. pasteurization, boiling, sterilization, smoking, concentration, drying, freeze-drying, quick freezing, milling, pickling, bleaching, preservation, souring, fermentation, etc. But the verb 'to process' is a maid-of-all-work in that it is used in ways taking it far beyond its original meaning, and modern usage applies it to almost any repetitive act or one which occasions change of any kind, so that the object of the act of processing may be anything at all. A report in the *Daily Telegraph* (28 Jan 1955) pointed out that London Airport officials speak of processing passengers, i.e. shepherding them through the formalities required for air travel. The ultimate semantic development of this verb was found in *Time* magazine when it mentioned how an oriental potentate had processed so many thousand women in the course of his reign. All this should not of course be linked with that verb 'process' in which the stress falls on the final syllable and whose meaning is 'go in procession'. An originally jocular formation from 'procession', this term is of surprisingly ancient vintage, going back as it does to the early nineteenth century.

With the spread of bureaucracy inevitable in the modern state and particularly in the *Welfare State* (one of those phrases that began as a jibe and ended as the standard expression) it is inevitable that human beings should not only be 'processed' but also catalogued, listed, and generally have their activities recorded in official files. KEEPING TABS ON THE ALIEN was a heading in *The Times* making use for this purpose of an expression transplanted from American to British usage from at least the mid-thirties so far as the spoken language is concerned, though this headline postdates that by a quarter of a century (15 March 1960). Keeping tabs (tabulations?) is not however something done to humans alone but to anything susceptible of inclusion in a filing system. 'The Home Office has just completed the first half of a £1 million-a-year project to keep tabs on fall-out,' announced the *Observer* in a typically modern sentence (22 Nov 1959).

A *Listener* article spoke of 'a small correspondence about

"working-class" literature, sparked-off by an editorial' (5 Apr 1956) and this technological metaphor has achieved great popularity in recent years, so that in commenting on her matrimonial trouble Miss Diana Dors once told press reporters that she did not know what had 'sparked it off'. As we all are aware, conjugal difficulties are liable to arise by 'chain reaction', an expression properly alluding to the fact that when a nucleus of uranium is split by a neutron, energy is released, and at the same time it emits more neutrons which in turn split more nuclei and so on. The reaction is self-sustaining, in fact. Nuclear physics is itself a splendid example of the imitation of art by life, since H. G. Wells used the phrase 'atomic bomb' in the *Century Magazine* in 1914 some thirty years before the first atomic explosion took place. Actually, until the bombardment of Hiroshima and Nagasaki in 1945 the idea of radio-activity was associated in the public mind with the treatment of cancer and was therefore beneficent in tone. Metaphorically it implied a sort of admirable energy. In 1927 Logan Pearsall Smith wrote of 'this radio-active quality of popular idiom' and C. E. Montague's *Disenchantment* mentioned 'the radio-activity of gifted teaching'. It is clear that the whole concept of radio-activity has changed since those days and now stands chiefly for a fearful threat hanging over mankind. And is it not extraordinary that even the elementary words 'cold' and 'hot' have had overtones of horror added to them by the present international situation? *Cold war* and *hot war* are to be found both in English and Russian, and also – one supposes – in every language in which such matters are discussed. 'Cold war' was coined in 1947 by the American commentator Walter Lippmann and 'hot war' was a natural sequel.

In like manner a new dimension has been added to such words as 'device', 'deterrent' and 'clean' (bomb) which became part of the nuclear vocabulary in 1957. Furthermore the method of counting backwards which is utilized in the launching of a rocket (new style) has given rise to the expression 'to count down' and also 'the count-down', which latter can for obvious reasons easily acquire gloomy implications. 'Whatever the future holds, there is no sign that a sinister, doom-fraught count-down is in progress' (*Sunday Times*, 31 Jan 1960). Let us hope that this continues to be so and that nuclear warfare will remain for ever in the realm of *science fiction*, a term invented in 1926 by the American Hugo Gernsback. Meanwhile the existence of a mode of warfare totally different in kind from any used until 1945 has caused such traditional weapons as artillery and infantry to be labelled 'conventional', which is surely a most unforeseen fate for this inoffensive word.

A curious and pleasanter by-product of experiments in nuclear weaponry (to use a modern word sounding like a cross between 'weapon' and 'armoury') is the name of the *bikini*, aptly described in Mary Reifer's *Dictionary of New Words*[1] as 'A type of very scanty woman's bathing suit', and named after the atoll in the Pacific on which an atomic explosion was staged in 1946. Some recent commentators do not seem to have adequately grasped the motivation of this word, however. Thus J. A. Sheard in his book *The Words We Use*[2] says that 'The connection here is not immediately obvious' (p. 90), while John Moore in *You English Words*[3] also seems puzzled by *bikini* (p. 211). The simple explanation is of course that the sight of a shapely young woman clad in this costume is supposed to set off in the male spectator an emotional reaction equal in force to that of the atomic explosion at Bikini. Such is the ability of modern advertising experts to make capital out of a dangerous situation. ('Bikini' is naturally one of those international words having currency in many languages, and at this point it is impossible to pass over in silence the strange derivatives developed from it in France in the year 1964 when there was much talk of a topless bathing suit, immediately known as the *monokini*. Here we have a splendid specimen of what etymologists call 'popular etymology'.)

One hopeful possibility in a century that has had more than its share of war is that man's innate aggressiveness will find a satisfactory outlet in the competitive exploration of space. Now that the first steps in this direction have been taken there exists already

[1] Peter Owen, 1957.   [2] André Deutsch, 1954.   [3] Collins, 1961.

a whole technical vocabulary that is being created in answer to the demands of the new science of space travel, itself dependent on *rocketry*. The *cosmonaut* (a word invented by the Russians and displayed by them on placards and banners on the day of Gagarin's first flight in 1961) travels in a *capsule* (like *probe* this is an old word put to a new use) *blasted off* from a *launching pad*. The *space suit* he wears had a name in science fiction even before it existed in reality. At present these *spacemen* have confined themselves to *orbiting* round the earth but they hope in due course to set up *space platforms* or *space stations* from which to conduct explorations of the moon and planets. All this vocabulary really forms a subject in itself, ranging from the *retro-rocket*, which so to speak puts on the brakes for the space traveller, to the *emotional indoctrination training* which teaches him to endure both fear and endless boredom as he hurtles towards Venus or Mars. Meanwhile television fantasies of adventures in space are sometimes known as *space operas* on the analogy of the so-called *soap operas*, the adventure programmes whose ultimate purpose is to help to advertise soaps and soap powders.

Recent dramatic developments in the technical sphere may have somewhat clouded our awareness of the neologisms arising from the war of 1939–1945, e.g. *airborne* (and the jocular 'chairborne'), *aircrew, airfield, airgraph, airstrip*, etc., to name only a few taken from the compilation of Professor R. W. Zandvoort already quoted. Indeed it is astonishing nowadays to read in the supplement of the *O.E.D.* a definition of *aircraft* stating that the word was used of flying machines collectively and only rarely of an individual aeroplane. Even the main body of the *S.E.D.* of 1955 explains the word solely as meaning 'Flying machines collectively'! This is a truly remarkable example of an incomplete definition, for during the war it was officially laid down that it could apply to a single machine, and in fact this was the usual sense.[1] Here we have a modification of meaning rather than the creation of a new word (the word itself antedates the 1914 war) and it is well-known that wartime conditions frequently give a

[1] By analogy with 'aircraft' we now have *spacecraft*.

new twist to an existing term, e.g. 'austerity, pool (as in 'pool petrol', the unbranded petrol of wartime days), expendable, collaboration, intake (new man or group of men being admitted to military depot, hospital, jail, etc.), siren, infiltrate, screen' (investigate credentials of potential suspects). In this sense 'screen' is usually taken to be of American origin. It is a word which sometimes puzzles people who find it difficult to grasp that to screen a suspect is not to gloss over his activities but on the contrary to subject them to a searching examination. But the point is that this verb has nothing to do with the screen which is a device for shielding from view, but must rather be connected with the old-established verb 'screen' meaning to sift by passing through a screen, i.e. an apparatus utilized for the sorting of coal, grain, etc. To this day coal is said to be screened in the colliery when it has stone and other impurities removed from it. In like fashion a group of persons is screened when they are sorted out into the innocuous, the suspect and the definitely guilty.

Radar (radio detection and ranging) is an originally American expression which rapidly ousted the British name of *radiolocation* (still enshrined, however, in its Russian derivative *radiolokatsiya*). First used as a means of detecting German planes approaching Britain this device was for some time a military secret and official propaganda accounted for notable success in locating enemy night-bombers by stirring accounts of R.A.F. fighter pilots devouring huge quantities of carrots in order to take in massive doses of the vitamin which improves vision. This and other inventions were the work of *boffins*. This odd word denoting scientists working more or less behind the scenes is difficult to account for. Perhaps it is to English literature that we must look for a clue. In *Our Mutual Friend* there is a Mr Boffin known as 'the golden dustman', and having a reputation for disinterested duty and service, though in appearance 'a very odd-looking old fellow indeed'. But in his *News From Nowhere* William Morris presents another Boffin, a dustman interested in mathematics. These descriptions might well have been applied by some elegant civil servant in wartime days to those devoted but informally dressed scientists with whom he came into contact. At all events the word is supposed to have been first applied to scientists working in conjunction with the R.A.F.

Another expression for experts working behind the scenes and shrouded in official secrecy during the 1939–1945 war was – and is – *backroom boys*, a phrase attributed to Lord Beaverbrook's wartime tribute to the 'boys in the back room' who were responsible for inventions intended to discomfit the enemy. One wartime invention did however bear the name of its maker, and that was the *Bailey Bridge*, consisting of prepared sections of light and easily transportable bridgework. The name is dated 1944 by the *S.E.D.* though this must be a little late, for I remember hearing it when I saw my first Bailey bridge at Medjez el Bab in Tunisia in late 1942, and this memory is confirmed by the statement of the American historian George F. Howe in his *Northwest Africa: Seizing the Initiative in the West*.[1] 'Defenses were organized and during the night a Bailey bridge span was erected over the gap in the broken bridge . . .' (p. 303), this being an allusion to Medjez and the night of 26–27 November 1942.

To a great number of people still alive the expression 'pre-war' was at one time an allusion to the period before 1914 but the semantic content of this term has been changed by the war of 1939–1945, with the practical result that it now normally refers to the time before September 1939. For absolute clarity people sometimes speak of the *inter-war years* when the narrower period of 1918–1939 is meant. What is interesting about 'pre-war', however, is its enlarged function. It had long been an adjective, as in 'the pre-war years' but of late it has been doing the work of an adverb in addition. 'Pre-war he hardly existed,' said an article in the *Spectator* (16 Mar 1956) while in the *Universities Review* of October 1959 we read that 'The plain fact is that the universities now need much larger staffs than they did pre-war' (p. 35). Stranger than this is a sort of substantival usage found in a speech by Mr Heathcoat Amory, then Chancellor of the Exchequer. 'The country must get used to fairly frequent changes

[1] Washington D.C., 1957.

in Bank Rate and credit restrictions to avoid the slumps and
booms of pre-war' (25 Jun 1960).

Mention of a Chancellor of the Exchequer reminds one that the
curious investigator of the history of words is constantly being
surprised by the venerable age of some of our modern-sounding
expressions, for 'the balance of trade' does not look out of place
among the up-to-date vocabulary of political economists, yet as
long ago as 1699 a certain Charles Davenant was writing an
essay whose title included what he called 'the ballance of trade'.
(*Imbalance*, on the other hand, is a recent acquisition.) Likewise
Coca-cola was first heard of in 1887, albeit in the United States,
and even its familiar abbreviation *coke* is dated 1909, though of
course this drink became known in Britain only in the post-war
era. To turn to another sphere, the dictators of fashion often
give sensational names to modern versions of clothes which are
merely the latest adaptations of styles of three or four decades
ago, but sometimes it has happened that even the new name
unwittingly repeats one that was in use many years back, and in
this way the name of the *sack dress* of the late nineteen-fifties was
anticipated by the ladies of the seventeenth century for Samuel
Pepys's diary duly noted 'My wife this day put on first her
French gown, called a Sac'. But perhaps only the name is the same.

In the cynical atmosphere of the nineteen-forties such words as
ponce and *spiv*, long established in underworld slang, suddenly
became known to the public at large. The spiv was the man of
the hour because of his talent for producing large quantities of
scarce and rationed goods for a financial consideration. These
commodities were obtained by theft or, more mysteriously, by
fiddling (often much the same thing). 'Fiddling' is now a highly
elastic term meaning anything from large-scale fraud to lapses of
memory in making income-tax returns. At all events the word
itself began to rise in the world, no doubt as a sign of the times,
and was soon to be found in respectable organs of the press.
'Expense allowances are apt to mean fiddling,' observed the
Manchester Guardian Weekly (10 Jun 1954). By 1963, however,
Hugh Brogan gave it as his opinion in the *Yale Review* (Autumn

number, p. 151) that ' "Fiddling" and "spivs" are words no longer current; they disappeared with the phenomenon they describe, which were features of the wartime and postwar black market'. But this is inexact; for only a few weeks later *The Times* Law Report recorded that 'The lorry driver instigated a fiddle whereby a smaller amount was put in the tank than shown on the invoice . . .' (20 Dec 1963). It would seem in fact to be the case that while 'spiv' has shown some decline in frequency the all-embracing 'fiddle' is to be with us for a long time to come. Certainly there is a magnificent solemnity about the phrase 'instigated a fiddle', as used by *The Times*.

Not so widely known as most of the words mentioned in this book is the adjective *camp* (or, as the name of a cult of sensibility, the noun *Camp*, spelled by some writers with a capital). The adjective can be found in the early twentieth century in the sense of 'addicted to actions and gestures of exaggerated emphasis' and 'pleasantly ostentatious, or, in manner, affected', as may be seen in Eric Partridge's *Dictionary of Slang and Unconventional English* (5th ed., vol. 1, 1961). In his *Passing English* (1909) J. Redding Ware assumed that it was 'probably from the French', but this can be dismissed as a shot in the dark. Partridge draws attention to the dialectal adjective 'camp' or 'kemp', meaning 'uncouth, rough', and suggests that it could have been this word which led to slang *camp* meaning at one time 'slightly disreputable, bogus'. By the nineteen-twenties it had come to signify 'homosexual', at least in London homosexual circles. In this connection there is an interesting allusion in Christopher Isherwood's *The World in the Evening*[1] where a character named Charles Kennedy asks in a scene set in the second world war 'Did you ever run across the word "camp"?' Affording the novelist a pretext for a two-page disquisition he goes on 'You thought it meant a swishy little boy with peroxided hair, dressed in a picture hat and a feather boa, pretending to be Marlene Dietrich? Yes, in queer circles, they call *that* camping. It's all very well in its place, but it's an utterly debased form . . .' (p. 125).

[1] Methuen, 1954.

There follows, in contrast to this, known by Isherwood as 'Low Camp', a discussion of what he calls 'High Camp', that is a mode of sensibility, exemplified, so he says, in the music of Mozart.

The best treatment of the subject is to be found in Susan Sontag's article entitled 'Notes on "Camp"', in the *Partisan Review* (XXXI) of 1964 (pp. 515–530).[1] These notes consist mainly of 58 numbered paragraphs which it is obviously difficult to summarize in a few lines, especially as Miss Sontag's main theme is that the term is almost incapable of exact definition. A relevant point, however, is that she shows that while Camp taste is not solely and simply homosexual taste 'there is no doubt a peculiar affinity and overlap' (p. 529). This she sees as stemming from the fact that 'Camp is a solvent of morality. It neutralizes moral indignation, sponsors playfulness'. It is therefore to some extent of propagandist value for those who are out of step with society. It is also an assertion of individuality. 'Camp is the answer to the problem: how to be a dandy in a mass age' (p. 527). The distinguishing feature of the cult is a spirit of extravagance and the attempt to do something extraordinary. Examples furnished by Miss Sontag are the drawings of Aubrey Beardsley, *King Kong*, *Swan Lake*, Jayne Mansfield and de Gaulle. One begins to suspect (entering into the spirit of the thing) that any attempt to define this word is likely to be itself somewhat camp. Those interested are advised to read Miss Sontag's article and also a short note on ' "Camp" as adjective, 1909–66' (*American Speech*, XLI, 1966) by William White of Wayne State University, to which some of the above references are due. The word has been touched upon here since it is somewhat remarkable that a term belonging to the slang of a secret minority group should become the name of an esthetic concept.

The materialist outlook continues to dominate western society and one unfortunate result is that the pace of life is constantly accelerating. A businessman who has saved several days of

[1] Now included in her collection *Against Interpretation* (Eyre and Spottiswoode, 1967).

travelling time by using an air liner instead of a ship is not conscious of having any more leisure as a consequence, and once his business is concluded he is required by his superiors to dash back to the airport to undertake some other trip taking him hundreds or thousands of miles away. As aggressive professionalism is highly regarded in the competitive world of modern commerce where words like 'amateur' and 'dilettante' are terms of abuse it naturally follows that breakneck activity is considered an end in itself. Inside or outside of the business community it is all but impossible to find anyone who will ever admit to being anything but frantically overworked. To announce with smug satisfaction 'I'm a busy man!' is nevertheless to make a boast rather than to complain, while to 'have no time for something' is to condemn it utterly. (Things must have been different in the eighteenth century, judging by Sheridan's *A School for Scandal*, where 'busy people' were interfering troublemakers – busybodies, in fact.) Even the words indicating leisure-time activities are somehow reminiscent of work – 'relaxing' sounds very much like a process intended to promote future efficiency, while even 'resting' has overtones of a well-deserved respite from noble labours. 'Doing nothing' is no longer heard, and even winners of the football pools publicly announce their intention of carrying on working just as before. It logically follows that the most complimentary adjectives in modern English are those implying capacity for great speed and a love of movement, so that a particular institution will now be said to be 'streamlined', 'high-powered' or 'forward-looking' and individuals who lag behind are urged to 'get with it' as though running for a moving bus.

Fortunately there are signs that the frenzied activity of the modern world is to some extent self-defeating and that society may have leisure thrust upon it by the increasing use of *automation*, i.e. the control of machines by other machines. This key-word appears to have been coined by a New Yorker named Diebold in 1952 as a replacement for the tongue-twisting *automaticization* and was well-known in Britain by 1955 or so. But a curious point about it, and one which goes to show that students of language may tend to overestimate the rapidity with which a given neologism becomes known to the mass of the population, is that when automation was discussed during the meeting of the T.U.C. in September 1955 it transpired that one half of the delegates were ignorant of its meaning, although it had been extensively mentioned in the press. Even in June of the following year the naming of the process was still considered as an open question by the *News Chronicle* which held a competition whereby readers were invited to submit variants of it. One of the winning entries was the ingenious *switchcraft* which unfortunately has not been heard of since.

The verb 'switch' meaning 'exchange' or 'transfer' has made rapid headway in Britain in recent years. WIVES' PACT TO SWITCH BABIES (*Daily Herald*, 18 Feb 1956) did not mean that there was an agreement to subject infants to corporal punishment, but merely that there was a promise to exchange them. However when the word appeared in this sense four years later in the *Sunday Times* it was enclosed in inverted commas (10 Jan 1960).

Another more important word taken over from the American continent by British housewives is *chore*. In the 'twenties this word was unknown to the mass of people in Britain, but it appears in a letter of 4 April 1926 written by Rose Macaulay, where it is a question of '... some dull household chore...'.[1] And in Galsworthy's novel *The Silver Spoon* there is mention made of '... washing, mending, games, singing, dancing and general chores'.[2] This word, incidentally, is etymologically related to the first element of 'charwoman' (modern *home help*, also from the United States). In the 'thirties it continued to be little-known. Having lived for many years in the States the novelist John Cowper Powys said in his *Autobiography* of 1934 that '... I did every mortal thing that had to be done in the way of what Americans call "chores" ...'.[3] In his *Boy with a Cart*,

[1] *Letters to a Sister* (Collins, 1964).
[2] The Grove edition of 1928, part II, vi.
[3] p. 634 of the 1949 reprint.

printed in 1939, Christopher Fry introduced this word into poetry.

> *Turning it over in our minds as we went*
> *About our chores.*

Certainly at the present time this useful word can be regarded as belonging to standard usage in Britain and the reason is not far to seek. To go back to the inter-war years, the various household tasks such as sweeping up, peeling the potatoes and so on were simply known as 'jobs', but nowadays changed social and economic conditions have to some extent altered the linguistic and emotional context of this word, taken to be a colloquialism in the 'thirties, if not downright slang. Since then it has gained greatly in prestige and is capable of being used in quite dignified circumstances, a process perhaps begun by Churchill's famous appeal to the then non-belligerent Americans, 'Give us the tools and we'll finish the job'. Yet once upon a time school-teachers were wont to warn their adolescent pupils against the inclusion of the word 'job' in their written applications for employment, which should mention only 'post' or 'situation'. But the fact is that at the present day a great deal of paid work is not so much connected with posts and situations as with temporary, part-time, more or less casual employment which is in any case better covered by 'job'. Again, the spread of the idea that to undertake paid employment is in itself virtuous has helped to endow this word with a new-found dignity. This upward movement of an originally slang word has left a gap for a term describing household tasks (what the military authorities depressingly call 'fatigues') and this has been filled by 'chores'. The two usages are unconsciously contrasted in a letter to the *Daily Telegraph* from a clergyman who explains 'We do our own chores' and then goes on to speak of the 'jobs' undertaken by vicars' wives, i.e. office work, teaching and so on (20 May 1954).

As a matter of fact 'chores' include monotonous and routine duties in general, as is seen in a *Daily Telegraph* article where we read of '. . . an interpreter who has just concluded his chores at an international beauty specialists' congress' (22 Mar 1954). But the root cause of the popularity of the word is the chronic shortage of domestic servants which characterizes the affluent society and the resulting awareness of the existence of manual work by people hitherto unburdened by it.

Meanwhile the period since 1945 has also been marked by the strength and confidence of big business and its attendant aptly-named advertising industry. Materialism is not of course an invention of the twentieth century but it is indisputable that the 'getting and spending' deplored by Wordsworth has now become a veritable way of life with its own techniques and mystiques. It is true that certain new words merely carry on old traditions in a new guise, so that the *pressure groups* of our time correspond to the eighteenth-century 'interests'. But the *public relations officer* (P.R.O. to initiates) is a relatively new phenomenon and an off-shoot of that increased sensitivity to criticism that is one of the hallmarks of our supposedly tough and vigorous age, making it hardly possible to comment objectively on any saleable com-modity without provoking reaction in the form of a sorrowing letter expressing the deep concern and wounded feelings of the P.R.O. of some organized group or other.

The term itself was evidently invented in the U.S.A. in 1920 by a Mr Ivy Lee (surprise is sometimes evoked by this unusual masculine name. But it is old-established, for in or about 1770 the head of a dancing school in Newcastle upon Tyne was a man named Ivey Gregg, according to Bewick, the famous engraver).[1] In Britain the first P.R.O. appears to have been Sir John Elliot, appointed to the Southern Railway in that capacity in 1924. One of the duties of such an official is to watch over the *image* of the enterprise he serves – in other words, over the impact made by his employers upon the public mind. In itself this shows an admirable awareness of a truth long known to students of language and philosophy, namely that a man's actions and

[1] p. 54 of Montague Weekley's abridged edition of *A Memoir of Thomas Bewick by Himself.*

beliefs are guided not so much by facts as by what he believes to be the facts. Such an 'image' is in the nature of things a simplified stereotype which may be untrue, partly true or else out-of-date or otherwise misleading–e.g. the names of the three main political parties in Britain. The existence of the usage is at any rate a healthy recognition that appearance and reality are not the same thing. It comes, then, from the jargon of advertising (*brand-image* in full) but has rapidly been transferred to politics and indeed any other sphere of human activity. 'Nothing has done more harm in Asia and Africa to the image of the Western world than the spectacle of the French Army in Algeria ...' (*Observer*, 30 Oct 1960).

When the chairman of the Amalgamated Press stated in 1955 that 'over the year our outlay on publicity and promotion rose by 11 per cent' the shareholders were expected to understand this 'promotion' as the furtherance of the company's activities and not the appointment of some employees to higher posts. That sense of promotion as 'furtherance' has a long and respectable ancestry stretching back to the Middle Ages, but only recently has it come into prominence as a technical term of commerce, via American usage. The rather curious result is that the two meanings of this term are liable to be confused in certain contexts, or rather, when the surrounding phrase is quoted out of context. So in the absence of any other explanation it would be difficult to determine the significance of a statement by Anthony Sampson that '. . . it is accepted that success without promotion is unthinkable' (*Encounter*, Dec 1959).

Mention of the Amalgamated Press is itself a reminder of the slight decline in fortune of the 'amalgamate' family of words which was very prominent in the 'thirties when many firms tried to combat adverse trading conditions by combining with each other in an attempt to cut overhead costs and what the advocates of a free economy call 'wasteful competition'. Much earlier than that the root word 'amalgam' appeared in the vocabulary of medieval alchemy in the fifteenth century, when it was applied to the combination of some substance with mercury.

The general use of 'amalgamate' for the combination of two elements in a homogeneous whole appeared around the year 1800, but the *S.E.D.* considers that the verb now particularly applies to 'bodies of people, societies, or organizations' and instances the Amalgamated Railway Servants of 1894 as an early example of this tendency. What is interesting, however, is the increasing use, in this sense, of *merger*, a noun existing since the early eighteenth century in the legal sense of 'Extinguishment of a right, estate, contract, action, etc., by absorption in another', but which is now freely used in Britain in the originally American sense of 'The consolidation of one firm or trading company with another' (*S.E.D.*). In the United States 'merger' has been preferred to 'amalgamation' because the latter has special reference in that country to 'the racial admixture of whites and Negroes' (Horwill) and in Britain 'merger' has made headway presumably because of the prestige of American usage and also because many transatlantic firms have British subsidiary companies which naturally tend to use American nomenclature. At all events, one might say that the growth of 'merger' in Britain at the expense of 'amalgamation' is ultimately linked with the question of racial discrimination, albeit across the ocean.

American terms have been generously used in Britain by the manipulators of the world of commerce and advertising, but *store* in the sense of *department store* is something of a special case, for in the United States the word is used for any shop however small. It is not altogether clear whether the present British usage (normally in the plural) is simply a straightforward abbreviation of the fuller American expression or a continuation of an old British usage. Certainly the Co-operative movement used 'store' from its inception over a century ago in Rochdale as is proved by a photograph of the original establishment bearing over the shopfront the single word STORE, and in some parts of England the 'Co-op' is invariably known simply as 'the store' *par excellence*. By the way, an early mention of 'store' in British writing is due to the adventurer William Hickey, who in January 1776 visited Kingston, Jamaica, where '. . . we lounged amongst the different

stores (shops or warehouses where trade is carried on) . . .'
(Vol. 2, p. 45).[1] The *Concise Oxford Dictionary* points out 'Co-
operative store or stores' and 'Army and Navy Stores', reminding
us that they originally sold only to members. Possibly the present-
day use of *store* is considered subjectively by its users as simply a
shortened form of *department store* and this assumption may well
be correct, especially as it seems to the present writer that this
use has become much more widespread since the nineteen-
thirties.

The business of commercial firms is to sell as much as possible
in order to realize large profits. In their endeavours to do so they
inevitably attempt to influence the spending habits of the public
by the manipulation of language and in some cases the result is
the creation of a new expression. There is nothing inherently
sinister about this and the process is illustrated in another sphere
by a Churchillian wartime memorandum given in the appendix
of *The Grand Alliance*. It was a question of finding a name for the
newly-created establishments which were to provide cheap,
plain meals in somewhat austere surroundings. 'I hope the term
"Communal Feeding Centres" is not going to be adopted. It is an
odious expression, suggestive of Communism and the workhouse.
I suggest you call them "British Restaurants". Everybody
associates the word "restaurant" with a good meal, and they may
as well have the name if they cannot have anything else.' This
admirable principle for the furtherance of human happiness is
perfectly familiar to businessmen and advertisers. The present
author has had the pleasure of consuming in pleasant and expensive surroundings a delicacy entitled 'game chips' which on
closer inspection proved to bear a suspicious resemblance to
potato crisps. As a general rule the word 'chips' tends to be
avoided in elevated circles even when referring to the genuine
article, which now becomes *French fried potatoes* in many restaurants as a result of American influence. This designation is a model
of ingenuity, possessing the double advantage of evoking thoughts
of a country skilled in the culinary art while at the same time

[1] Hurst and Blackett, 1918.

banishing all hints of that plebeian product sprinkled with vinegar, wrapped in newspaper and preferably eaten during the course of an evening walk. (Without using the American phrase, some restaurants list 'Fried fish with chips' – anything to avoid the taboo 'Fish 'n' chips'.) Actually eating habits can vary a good deal over the centuries. In the early nineteenth century the dogfish appears to have been regarded with some disdain, judging by a statement published in 1837 to the effect that 'It must not be concealed that the dog-fish was an article of food with our ancestors . . .'[1] This fish is once again eaten today but is dignified by the name of *rock-salmon*. Similarly butchers somehow never seem to speak of 'mutton' nowadays, but always 'lamb', so that the old jibe about mutton dressed as lamb is now literally true.

In some cases the metamorphosis affects not age but sex. On learning that during a holiday in Spain 'I needed only to wear a suit and a thin shirt' the unwary reader might assume he is reading about masculine matters, though in fact this quotation is taken from an article by Mrs Nicholas of the *Sunday Times* (27 Nov 1955). The American *suit* has ousted the older 'costume' with astonishing rapidity (due to woman's fear of being considered old-fashioned, or even old), while *shirt* is really a blouse, ultimately an off-shoot of the American *shirtwaist*. Some psychologist should really tell us what envies and unfulfilled longings cause women to steal the names of men's clothes. Even a blouse was once a peasant's smock and 'knickers' represents a shortening of 'knickerbockers'. 'Knickers', by the way, seems to be abandoned by the younger set in favour of the appallingly masculine *pants*, admittedly by way of the diminutive form *panties* (*pantees*) which the *S.E.D.* dates from 1905 in the main body of the work, but more realistically from 1926 in the Addenda, under *scanties*. As a practical example of the regrettable obsolescence of 'knickers' as a general term we may mention the surprise of Kenneth Tynan, the drama critic, at its use by John Osborne in his play *Under Plain Cover*.[2] If it may be mentioned in the same breath, the

[1] *Glossary of Finchale Priory* (Surtees Society, 1837).
[2] Faber, 1963.

ecclesiastical vestment known as a *stole* has also given a name to a sort of evening wrap which in some cases is curiously reminiscent of the shawls which working-class women sometimes wore in the nineteen-twenties, matched by a spare cap of their husband's.

Synonymous with 'scanties' is *briefs*, equally self-explanatory. This latter did not catch the eye of the compilers of the 1955 *S.E.D.*, though it was certainly extant well before that date. By a curious reversal of the usual tendency 'briefs' also became a masculine garment in the early nineteen-sixties. A far cry indeed from the long woollen underpants of the earlier part of this century. To return to feminine fashion, *bra* was recognized in 1955 by the *S.E.D.* albeit as 'Slang abbreviation of BRASSIÈRE'.[1] In fact it now seems to be a general term, but we are reminded thereby that *falsies* ('Coax your figure into shape') is omitted from the *S.E.D.* though it gained currency in Britain about 1950. Like 'bra' it is of transatlantic origin. A curious linguistic – or psychological – feature is that so many names of women's garment exist in a diminutive form (philologically, that is) ending in -*ie*, or -*ies* in the plural. Thus 'nightie', 'cammie' (a spoken form current up to the nineteen-twenties for 'camisole', enshrined in the compound 'cami-knickers'), and the unlovely 'combies', in addition to those incidentally mentioned above. The underlying and unconscious motive is possibly to lend an air of childish artlessness to words which are felt to have some element of taboo attached to them. Smallness in itself is of course supposed to be highly desirable by women in anything concerning their figures, hence corselette, which shows signs of replacing 'corset', and incidentally reminds us of the old word 'corslet' meaning a piece of defensive armour covering the body of a fighting-man.

Some slight variation or innovation in design is often the pretext for the renaming of a woman's garment. So the *girdle* (from the U.S.A. and omitted in this sense from the 1955 *S.E.D.*) is a lighter, and abbreviated, and generally less impressive affair than its creaking predecessor of the 'thirties, the corset (more

---

[1] 'Bra' goes back to 1937 say C. Willett Cunnington and Phillis Cunnington, in their *History of Underclothes* (Michael Joseph, 1951), p. 242.

usually in the plural at that time), itself the supplanter of the earlier 'stays'. At that period a girdle was in British usage simply a belt or cord engirdling the waist, for example the girdle of a schoolgirl's tunic. In an earlier convention it was also a masculine accessory, as in Francis Bacon's essay *Of Marriage and Single Life* where he speaks of men who 'will go near to think their girdles and garters to be bonds and shackles'. It may be appropriate at this point to recall how the *New Yorker* once extracted amusement from a British recipe for the baking of scones 'on a greasy girdle'. The editor did not know (or professed not to know) that in Scottish and northern English use this is a variant of 'griddle' – hence 'girdle cakes' as an alternative name for scones. In 1957 a firm was advertising its 'Corset Bank' ('AT ALL TIMES we have in stock a complete selection of models and sizes in these famous makes'). This is of course a variant of the modern use of 'bank' as a store or reserve, like *blood bank* or *eye bank*. 'Bar' has likewise passed into commercial use with reference to a counter given over to a particular product, probably on the analogy of 'coffee bar'. So a 'Bra Bar', a 'Slipper Bar' in a shoeshop, along with a 'Heel Bar', a 'Carpet Furnishing Bar' and – seen in 1958 – a 'Furnishing Pattern Bar' giving a selection of patterned materials for furnishing. Finally 'Hat Bar' in 1965.

Edith Bone, a political prisoner released from a Hungarian jail during the abortive uprising of 1956, was puzzled by many words used in the British shops she had not visited since she left England in 1949. 'When after a few days I went shopping, I often did not understand what the saleswoman said to me; I did not know whether I wanted 15, 30 or 60 denier nylons, stretch or non-stretch; I had never heard of polythene bags, Terylene . . .'.[1] Actually 'denier' is a long-established word dated 1839 by the *S.E.D.* and defined as 'A unit of weight, equal to about $8\frac{1}{5}$ grains, by which silk yarn is weighed and its fineness estimated', but it has become known to the public only since the introduction of nylon stockings (oddly known as 'nylons' though silk stockings were never described as 'silks'). *Nylon* is itself a word of some

[1] *Seven Years' Solitary* (Hamish Hamilton, 1957), p. 211.

linguistic interest. It is dated as early as 1932 though quite unknown to the public at large until the ending of the Second
World War, being officially authorized for sale in Britain in the
form of clothing from 1 December 1946. Writing in the review
English in the autumn number of 1954 A. M. Macdonald assumed
that the origin of the word was unknown. 'One would have
thought that the history of a word like *nylon* would be easy to
trace. But not so. The man who made the first nylon is dead, and
he has left no record of what happened at the christening. New
York (N.Y.) and London (Lon.) have been suggested...'
(p. 95). On the other hand the distinguished Swiss scholar
Walther von Wartburg states in his *Etymologica*[1] that Du Pont
de Nemours asked personnel to suggest an easily-remembered
name for the new substance which would also be suitable for
various languages (p. 592). *Nylon* was accepted, and by its ending
it falls in line with cotton and rayon while the first syllable recalls
the second part of *vinyl*, a substance which is the basis of numerous
synthetic fibres. *Terylene*, another of the words that puzzled Miss
Bone, is also a synthetic clothing material.

Even at the time of publication of Miss Bone's book in 1957
there was a whole series of such artificial fabrics in existence but
their names cannot be said to have become household words,
except for the older 'rayon' and 'Celanese', dating from the
middle nineteen-twenties (a period, moreover, when mention
of 'crêpe de chine' – now never heard of – was as common as
that of nylon nowadays). Celanese is properly a proprietary name
for the artificial silk made by British Celanese Ltd and echoes the
'cellulose' from which it is made. Rayon is likewise an artificial
silk made from cellulose. The *Concise Oxford Dictionary* gives
the origin of rayon as French but the boot is on the other foot,
because French *rayonne* did not appear until 1930. As an example
of a few of the synthetic fabrics available in 1958 one might quote
from a very brief glossary published in the *Observer* (12 Jan
1958) which mentions *Acrilan, Dralon, Dynel, Lurex, Orlon* together
with such processes as *Agilon* ('giving the nylon greater elasticity'),

[1] Niemeyer, Tübingen, 1958.

Banlon ('used mainly for nylon, to crimp the fibre, making it bulky, and so able to keep warmth') and *Taslan texturing* which also makes the fibre warmer.

'Jeans' is now the name of a particular type of trousers, or overalls, worn by either sex, but is derived from the material involved and this in turn ultimately reflects the town of Genoa by way of the medieval French version *Janne(s)* (just as the *duffle-coat*, which in recent times has spread from the Royal Navy to the general public, is called after Duffel near Antwerp). The traditional British form was 'jean', dating from the fifteenth century. In the 1922 edition of his book *The Romance of Words* Ernest Weekley pointed out in a footnote that 'The form *jeans* appears to be usual in America' and quoted an American reference to 'a gray jeans coat' (p. 43 in 1949 reprint). This was in fact an old-established American form, dating from the sixteenth century as we see from the *S.E.D.* which gives 1879 for its first recorded use in Britain ('Overalls, latterly slacks'). But it is possible to cite an earlier British dating than this, for 'jeans' is found in *Handley Cross* by R. S. Surtees. '. . . Septimus arrived flourishin' his cambric, with his white jeans strapped under his chammy leather opera boots . . .'. This was first published in 1843. The 1854 edition includes an illustration by John Leech showing that the jeans are trousers (p. 139). In present-day usage the word certainly came from America, however, around 1950 and can in practice be said to rank as a neologism from the point of view of the British public.

An important word in the vocabulary of feminine fashion is *accessories*, consisting in the main of gloves, shoes and handbag, though jewellery and other ornaments are sometimes included. This concept is not found in the *S.E.D.* though Mary Reifer's *Dictionary of New Words* duly notes a verb *accessorize* 'to provide with dress accessories, such as handbag, gloves, shoes, etc.' The male reader will recall that these items are supposed to form a matching or at any rate harmonious whole.

As new words come into fashion some old ones are casualties. 'Mannequin', which entered the language at the beginning of the present century, is tending to fall out of favour, possibly because of an unconscious association with 'man' which lends an inappropriate aspect to this very feminine word. In fact this impression is etymologically correct, since 'mannequin' was a borrowing via French from a Dutch word literally meaning 'little man' and which has itself been taken directly into English as 'manikin'. The special meaning of 'mannequin' in the world of dress designing stems from the earlier use in French whereby the word was applied to the dummy made for the display of clothes. *Model* is now ousting it and is a neologism in this sense though the older meaning of an artist's model posing for sculpture and painting goes back to the seventeenth century. The *S.E.D.* assigns no date to the newer usage, although the verb *model* in the sense of showing off clothes to prospective customers is dated 1927. This verb is decidedly to be found in very good company nowadays. 'Five-year-old Margaret Fash and six-year-old Andreas Faefel modelled fashions from Switzerland,' writes *The Times* (7 Oct 1959). There is some danger that the noun may be short-lived, since in court proceedings attractive young women without visible means of support are in the habit of claiming to be professional models. There may consequently be a movement away from the ambiguity of the word in favour of some new creation.

One of the aims of modern advertisers is to bring into being as many occasions as possible for the more or less obligatory giving of expensive presents, thereby increasing commercial sales. On the American model *Mother's Day* and *Father's Day* are now part of the salesman's calendar although the British public has not responded with universal enthusiasm to these new opportunities for spending money. In particular 'Mother's Day' has met with opposition on the grounds that the traditional name is Mothering Sunday and in 1956 it was unexpectedly revealed that the rules of the Society for the Promotion of Christian Knowledge (S.P.C.K.) preclude the use of this neologism. The ensuing controversy induced one leading religious card dealer to state that his chief reason for using 'Mother's Day' was to ensure his products a place in the American market. This consideration presumably does not apply to the ever more frequent clipping of 'wedding anniversary' to *anniversary*, a straight-forward imitation of American idiom by the younger speakers in the first instance.

Fortunately for many millions of mothers there are some changes in the English language which mark a lightening of their daily burden. Gone are the days when Monday morning was marked off from all other mornings by the collective thumping and thudding proceeding from all the washtubs of the neighbourhood, and perhaps the time will eventually come when even the word 'washtub' will be listed as obsolescent in the dictionaries, ousted by *washing machine*. The humble Kitchen Sink, the very badge of feminine servitude, has become the title of a theatrical movement, leaving a gap to be filled by *sink unit*. 'Unit' is in fact a hardworking little word at the present time, doing service in *unit furniture*, *garbage disposal unit* and *accommodation unit*. ('Accommodation unit, sweet accommodation unit!'). The *spin drier*, *pressure cooker*, *immersion heater* and *deep freeze* all co-operate to aid the housewife. Shopping is frequently done in a *supermarket* (the name comes from America) with its *self-service*.

Large multiple shops and increased foreign holidays have gone some way towards popularizing the more exotic foods hitherto little known in Britain, such as scampi and ravioli. In some cases, though, experience has shown that unaccustomed products sell better under a homely name and so ravioli becomes '*cheese flaps*'. A sign of the times is to be seen in the fact that fruit is often known as 'fresh fruit' to make it clear that it is not a question of the canned variety which is in danger of being regarded as the norm, as in the case of pineapples in particular. 'Canned' and 'tinned' are very nearly synonymous in British English, though the former is gaining ground to some extent in actual usage by virtue of its American background. Beer is almost invariably said to be canned rather than tinned, as befits a specifically American invention, though even this rule is not absolute and in Sid Chaplin's novel *The Day of the Sardine* there is to be found an example of tinned beer.[1] Music, on the other hand, is meta-phorically said to be canned, never tinned. Like other products, it is rarely to be had in its natural state, just as entertainers only exceptionally make what they call a personal appearance. A similar shift in the usual perspective seems to be operating in the realm of contrasted natural and artificial substances. A letter in *The Times* recounts that a gentleman asking for a sponge in a large store was shown 'an article seemingly composed of porous rubber' (23 Oct 1957). When he remonstrated he was told 'That is a sponge, sir, but perhaps you want a natural sponge'. The assistant then produced a sponge in a cellophane bag boldly labelled NATURAL SPONGE. The writer of this letter then pertinently asked whether we must now call a spade 'a natural spade'. Five years later the *Spectator* more or less unwittingly answered this question by announcing that the playwright Brendan Behan had a few simple themes, like religion and 'natural sex' (21 Dec 1962). And in fact the adjective is becoming a real necessity on occasion. CHANGE IN LAW ON SEX OPPOSED, a headline in the *Daily Telegraph*, is misleading to an older generation in that the subject-matter proved to be homosexuality (22 Oct 1955).

In the world of publishing, where with typical conservatism it was for many years considered that *paperbacks* could not be a commercial success, there is now a frequent need to refer to *hard-cover books* in order to differentiate these from the paper-backed variety which many readers regard as the norm. In demotic English, indeed, 'book' has been extended to any magazine or 'comic'. As a semantic curiosity *horror-comic* is worth a second glance, being a remarkable contradiction in terms. It has been distinguished, incidentally, by inclusion in 1959 in the *Dictionary of English Law*,[2] together with the overdue entry 'fish, fried'.

A very striking feature of contemporary English is the way in which almost any profit-making activity is termed an 'industry'.

[1] Eyre and Spottiswoode, 1961.
[2] Sweet and Maxwell.

Now the application of this word to what the *S.E.D.* calls 'a particular branch of productive labour; trade or manufacture' is an ancient one, but there is no doubt that it has become a vogue and shows strong signs of triumphing over the less impressive 'trade'. A century ago it was perfectly possible to speak of agriculture as a trade, though this would strike most of us as rather odd nowadays. '. . . agriculture, like any other trade, is in a state of progress . . .' said *The Times* on 4 November 1863. Agriculture is now regarded as an industry, i.e. 'the farming industry', just as the agricultural labourer survives as such only in the vocabulary of older speakers now that he has become a 'farm worker'. Likewise we hear frequent references to the 'horticultural, pig, catering, clothing, toy, film, record, insurance, popular music, railway, handknit, newspaper, holiday, gambling (what economists call an 'extractive industry'?), aerospace, banking, tourist, hotel, garage, magazine' and . . . book industries. *The Times* drama critic, without any ironic intention, wrote of 'the theatre industry' (26 Feb 1965). In the Unilever quarterly entitled *Progress* (1966) a lengthy article was devoted to the 'football industry'. Clearly, no tangible product is needed to qualify for the appellation. Sir Gordon Richards has spoken of the 'racing industry' and during the London bus strike of May 1958 there was constant talk of bus transport being 'a public industry'.

Envy and rivalry have no doubt always existed among members of different trades and industries but in these days of wide publicity for and against sectional interests it is easier for some random word from a ministerial speech to be pounced upon by the press and thereby to achieve new status in the language. Farmers have never forgotten the celebrated description of themselves as *featherbedded* by subsidies and tariffs, nor has the *S.E.D.* which dates the corresponding verb as arising in 1950 – 'to provide with advantages or conveniences, as if with the soft and yielding comfort of a feather bed'. The expression has taken a good hold in the British vocabulary and evidently has a long future ahead of it. In the American context there is yet another meaning involved, according to Mary Reifer's *Dictionary of New Words* under 'featherbedding' – 'Employment of more personnel than is actually necessary for one particular job, resulting from pressure from labor unions'.

Because of a parliamentary speech fresh life may be given to an expression long dormant in the dictionaries, and this has happened to the rather technical phrase *as of right* which had theoretically been in existence since the nineteenth century but leapt to prominence as a result of the debate on Old Age Pensions at the end of 1954 when some parliamentary speaker claimed that they should be given 'as of right'. Most people had never heard this before but in a matter of weeks the *New Statesman* was using the phrase in connection with the right to carry out work at museums (22 Jan 1955), while in the following year *Horizon* was saying 'An adequate grant is expected as of right' (May 1956). 'As of right' has been a firm favourite with politicians and journalists ever since. Similarly for the 'attachment' of wages of men bound by maintenance orders. The term is centuries old, but was brought to public notice only in early December 1957 by parliamentary discussion.

Much is now heard of the *fringe benefits* enjoyed by some employees.[1] These include all the benefits granted by the employer which are additional to wages or salaries, such as *luncheon vouchers*, sick pay, holidays with pay, superannuation, assistance with housing and children's education, etc. In theory the notorious *expense account* (or *expenses account*) ought not to be regarded as a fringe benefit since it supposedly applies only to the reimbursement of money necessarily spent in the course of the firm's business ('Here's expenses for thee' as Shakespeare had it) but even if this were invariably the case there is doubtless some pleasure to be obtained from wining and dining with clients in luxurious surroundings. The importance of all these perquisites is that they represent a disguised form of income particularly welcome in a society where wages and salaries are subject to very stringent taxation. Fringe benefits therefore seem likely to remain

[1] This expression is the title of a book published in 1959 by F. M. Wistert.

with us for some time. The expression was first recorded in an announcement by the United States Labor Board during the Second World War.

Recent years have seen a quickening of public interest in university education and an unprecedented expansion of facilities in this direction. Not so long ago the great mass of the British population knew vaguely that universities were something to do with a boat race and undergraduates were considered to be rich young men with a talent for organizing spectacular breaches of the peace. Now that secondary and university education is more widely available there has been a corresponding popularization of the appropriate jargon. Noteworthy here is *Oxbridge*, often imagined to be a modern coinage and sometimes ascribed to H. G. Wells, but in reality it comes in the first place from the pen of Thackeray, who sent his hero Pendennis to that imaginary seat of learning. What is true is that it has only recently come into fashion as a convenient abbreviation for 'the universities of Oxford and Cambridge', as in the *Times Educational Supplement* where the heading A W A R D S A T O X B R I D G E (30 Dec 1960) refers to the two ancient universities and not to the place of that name in Dorset. In 1928 Oxbridge was alluded to by Virginia Woolf in a series of lectures published in the following year as *A Room of One's Own*. Later it was mentioned by Dr Joad and others but only in the fifties did it achieve real popularity, perhaps as a result of the polemical writings of 'Bruce Truscot' (Professor Allison Peers) who opposed to Oxbridge the collective idea of Redbrick, denoting the modern universities – with the signal exception of Durham – since at that time the weather-beaten stone of the ancient universities contrasted with the brickwork of the civic universities, though by the early nineteen-sixties the really modern university was beginning to look more like a collection of blocks of *multi-storey flats.*

Now that the universities are big news and big business it is disheartening to have to report the increased tendency of the public to apply to the adjective 'academic' the sense of 'impractical, ineffectual', though in fairness it must be conceded that some

Educatio colour is lent to the attitude that prompts this usage by the typical academic taste for preferring to consider the curious and unlikely possibility rather than the humdrum probability which interests the average man. In gambling terms, it is almost incredible that a scholar should back the favourite, for he will always produce convincing reasons why an interesting outsider will walk off with the race. Still, it is slightly unjust that 'academic' should ever come to indicate something dangerously near to thoroughgoing stupidity as in the following sentence from the *Guardian*. 'The more experienced negotiators on the staff side realise that it is academic to hope for all-round increases so soon after the Industrial Court award . . .' (12 Nov 1963).

From the (American) university world there comes the curious formation *teach-in*, which became well-known in Britain during 1966 in consequence of the reporting of teach-ins about the Vietnam war conducted by members of the University of California. Similar functions were arranged in British universities. It is often assumed that the word was a device created to attract attention, but the fact is that it was already in good use in the U.S.A. as an alternative name for a university seminar, i.e. a class meeting for the purpose of instruction and discussion. Certainly in journalistic usage this word has acquired an air of defiance and shows signs of being the starting-point for a series of neologisms denoting activities connected with mass passive resistance or protest, as for example 'kiss-in', actually reported from an American seat of learning as the name given to a practical form of counter-demonstration against the decision of the authorities to discourage tangible signs of affection among students.

By an unexpected paradox there appears to be a tendency for rising standards of education to be accompanied by a general coarsening and toughening of linguistic expression in Britain, though it would be wrong to ascribe this lowering of standards to any one cause. Certainly the effect of fighting two major wars within thirty years cannot but have removed a number of restraints from spoken usage, while in the literary sphere the desire of modern novelists to depict everyday life with a maximum of realism has inevitably led to the inclusion of expressions in their written vocabulary which in earlier years would never have appeared in print and which were in any case more or less unknown to a great many readers. Monica Baldwin, whose book *I Leap Over the Wall* has already been referred to in these pages, stresses how this point struck her on returning to English society after spending the period 1914–1941 in a convent. 'Perhaps what startled me most was the constant recurrence of words which not even a man would have used before girls when I left school. "Lousy", for instance, and "mucky", "guts", "blasted", "bloody" and "what the hell"' (p. 123). All this is in line with the general revolt against restraint of any kind and with the belief that boldness in self-expression is somehow democratic and a guarantee that the speaker is not putting on airs. So when opening the 1963 Campaign for Education exhibition Lord Boothby declared 'I was bloody nearly mental till I was nineteen....'. Another public speaker, none other than the then Minister of Education, asked 'How the hell can you do that?' when considering a particularly thorny problem at the annual meeting of the National Foundation for Educational Research on 12 October 1955, while in January 1958 a well-known Conservative M.P. explained on the Home Service of the B.B.C. that '... keeping a matter under constant and careful review means doing damn-all about something awkward'. Speaking two years earlier than that, on 17 April 1956, Mr Harold Macmillan had informed the House of Commons as Chancellor of the Exchequer that nationalized industries had not '... a cat in hell's chance' of borrowing from the money market. The future Prime Minister had indeed already distinguished himself as a manipulator of colloquial English on his return from the Geneva Conference in July 1955 when he announced 'There ain't gonna be any war'. This prediction was studiously ignored by *The Times*, presumably on account of the vulgarity of its form. (This is not to say that the august columns of that newspaper are never sullied by improper words, for earlier in the same year it had duly reported the characteristic advice of a policeman: 'Don't argue – get those buggers out of here' (27 Jan 1955). Evidently *The Times* considers that vulgarity is only to be expected from the lower strata of the body politic.) Actually Mr Macmillan's sentence was slightly infelicitous from the proletarian point of view since it violates the rules of sub-standard English and should have been 'There ain't gonna be *no* war'. Better informed in these matters, the press was soon quoting the much-publicized remark in this form, so much so that by 17 October of that same year, when addressing no less a body than the members of the Conservative Conference at Bournemouth an unrepentant Mr Macmillan repeated – in the amended form – 'There ain't gonna be no war'. Whether this was because of the frequent use of this version in the press or whether he by now thought that this is what he said in the first place would be difficult to determine. A more interesting point for the student of language lies in the source of Mr Macmillan's inspiration. The *New Statesman* took it to be transatlantic and a contributor wrote a parody of some length, beginning as follows:

> *'I'll tell the world' sez Kid Macmillan*
> *'Everything's gonna be grand!*
> *Washington's willin', de Kremlin's willin',*
> *De whole situation's in hand.'*

But in the end it transpired that the allusion was characteristically to an Edwardian popular song.

With increased laxity in sexual matters it was inevitable that the relevant vocabulary should start to appear in public. *Sexy* is dated 1928 by the *S.E.D.* though the present writer must confess in all humility that he had never heard of this word until 1946 on returning to the United Kingdom after service with the armed forces. Certainly it is now a key-word in the vocabulary of the second half of the twentieth century and as such it admirably illustrates the truth of the dictum that it is not so much the first dating of a word that matters so much as the time when it first gained general currency, thereby showing itself to be responding to a need of a given society. Incidentally it is perhaps worthy of remark that Shaw himself included this word in *On the Rocks* (1933) where Aloysia in Act 2 says 'Then all of a sudden you pick out one and feel sexy all over'. Here the meaning is presumably that of the definition of the *S.E.D.* and implies immoderate interest, but there is now a secondary sense, that is, 'sexually attractive to an immoderate degree'. But to return to the question of the earliest dating of the word, it is clear that the date given by the *S.E.D.* is not the final word on the subject, since 'sexy' appears in a letter of 20 January 1925, written by Ernest Boyd from New York and published in a Parisian periodical, *La Nouvelle Revue Française* (1925, p. 313). The subject was Joyce's controversial novel *Ulysses*, and Boyd's argument was that people were buying the book because they thought it was 'sexy'. Though his letter was couched in French, Boyd used the English word in inverted commas, considering that it had no French equivalent.

Sex life has similarly been in existence since the 'twenties, as recorded by Robert Lynd in 1927 in an essay reprinted in *Books and Writers* where he said on p. 216 that '. . . the interesting thing about Helen was not what people nowadays call her "sex life"'.[1] Yet not until some twenty years later did it really become an overworked member of the vocabulary. The clinical-sounding *to have sex* seems to be more recent, and no doubt had to come into being in order to cater for the needs of a society in which many people seem to regard the process as a necessary therapeutic measure to be carried out in as abstract a manner as possible, surrounded by all scientific aids. (One of these, The Pill, threatens to monopolize the use of that name, so that before long all other pills will have to be known as tablets, or something of the sort.) To characterize this activity one prefers the two words of the variety now known as four-letter which caused all the trouble for the defence in the famous Lady Chatterley case of November 1960, and which were duly printed in full by the *Observer* and the *Guardian*, something that even dictionaries had hitherto

[1] Dent, 1952. The essay is 'The Bounds of Decency'.

hesitated to do. Since that time, Kenneth Tynan has achieved some notoriety by pronouncing one of them on a B.B.C. television programme, thereby making linguistic history on 13 November 1965. In the Lady Chatterley case one of the witnesses was Professor Richard Hoggart (as he now is), whose own impressively-titled book *The Uses of Literacy* had already introduced readers to words rarely or never seen in print before that time. Various words also taboo in earlier years are now to be seen from time to time in the intellectual press, though never in the popular newspapers.

There has however been one unexpected reaction to all this, and that is the veering away of official terminology from the time-honoured phrase which tells of some exalted personage 'cutting the first sod' on the site of a future building. The process began in April 1954 when Princess Margaret was widely reported as 'cutting the first turf' of a new mine near Nottingham. By February of the next year *The Universities Review* was describing how Sir Frank Stenton had cut the first turf of a new Faculty of Letters.

A word which has moved up in the world as an expletive while losing ground in serious use is 'ruddy'. The profane use of this word is British in source, though rather surprisingly the American character Robert Jordan utters it in Hemingway's *For Whom the Bell Tolls* as early as 1941. 'You ask for the impossible. You ask for the ruddy impossible' (chapter 13). To revert to the traditional meaning, in act II of *Julius Caesar* Shakespeare makes Brutus say—

> You are my true and honourable wife;
> As dear to me as the ruddy drops
> That visit my sad heart.

During the screening of the film version some titters arose from the groundlings at this point, obviously because they were reminded of the use of 'ruddy' as a colloquial substitute for the expletive 'bloody'. The original link between these two is easy to understand, being connected with sound and meaning at the same time. In demotic speech the expletive function of 'ruddy' antedates our period in its origin, but in recent times it has made striking inroads into the speech of social classes that would have disdained it in earlier days. The final blessing came from the Duke of Edinburgh in a newsreel of May 1956 when he uttered the phrase 'ruddy well'. The practical result of all this is that 'ruddy' is retreating from serious contexts (like 'blooming', that other substitute for 'bloody'), witness a B.B.C. programme of 25 June 1957 when Hitchcock apologized for alluding to the 'ruddy hue' of some colour films. One wonders what he would make of Browning's lines in *Pauline* –

> *And when he woke 'twas many a furlong thence,*
> *At home: the sun shining his ruddy wont.*

Though a certain coarsening of speech and writing is typical of our times it would be wrong to think of this movement as unhampered by any opposite tendency to avoid particular words seeming to betray attitudes now considered anti-social or undemocratic. So though the poor are always with us they are now, in accordance with American example, the *underprivileged*, or *lower income brackets*. Physical and mental afflictions are now known by less forthright names than twenty or thirty years ago. The result is that in some cases the names of certain welfare societies have had to be adjusted to the new trend. 'Crippled' becomes 'handicapped', for example, and the famous 'Waifs and Strays' are now 'The Children's Aid Society', which is no doubt a kinder name but harder to remember. Similarly 'drunkards' are now *alcoholics* and the insane are the *mentally ill*. It is traditional for students of language to deride euphemisms on the grounds that softened names do not alter hard realities, and of course if they serve only as a pretext for doing nothing to help the weaker members of society they should indeed be a target for derision but on the whole it cannot be denied in these cases that the less harsh vocabulary of the present day is indicative of a desire, however vague and groping, to ameliorate the lot of others.

This having been said, it is nevertheless a little difficult to avoid jibbing at certain exaggerated cases brought about by this attitude. The word 'slum' is not a nice word and should not appear in official reports, Worthing Town Council have decided. Instead, the phrase 'unfit houses' will be used. So reported the *Evening Standard* (30 Jul 1955). Curiously enough the word 'street' has become associated in many people's minds with slum property, possibly because of the widespread tendency in the 'twenties and 'thirties to use other words for the designation of new thoroughfares resulting from the great amount of house-building carried out in that much maligned period. This in turn has caused 'street' to be left attached to the older property, as against the more modern designations, so that 'Coronation Street' cannot compare with richer relatives such as Coronation Road, Drive, Way, View, Avenue, Crescent, and – who knows? – perhaps some day even Boulevard. 'Terrace' is more of an unknown quality, if only because of the (chiefly southern) prejudice against terraced housing. It is noteworthy that such illustrious cases as Downing Street, Harley Street and so forth have not been able to stem the general movement of the popular tide that has left 'Street' high and dry.

The associations clustering round a word can in fact change very rapidly. In spite of Palmerston's *Civis britannicus sum* the term 'citizen' always had a faintly un-British flavour until recent years. It was good enough for literary use, as in St Paul's 'citizen of no mean city' or the 'Sweep on you fat and greasy citizens!' of Shakespeare's melancholy Jacques, or for the French revolutionaries of the history books, and, in our own time, Americans. But its application has now imperceptibly spread with the weakening of the old word 'subject' consequent upon the modern idea of the monarch as the personification rather than the ruler of the nation. In the sphere of international affairs we therefore often hear nowadays of 'British nationals', a somewhat uninspiring term, formed by analogy with such existing phrases as 'French nationals' and 'German nationals', i.e. where the nationalities in question do not entail subjection to a sovereign.[1] More far-reaching in its possible future consequences is the Americanism *second-class citizen* that has been implanting itself in British usage since about 1960, and which simply means someone who is treated worse, or else seen in a worse light, than other members of the community. An unforeseen result was that by 1964 the British Railways Board was considering abolishing 'second-class' from its official terminology and applying to carriages other than first-class ones the designation 'standard', since 'second-class' sounded derogatory. (On the same principle there are no small eggs in shops, only large, medium and standard.) On reflection, it is rather regrettable that British Railways ever reintroduced the name 'second-class' for the category of travel known for many years as 'third-class', for there was a certain noble eccentricity about a railway system endowed only with first- and third-class coaches.

As a matter of fact, now that British life has become more egalitarian in numerous ways than before, it is evident that questions of status are of increased importance for individuals and Britain is thereby joining the American system in this respect. Only a generation ago such matters were settled by social class but now there is an increased emphasis laid on conspicuous consumption as a source of prestige, and this process is symbolized by the *status symbol*, whether this be a second car, an *au pair* girl, or continental holidays. The egalitarian trend has not prevented people from thinking that there is, and always will be, some well-entrenched group manipulating society from behind the scenes, whatever political party may be in power. To this is given the name of the *Establishment* (with or without a capital letter), supposedly popularized by Mr Henry Fairlie. The history of the word is admittedly somewhat obscure, though what is certain is

[1] e.g. the phrase 'to protect our nationals', heard in the House of Lords (1 Nov 1956). During the previous year the B.B.C. news bulletins had already introduced the usage when speaking of 'British nationals hurt in rioting at Singapore' (13 May 1955).

that it has lately come to the fore in response to a need, and as the matter is put by Professor Galbraith 'The word "Establishment" did not just happen; it gained currency because it describes something'. (The professor is something of an authority on these questions since it was his book which launched the name of the *affluent society*.) Perhaps the answer is that while there have always been establishments in Britain they tended in former times to correspond more closely than at present to the nominal ruling circles, whereas at present the discrepancy between the two is more clearly visible and so creates a need for a specific name not required hitherto to the same degree. So, 'The Establishment, instead of retiring to its tent, has thrown itself into the task of training scientists . . .' (*New Scientist*, 6 Jun 1957). Henry Fairlie was not exactly the inventor of the word, as was made clear by the *Spectator* (in whose pages he had popularized it) in the number of 20 November 1959, where Hugh Kingsmill stated in an article entitled 'Establishments I have known' that it had been bandied about in 1935 by Hesketh Pearson, Malcolm Muggeridge and himself. Yet even this is not the end of the story, for in that same number there was a letter pointing out an occurrence of this sense of 'establishment' in Dr Charles Burney's account of his 'Musical tour' of 1770! 'There are, however, schisms in this city as elsewhere, but heretics are obliged to keep their opinions to themselves while those of the establishment may speak out.'[1] Here we clearly see the religious origin, and in fact 'Establishment' was used as a synonym of the Established Church in the nineteenth century, e.g. by Dickens in *Dombey and Son* (chapter 32), though of course it is quite possible that the word was re-invented in the twentieth century after a period of disuse. It would clearly be easy to form it by analogy with the 'Established Church' of England.

Social mobility has at the same time given practical urgency in the minds of many individuals to questions of speech. (Here we are concerned for the moment with vocabulary and not

[1] The original is Percy Scholes' edition of Dr Burney's *Musical Tours in Europe*, vol. ii, p. 207.

pronunciation.) This has presumably been an important social matter ever since at least 1066, but received no publicity until Professor A. S. C. Ross of the University of Birmingham published a paper entitled 'Linguistic class-indicators in present-day English' in 1954.[1] To be exact, this article appeared in the *Neuphilologische Mitteilungen* at Helsinki, and formed the basis of another article, written by Miss Nancy Mitford in *Encounter* shortly afterwards.[2] This second article gave rise to a sensation in the sense that *Encounter* was deluged by requests for off-prints of it, and soon the whole country had heard of the U and non-U affair. (Though it has been said that 'It is non-U to discuss U and non-U', surely the last word on the subject!) In 1956 Hamish Hamilton published a volume of essays including a modified form of Ross's article, together with the ensuing discussion aroused thereby, and in 1959 this appeared in Penguin Books as *Noblesse Oblige*, edited by Nancy Mitford. Ross's thesis is a simple one, namely that the upper class nowadays is clearly marked off from the others only by its speech, not necessarily being richer, cleaner or better educated. Forms of address, vocabulary and pronunciation are investigated by him on the basis of U (upper-class speaker) versus non-U – gentlemen versus the rest, in fact. Like all simplifications this is a mixture of true and false but at any rate it caught the imagination of the public. This is not the place to discuss in even the most cursory fashion the contents of Ross's article. Some of his items are strikingly true, e.g. U 'bicycle' as a verb, but often the distinction made seems to be incorrect as a question of fact, as in 'Non-U note-paper/U writing-paper'. At all events the former is to be found in a letter written by Lord Gladstone, who speaks of 'Bath club note-paper' (1926).[3] Likewise 'writing-paper' is part of the vocabulary

[1] Cf. 'U and Non-U: an Essay in Sociological Linguistics', by Alan S. C. Ross, pp. 91–106 of *The Importance of Language*, edited by Max Black (Prentice-Hall Inc., 1962).

[2] *The English Aristocracy*, in the September number, followed in the December number by *U and non-U* by Professor Ross.

[3] *Hatred, Ridicule and Contempt*, by Joseph Dean (1955 edition, Pan Books), p. 94.

of a great many people who are not members of the upper class. A more promising method of research would be to investigate P (prole) language, but presumably this would not be of the same interest to the public.

Still, *U* and *non-U* are now elements of the English vocabulary. On 4 June 1957 the Prime Minister, Mr Harold Macmillan, was asked the following in the House. 'Will you look into this question as to whether it is only the U-people in this country who have brains?' Then on 22 January 1958 Mr Glenvil Hall (Colne Valley) complained in the House that he and others who had approached the Leader of the House, Mr R. A. Butler, 'felt definitely non-U when we were in his presence'. But this must have been considered as verging on unparliamentary language, or at any rate very non-U, for Mr Butler expressed his astonishment and Mr Hall had to withdraw his remark.

Also in 1957 a very fruitful line of research was suggested by P. N. Furbank in *The Twentieth Century* (originally known as *The Nineteenth Century*, a title retained until half-way through the present century), for in the April number of that year there appeared his article 'On the idea of an ideal middle-class speech'. This time the subject is the speech of the 'lower regions of the upper middle class' whose unconscious aim is 'not freedom from certain awkward facts but from all facts; a total divorce of words from things'. The typical example cited by the article is that of a young woman disturbed during her reading of a book from which she is learning Italian. After a while she asks the question 'Do you mind if I sink back into my Italian?' Here, indeed, various categories of human activity are verbally jostled together in a manner which is doubtless strange to anyone unaccustomed to this type of speech. The result is by no means a total divorce of words from things as suggested by the author of the article, but there appears in this sort of self-expression a kind of ease of metaphor which at least jolts the language out of its accustomed grooves. To what social class, if any, this style should be assigned is a moot point, but it is certainly very widespread in academic circles. To take at random a sentence recently heard in a university refectory: 'Would there be any possibility of having breakfast on the train before we are decanted at Munich?' Here we have a totally unexpected image which is nonetheless perfectly understood by the listener. From the point of view of the speaker there is both an avoidance of banality and a lack of any straining after the conventional expression, whatever it may be.

During the 'twenties and 'thirties of this century the term 'nigger' was quite normally heard in Britain with a more or less neutral connotation that was meant to be as inoffensive as 'Negro' or 'black man'. It would consequently not have occurred to the average reader of Agatha Christie's *Ten Little Niggers* (1935) that there was anything unusual or objectionable about this title. 'Nigger brown' as the name of a particular colour of silk stockings was simply a technical term, probably less striking in the pacifist 'thirties than 'gun-metal grey' in the same catalogue. By 1963, on the other hand, the *Drapers' Record* noted that while the British Colour Council no longer used 'nigger brown' in its nomenclature many retailers and manufacturers did so, thereby risking the loss of business from coloured people. Whether as the result of an increased regard for the susceptibilities of others or because of business acumen it seems likely that this part of the British vocabulary is due for a change. But a curious sequel to the increasing reluctance to describe a coloured person by any racial term is the use of geographical names in this connection even when these are patently absurd, such as 'A West Indian born in London', 'an African born in this country' and so on. But perhaps after all this is no more curious than the Irish habit of determining Irishness by ancestry rather than by habitat.

Nothing is more difficult to be certain of than the death of a word, so that even the most ailing member of the vocabulary may take upon itself a sudden new lease of life. This has happened to *Asian*, until recently stigmatized by dictionaries as 'archaic', because a feeling has arisen that 'Asiatic' is somehow pejorative and 'Asian' is more acceptable. A reader of the *Daily Telegraph* pointed out in the correspondence column of that newspaper how in Australia the distinction is quite explicit and that 'for some time Australians have been most careful to distinguish between "Asian" and "Asiatic" . . .' (4 Oct 1957). In Australia 'Asian' is the polite word. In British official terminology it certainly has replaced its synonym, while it is a sign of the times that *The Asian Review* now incorporates *The Asiatic Review* and not the other way about. Perhaps most striking of all was the notorious *Asian flu* of the latter half of 1957 which was never spoken of as 'Asiatic flu', though whether that was a case of a polite word is a very nice point!

Even in the sphere of illness and injury there are changing fashions and the omnipresent *slipped disc* is duly noted by the makers of dictionaries, but it will come as a surprise to discover that as late as the 1950 edition of the *Concise Oxford Dictionary polio* was defined as '(Person suffering from) poliomyelitis' and it was not included in the main body of the *S.E.D.* (1955) but only in the supplement of additions where it is explained as a 'colloquial shortening of POLIOMYELITIS, originally U.S. 1931'. Though dating back to the nineteenth century as a medical term 'poliomyelitis' was itself quite unknown to the public in general as late as the thirties of the present century, when the usual term for this affliction was the misleading 'infantile paralysis'. As a matter of fact the disease in question has become better known since that time so it is not surprising that a shorter and more exact name has in the long run been preferred. 'Diphtheria' and 'scarlet fever' are happily no longer household words as they were in the 'twenties when the latter was often simply known as 'the fever' by reason of its prevalence. At that time tuberculosis was always known as 'consumption' (technically 'pulmonary consumption') but in the 'thirties this was replaced amazingly rapidly by the more scientific-sounding *T.B.*, itself springing from medical jargon where it really stood for 'tubercle-bacillus'. In one sense the substitution of T.B. for 'consumption' was rather fortunate linguistically, since otherwise such later phrases as 'mass consumption' might on occasion have been ambiguous. T.B. was already in existence in 1925, appearing in the *Modern*

Language Review for that year (p. 105) and significantly glossed as 'tuberculosis' in brackets.

The *kiss of life* became well-known in the early 'sixties as a method of reviving unconscious persons by breathing directly into the patient's mouth. As a matter of fact this is an ancient practice which had been allowed to fall into disuse, and for example we find a record of this technique in the *Gentleman's Magazine* for 1746 (p. 284). At Alloa in Scotland a miner had been rendered unconscious and apparently lifeless by noxious fumes. When he had been brought up from the pit a surgeon '. . . applied his mouth close to the patient's, and, by blowing strongly, holding the nostrils at the same time, raised his chest fully by his breath. He immediately felt six or seven very quick beats of the heart, the thorax continued to play and the pulse was soon after felt in the arteries.' In fact the word 'kiss' is something of a misnomer, and the French are more literal when they describe this technique as *bouche à bouche*. Why then is it not similarly 'mouth to mouth' in English? The answer probably is that it is a case of analogy with the semantically unrelated *kiss of death* which in any case is purely metaphorical, and implies 'an apparently advantageous action which in reality will bring trouble or destruction'. This in itself seems to be a fairly new expression, current in speech for some time before it was met with in writing. A recent instance from the *Observer* supplement clearly illustrates the meaning. 'Allying with Churchill was regarded as the political kiss of death even in 1939' (18 Sep 1966).

It is likely, then, that the mere existence of the *kiss of death* opened the way for the creation of a *kiss of life*, not necessarily with any logical link, for the speakers of the language often, as it were, 'fill in' a gap which can be considered to exist in the vocabulary, and so in such cases the creative process begins with the phrase and not with the concept which it describes, thus reversing the usual order of things.

In Britain the period from 1965 onwards has been marked by a sudden increase in drug addiction, especially among young people. The most easily obtainable narcotic is *marijuana* (or *marihuana*), a variety of hemp, Cannabis sativa, smoked in cigarettes known as *reefers*. This drug has a number of slang names, the best-known one being *pot* (though the 'Mary Warner' of the 'thirties is heard no more). *Marijuana* is Spanish in form but is of native Mexican origin. According to A. J. Bliss's *Dictionary of Foreign Words and Phrases in Current English*[1] there is a likelihood that its phonetic shape has been influenced by the Spanish girls' names *Maria* and *Juana*. This word is dated 1923 by the *S.E.D.* but has become known to a wide public in Britain only in the last few years. A much more recent creation is the adjective *psychedelic*, coined in America. *Psychedelic* ('revealing the soul', evidently from Greek *psyche* 'soul' + *dēloō* 'show') is unusual in form since English words compounded from *psyche* normally appear as derivatives of *psycho-* (thus psychology, psychosomatic, psychopath, etc.). Psychedelic drugs are those which modify perception, sensation, thinking and emotion, and lysergic acid (L.S.D.) for example, will afford a 'psychedelic experience'. A California-based cult attaches great importance to the use of such drugs as a means of increasing perception and extending human awareness ('the psychedelic revolution'). Incidentally the best discussion of these matters is still Aldous Huxley's *The Doors of Perception* (1954), in conjunction with his *Heaven and Hell* (1956). The word 'psychedelic' was first used (by Huxley and Dr H. Osmond) in 1957.[2] In fact this adjective can be used in a way which does not imply the taking of drugs, since in Britain as in the U.S.A. various devices entailing the use of rapidly changing patterns of sound, colour and movement have been used in such a way as to create a semi-hypnotic state in the victim. In southern England there is at least one 'psychedelic restaurant' where the enjoyment of diners is supposedly heightened by the presence of changing colours and sound effects. Men's underwear can now be obtained in vivid psychedelic patterns, though the adjective does not yet seem to have been applied to female lingerie, possibly because it is taken for granted that this has long been calculated to

[1] Routledge and Kegan Paul, 1966.
[2] I am indebted to Mrs Elinore J. Marvel for this information.

heighten the perception of the beholder, so that no explanatory adjective is required.

Clearly 'psychedelic' is becoming less of a technical term and more and more of a fashionable word, so that as time passes it will progressively lose its strict meaning. Indeed the process is well under way in both Britain and America. In the spring of 1967 there was a cartoon in the *Daily Express* showing an ultra-modern young curate being closely questioned by his ecclesiastical superior in connection with reports of his 'psychedelic sermons', while in the U.S.A. the issue of *Newsweek* for 1 May 1967 included a mention of news that '. . . hippies are smoking dried banana peels to get a psychedelic kick'.

On the more technical plane, *Psychedelic Review* is the publication of an American movement led by Dr Timothy Leary, a former Harvard faculty member, which claims to achieve spiritual discovery through the use of hallucinogenic chemicals such as L.S.D. and mescaline. The review was founded in 1963.

Ambiguity can arise from the most unlikely quarter. When in 1922 Dean Inge included in his Rede Lecture on 'The Victorian Age' the phrase *'vital statistics'* it is highly unlikely that he could have foreseen the fate which was to overtake this innocuous and somewhat forbidding expression in a later decade. It seems to have been invented in the first place in the first half of the nineteenth century with reference to births, marriages and deaths. Though the original sense theoretically continues, at the present time this has been quite overlaid in the public mind by a jocular extension of meaning, occasionally with curious results. Thus it was reported in the press in October 1964 that a letter arriving from abroad and addressed to the Vital Statistics Office (actually the district register office), Grantham, was taken by the postal authorities to a local corset factory. The habit of expressing a woman's bust, waist and hip measurements respectively in three groups of figures and calling the resulting expression her vital statistics was first publicly applied to film stars and other entertainers, though the present writer must confess to a surprising uncertainty as to when this began. (Theoretically a man also has vital statistics but they never seem to be of general interest.) We are told, though this is somewhat outside the scope of the present work, that ideally a woman's waist should measure 10 inches less than either the bust or hips. Observers of the continental scene are reminded that the relevant statistics are expressed there in centimetres and not in inches, for unless this is taken into account the figures appear unduly inflated. Certainly it is likely that the serious use of 'vital statistics' is going to be increasingly inhibited from now on.

It is a commonplace occurrence when two very different meanings of a particular word both struggle for survival in a fight which leads to the triumph of one sense or the other, but it is not often that it takes the lexicographers well over half a century to realize the existence of one of the meanings. This has happened in the case of *antibiotic*. In the main body of the *S.E.D.* it is dated 1860 and shown to be a rare adjective meaning 'Opposed to a belief in the presence or possibility of life' while only in the supplement of additions do we find any mention of this word as a noun and adjective indicating '(A substance) that destroys or impairs living organisms, e.g. bacteria'. The dating for this more modern meaning is 1892. In general English usage, of course, this word has become known only in more recent times precisely because of the enormous extension of the treatment of disease by antibiotics.

PURPLE HEARTS, read a laconic heading in a *Times* Law Report (27 Feb 1964). This was not a reference to the United States military award of that name, but to the notorious so-called Purple Heart tablets which were a source of drug addiction in teenagers in Britain from the early 'sixties, and which were heart-shaped and purple at that time. It is a fine point as to whether their name is to be ascribed solely to these latter features, or whether, at any rate in America, there was at first a punning allusion to that decoration given to American soldiers wounded on active service, though certainly this latter element would in any case be totally unknown to the mass of the British public.

Another – and more surprising example of how slowly even

the most authoritative dictionaries sometimes react to the changing usage of certain words is seen in the case of 'enemy' as an adjective meaning 'of or pertaining to an enemy'. In the main part of the *S.E.D.* this is marked as 'Now *rare*', and a quotation 'enemy goods' is given for 1793! Mercifully the supplement at the end of the volume corrects this by saying of that entry 'Delete "Now rare"', giving examples from 1891 (enemy world), 1915 (enemy territory) and 'modern' usage (destroyed by enemy action). It will be agreed that this correction is somewhat belated, especially after two world wars in which this adjective has had a good run, but let us hope that it will soon be marked 'archaic' as a result of changed world conditions.

In *English Social Differences* (1955) Professor T. H. Pear speaks of a public-school prefect as being 'at the most neurotic, irritable and exotic period of his life' (p. 206).[1] At first sight 'exotic' would appear to be a misprint for 'erotic' but experience reveals that *exotic* is frequently used in this way though the exact sense intended is difficult to define and seems to have little overt connection with the customary meaning, i.e. 'not indigenous, alien, barbaric'. Perhaps the latest implication is 'unusual' or 'whimsical'. Similarly the leather jackets and knee-boots of teenagers have been said to be exotic, though these adolescent fashions are by no means exotic in the traditional sense, being reproduced in many countries in the western world. This is in fact something of a vogue-word in certain circles, and may in a way be compared with the over-worked 'nostalgic' and 'nostalgia' which hitherto concerned melancholia induced by prolonged absence from one's home or country but now more often than not refer to time and bygone days rather than to place. The change of emphasis is natural in an epoch of unprecedentedly rapid change in almost every sphere of life, and at a time when the individual is more than usually prone to regrets for the vanished scenes of youth.

The technical vocabulary of engineering includes the phrase 'stresses and strains', now frequently heard in general conversation with an extended meaning, e.g. 'the stresses and strains of

[1] Allen and Unwin.

modern life'. But a curious point is that the order of words is frequently altered, giving *strains and stresses*, attested for example in Fitzroy Maclean's *Eastern Approaches* (p. 114) in 1949.[1] Again, in a Ministry of Education pamphlet entitled *Language* (1954) we find this word-order. '. . . it is interesting to note the strains and stresses that have existed almost from the beginning, between the English language here and in America' (p. 10). It is difficult to see any reason, phonetic or otherwise, for the modern reversal – in general parlance – of the order of words here, though possibly what is involved is an unconscious desire on the part of speakers to reproduce the alternation of strong and weak syllable accentuation so typical of English phraseology, hence *stráins ǎnd stréssěs* as against *stréssěs ǎnd stráins* (cf. *Jéw ǎnd Géntǐle* rather than *Géntǐle ǎnd Jéw*, *Kíng and Cóuntrў* rather than *Cóuntrў and Kíng*). This type of explanation will not, however, suffice to explain the change of 'the Havenots and the Haves', as used by Lord Lytton (died 1873), to the modern *Haves and Havenots*, since neither version gives the alternation of strong and weak accentuation.

Just as 'strains and stresses' (as well as the original version) is in general use nowadays, so the verb *stress* is quite normally intended to indicate emphasis on a fact or idea, although the S.E.D. continues to mark this sense as 'Chiefly U.S.'. Evidently the older sense in Britain was that pertaining to the laying of stress on a particular word or syllable when speaking. The more recent usage simply gives the verb a metaphorical meaning, in fact. Similarly for to *shore* or *shore up*, which is an old-established though at one time somewhat neglected verb in the practical sphere meaning to hold up with a 'shore' – a prop or beam set against a ship, wall or tree as an oblique support. To prop up, in commoner parlance. During the nineteen-fifties there was suddenly a tendency to make figurative use of this old expression, probably under American influence, and it became well-known in the end in connection with the 'shoring-up' of political parties, regimes, economic systems and so on, even though the literal

[1] Cape.

meaning had been half-forgotten, so that when a B.B.C. news bulletin of December 1959 mentioned this expression in connection with the removal of a wrecked bridge in a train disaster it transpired that many listeners had not heard it before. It will frequently happen that some word or phrase exists for years before events bring it into real prominence, and this is precisely why the study of changes in linguistic fashion sheds light on social attitudes, as well as changed conditions in society. Thus everybody knows the word *cosh* nowadays, though when Robert Graves used this word in *Goodbye to All That* in 1929 he felt it was necessary to explain it as 'a loaded stick' during an allusion to the trench warfare of 1916. It was in fact first attested in 1874 but became something of a 'household word' only in the nineteen-fifties as a result of the adoption of this weapon by young thugs, the so-called 'cosh boys'.

In some cases the word will not only emerge from obscurity but will undergo a modification of its meaning in order to meet new conditions. *Lay-by*, for a 'portion of road extended to permit a vehicle to stop there without interfering with traffic', may seem to be a neologism, and this is certainly the case so far as this precise meaning is concerned (hence the inclusion of the word and this definition in the addenda of the 1950 edition of the *Concise Oxford Dictionary*). But the same word meant a railway siding in the early years of this century, while there is a letter of 7 July 1826 which mentions a 'laybye' at Islington in the bank of the canal, intended for barges.[1] The modern application of this word has obviously been brought about by the tremendous extension of high-speed road travel. Needless to say a whole new vocabulary has grown up in the last generation or so around the motor-car and the ever-improved roads demanded by a car-owning democracy, a vocabulary containing many scores of words ranging from *traffic lights* to the more recent *flyover* and *underpass*. It is indeed a curious thought that 'parking' was one of the words that Monica Baldwin did not know on emerging from her convent in 1941. Nowadays NO PARKING is the most

[1] *Notes and Queries*, 1960, p. 148.

ubiquitous of prohibitions. To 'park' is in fact military in origin, and was being used with reference to wagons and guns as far back as the Napoleonic wars. Before that it simply meant to enclose in a park.

'Suburb' might sound rather as though it were a twentieth-century word, but in reality it is Biblical. 'The suburbs shall shake at the sound of the cry of thy pilots' (Ezekiel 27, verse 28). Earlier still it is to be found in Chaucer where robbers lurk 'In the suburbes of a toun'.[1] Even 'Suburbia' is dated 1896, and so antedates our period. *Subtopia*, on the other hand, is modern. It applies to ill-conceived building development disfiguring the landscape and is a rather ingenious word, combining as it does the allusions to 'sub-' (cf. substandard) and Utopia. A would-be Utopia that did not succeed, as it were. The term was invented by Mr Ian Nairn, a contributor to an architectural journal, in 1955. *Conurbation* dates back some twenty years earlier than that, and refers to a feature of the distribution of British population which becomes increasingly pronounced, namely the tendency for existing aggregations of urban districts to become even more densely populated. 'Conurbation' is a most useful word to describe these regions of great population, some half-dozen in number in England and Wales.

Like people, words are capable of migrating from the provinces to the fashionable metropolis. The *O.E.D.* lists *pot-hole* as local, relying on the *English Dialect Dictionary* which had assigned it to Northumberland, Cumberland, Westmorland and West Yorkshire. The more recent *pot-holer* is the everyday equivalent of the speleologist, aptly defined by a journalist in 1957 as 'a man who takes a walk inside a mountain'. *Intake*, which had a sudden rise to fame in the second world war in the sense of persons or things admitted, is an extension of other meanings of this word which is marked by the *S.E.D.* as 'chiefly Scottish and northern dialect'. The oldest meaning, reaching back to the six-

[1] The Canon's yeoman's prologue. But in Biblical and Chaucerian usage the meaning of 'suburbs' is simply 'surrounding country' and not 'outlying districts of a city'.

teenth century, is that of an enclosure, and this has not even now entirely died out in northern usage, as at Newcastle upon Tyne where certain enclosures of the Town Moor are officially known as Intakes, while a district of Sheffield is named Intake, presumably having been taken in from the surrounding countryside.

Sometimes an old word can be given a new interpretation by a modern generation, and one suspects that this has happened in the case of *raffish*, which was in the first instance a dialectal word listed in the English Dialect Dictionary and so antedating the creation of the R.A.F. ('raf') with which many speakers seem to connect it in its sense of 'dissipated, fast-looking'. (In a rather similar way, 'blowzy' is often connected with 'blouse', quite unjustifiably.)

Now regarded as part of the British national way of life are *elevenses*, whose name was originally dialectal. Though the expression has been in existence from the middle of the nineteenth century it has not been in general the standard language until fairly recently. *Natter* is dialectally of similar age, but began to pass into the language in general around 1940 or so. *Tatty* is from the Midlands and meant 'shabby' in the first place, probably being related to 'tatters'. During the 'fifties it rapidly became known, and Rose Macaulay included it in a letter of 3 August 1951 when discussing two church services. 'They seemed unreal and kind of tatty.'[1] This is colloquial style, but ten years later the adjective could be used in academic prose. 'It is these institutions that are now beginning to look somewhat tatty; the façades are cracking,' wrote a professor in the 1962 spring number of the *Wiseman Review* (p. 44). In the summer of 1966 the Leader of the Opposition, Mr Edward Heath, was able to deride the government's economic measures as 'a tatty ragbag of old ideas'.

But perhaps the most conspicuous regional recruit to standard English in recent years is *ploy*, listed in the *S.E.D.* of 1955 as Scottish and Northern, but included in the *Concise Oxford Dictionary* of 1964 simply as 'colloquial', with the definition 'Expedition, undertaking, occupation, job . . .' The origin is said

[1] *Letters to a Friend* (New York, 1962).

to be unknown. Though it has only recently gained general currency it is first attested in the eighteenth century, and of course may have existed in speech for centuries before that. In spite of the dictionary definition, the most common meaning nowadays is 'gambit', 'shrewd trick', and this sense, together with the word itself, was made known by Stephen Potter's books on *Lifemanship* and *Gamesmanship*.

Brash, 'rash, cheeky, saucy', is in the short run of American origin and is marked as 'originally or chiefly U.S.' in the 1950 edition of the *Concise Oxford Dictionary*, though it is interesting to compare this with the entry in the *S.E.D.* which calls it 'dialectal' and gives the dating 1824, presumably a reference to John Trotter Brockett's *Glossary of North Country Words* completed in that year and giving the same definition of this adjective as the *S.E.D.*, 'impetuous, rash'. Clearly it is a question of the same term, so that once again a word belonging to an English dialect has taken root in America during the settlement of that continent then travelled back to England in the twentieth century as an Americanism. The ultimate etymology is unknown.

Makers of dictionaries are inevitably trapped on occasion into stating apparently eternal truths to which time later gives the lie. Thus the preface to the first edition (1911) of the *S.E.D.* says that this dictionary includes 'many words and senses that are fossilized, having in them no life or capacity for further development, but kept extant by being enshrined in perhaps a single proverb or phrase that is still in use; of this sort are *coil* (confusion), preserved by "shuffled off this mortal coil", and *scotch* (wound), preserved by "we have scotched this snake, not killed it".' *Scotch*, well-known because of its use in *Macbeth*, has therefore long had the meaning of 'wound' as opposed to 'kill'. Yet astonishingly it can imply 'kill', if only metaphorically, in contemporary English. Here, taken from the press on the same day, are two instances of this reversal of sense. Writing in the *Sunday Times* (25 Sep 1966) Cyril Connolly spoke of a book on the assassination of President Kennedy '. . . with pages and pages devoted to the enumeration and scotching of every conceivable rumour, however grotesque . . .' while in the *Observer* John Wain stated of a book on Hemingway: 'One thing Hochner's book will do is to scotch the widespread belief that Hemingway shot himself because he had cancer.' In these cases, and especially in the latter one, it is evident that the meaning is not merely 'wound' but definitely 'kill, destroy'. True, there had been a tendency in the nineteenth century to use 'scotch' in this more radical sense, but evidently in 1911 it was considered that this was no longer the case and did not merit any mention. At the present time, however, *scotch* is readily used in that sense of 'kill' which originally was specifically excluded.

4

Word Structure

WHEN quiz-masters or schoolteachers require their victims to produce the opposite of a given word the correct answer is often a word of totally different root, e.g. as the opposite of 'artificial' we can say 'natural'. If the question were put the other way we could give as the opposite of 'natural' either 'artificial', or else, 'unnatural', according to the precise shade of meaning. On the spur of the moment we might well recall only 'unnatural', since obviously the use of a prefix is a convenient way of indicating reversal of meaning. In Esperanto this is in fact the usual way of forming contraries, so that *bona* 'good' has as its opposite *malbona* 'bad'; in other words Esperanto simply prefixes *mal-* to any word in order to obtain that word's opposite. To take another example: *amiko* is 'friend' therefore *malamiko* is 'enemy'. Of course it is by no means unknown for English to carry out a similar process with 'mal-' (also with 'mis-' and 'dis-') but here the technique is not always quite the same as in Esperanto, since these prefixes more often than not indicate not exactly an opposite but rather an element of imperfection or remissness, as in 'maltreat' or 'distaste'. It is 'un-' which so often expresses the negative or opposite of nouns, adjectives and verbs, but although this prefix has been used extensively in English since the earliest times it cannot be applied indiscriminately. Thus the opposite of 'white' is 'black' and not '*unwhite*' (the asterisk indicating that the form does not exist in English).[1] This having been established, it must next be said that in present-day English there is a strong tendency, in the written language at least, to extend the scope of 'un-' by applying it to words hitherto unaffected by its use. An example

[1] Though in South Africa the opposite of 'white' is 'non-white'.

that springs to mind is that of *unclear*, imported in recent years from America where in turn the ultimate origin was perhaps the German *unklar*, via American scholarship which is strongly influenced by German academic models and language. At all events, the position at present is that it is now possible to use 'unclear' as the opposite of 'clear'.

A peculiar difficulty arising in the study of the history of forms in 'un-' is that no dictionary has ever listed all possible words actually created by the use of this prefix because through sheer weight of numbers the lexicographer has perforce to restrict himself to the more frequent and important of them. Unfortunately the practical result of this state of affairs is that anyone saying that a particular word beginning with 'un-' has only just begun to appear in English lays himself open to the objection that it has probably been current for a very long time, and that the mere fact that it is not listed in a dictionary does not suffice to disprove its existence in earlier years. Two points can be made here; first, that the onus lies upon the objector to show an earlier dating in a text of the word in question – e.g. 'unclear' – and secondly that in the discussion of these prefixes we are speaking of very general tendencies affecting present-day English. So it may well be that 'unclear' was written in Britain once or twice in the early twentieth century, but the point at issue is that nowadays it is quite frequent and furthermore that words in 'un-' are formed much more freely than was the case hitherto, and seem less idiosyncratic as coinages, so to speak. Some are admittedly less striking than others, and when in *The Times* we find 'As men they are unalike' (26 Feb 1960) we may reflect that our own usage would probably have been 'not alike', without being very conscious of whether 'unalike' is a new word or not. But when I. A. Richards writes of someone's 'unwasteful life' the adjective is more arresting through being an obvious invention.[1] A literary critic refers to a 'contemporary un-hero, the desperately unfunny Archie Rice' (*Observer*, 29 Sep 1957) and the *un-hero* cannot but stand out starkly as a neologism denoting a modern concept.

[1] *Principles of Literary Criticism*, 4th ed. (Kegan Paul, 1930), p. 57.

Unfunny in this sentence also has something of a modern ring about it and certainly the precise shade of meaning is interesting, for it is not simply 'not amusing' – one would not bother to say, for example, that the multiplication tables are unfunny – but 'not amusing in spite of the desire to amuse', which is a good description of the broken-down entertainer mentioned here. A curious expression came to light in the now defunct *Truth* when it was said that 'during the pre-Christmas months a large number of *un-books* appear – books which are not bought to be read but to be given as presents' (4 Oct 1957). This may have been seen by a reviewer in the *Observer* who a little later that year spoke of the 'evocative and un-radio results' obtained by a television interviewer trying his hand at creating a whole programme (8 Dec 1957). The meaning here is 'uncharacteristic of radio'. Earlier in that same year *Truth* had alluded to 'Mr Macmillan's unsuccess in the "Little General Election"' (7 June 1957). In the previous year the *New Statesman* included in its pages the neologism *unpublicity* in a serious article. 'After six years of unpublicity, Bernard Shaw's 8000-word will has come into the news' (26 Jan 1956). Whether this is equivalent to 'deliberate silence' or simply 'lack of news' is not clear. The *New Statesman* was in 1961 to use the striking word *unfreedom* in 'He was strongly inclined to interpret it as the surviving clique of Stalinist toadies and deadheads in the Writers' Union trying to strike a blow for unfreedom' (27 Jan 1961). Here we have the familiar journalistic trick of standing a well-known phrase on its head, but the point is that in this case the requisite vocabulary was already to hand, for 'unfreedom' had been used in the *Observer* a couple of years previously (8 Mar 1959). This prefix 'un-' with its negative meaning is as old as the English language but at the moment we seem to be in a period when its application is less restricted by habit than, say, thirty or forty years ago, and it remains to be seen how far ᵗhis tendency will go in future times.

There is no doubt that 'un-' can be handled in such a way as to render subtle shades of intention going beyond a mere reversal of the positive meaning. Thus, in her memoirs Lady Diana Cooper speaks of 'unrobust health' and no doubt many of us recognize this physical state and admire this neat evocation of it. Similarly in '... at least half the cardinals came from unrich families' (*Observer*, 12 Oct 1958) there is no suggestion that 'unrich' means 'poor'. It merely implies an economic condition which though not necessarily poverty is certainly not wealth. On the other hand it is occasionally possible for a writer to manipulate an existing adjective beginning with 'un-' in such a way as to impart to it a new meaning. 'Unprofessional' is a familiar word in such phrases as 'unprofessional conduct' but the element of moral judgment is entirely lacking in the following sentence, dealing with the conductor, Bruno Walter. 'He was born in Berlin in 1876 – his unprofessional name being Schlesinger' (*Observer*, 18 Feb 1962). Here the sense is the neutral one of 'real, not adopted for professional reasons'. What is noteworthy is the fact that the prefix is used in a sort of mathematical way to reverse the meaning of the adjective without operating any value-judgment. In this case 'unprofessional' does not mean 'amateurish' nor does it mean 'immoral' but quite simply 'not professional'. Of course, from a purely theoretical point this is precisely what one might expect though in fact this word has in the course of its history acquired the other more complicated and emotive senses just mentioned. The significant thing in the present instance is that for once the adjective in its negative form has been given its negative meaning pure and simple, for this quasi-mathematical use of 'un-' in order to reverse a meaning is particularly characteristic of present-day English. Such a straightforward relationship, positive versus negative, cannot by any means always be taken for granted in the existing English vocabulary so far as words of this type are concerned, e.g. 'canny-uncanny', 'easy-uneasy', 'loosen-unloosen' and so on. What we are witnessing nowadays is a freer use of 'un-' as an automatic means of indicating an opposite.

A rare case going against this general stream is that of 'unbalance' ('lack of balance') which was being used as early as 1887 but seems likely to be ousted by the recent *imbalance*, much beloved of commentators on politics and economics. If 'un-balance' does in fact disappear for good then a curious pattern of words will be left behind, with the noun 'imbalance' corresponding to the adjective 'unbalanced', not that this discrepancy will shock any speaker of the English language, so rich in structural anomalies.

It is abundantly clear, at all events, that the prefix 'un-' is enjoying a sudden wave of fashion and can be applied in sophisticated circles to a great many words, though doubtless even now it would not occur to everyone to venture to use such forms as *unburnt-out*, *unbirdminded* or such Anglo-French hybrids as *unblasé* and *unbourgeois*. There is still the general tendency for the prefix to be attached to adjectives rather than to nouns, while verbs seem to attract it only rarely. 'The first World War did much to uncomplicate the state of courtship,' declares E. S. Turner in *A History of Courting* (p. 207). At first sight this 'uncomplicate' does not appear to be anything more than an elaborate synonym of 'simplify', yet perhaps on second thoughts it must be said that it may stand for more than that, for after all even 'uncomplicated' is not the same as 'simple' and a simple village maid (to follow Turner's choice of theme) is not necessarily uncomplicated.

A significant by-product of the vogue for this prefix has been the humorous creation of back-formations based on the roots of certain existing words in '-un', thus *kempt* from 'unkempt' and *couth* from 'uncouth'. It is thought that this vogue began among Oxford undergraduates and the two examples just given are admittedly humorous in intent, though what is curious about them is that they had already existed in the English language hundreds of years ago. 'Kempt' simply meant 'combed' and is listed as archaic, while 'couth' meant 'known' and is said to have survived in Scotland with the senses of 'kind, agreeable, snug, cosy'. But in the adjective *committal* we see a brand-new opposite of 'non-committal'. 'A hunched teen-ager, hair slicked flatter by rain, was more committal' (*Observer*, 30 Oct 1960). This avoids saying 'less non-committal', and the whole sentence is in fact a splendid example of contemporary English, especially in the use of 'flatter' without any term of comparison – not 'flatter than usual' or 'flatter than most' but just 'flatter' – like ***** WASHES WHITER. (This remarkable piece of syntax is incidentally in process of being introduced into the French language, to which it is totally foreign, by the way, via ***** LAVE PLUS BLANC, a literal translation of the English slogan.)

An unforeseeable fate has overcome the pair of adjectives 'inflammable' and 'non-inflammable', which have become, or at least are becoming, *flammable* and *non-flammable* respectively. This is not so much the normal play of linguistic development as a deliberate act of policy intended to lessen confusion and danger in the practical sphere. The practice of the new nomenclature seems to have begun in the United States and was first brought to the notice of the British public in the nineteen-fifties when petrol-tankers belonging to the U.S. forces were marked FLAMMABLE. In the *Economist* (25 May 1957) there was an article entitled 'Flammable clothing', and at that date the British Standards Institution had already used such words as *flammability* and *flammable* in a report on that subject. The situation now is that the Institution prefers *flammable* and *non-flammable* to 'inflammable' and 'non-inflammable'.[1] Considerations of safety must come before linguistic tradition and there is no doubt that in due course the newer usage (if indeed it becomes universal) will do away with the dangerous ambiguity hitherto arising from the possibility of some people misunderstanding the prefix 'in-' of 'inflammable' as having negative force as in such words as 'inaccessible' rather than as 'inhabitable'. The only danger is that in the short run a proliferation of forms may simply cause confusion all round!

When the opposite of a verb has to be created the prefix usually coming into play is either 'de-' or 'dis-', in spite of 'uncomplicate',

[1] Cf. *Notes and Queries*, January 1960, p. 2. Furthermore, the Fire Protection Association adopted 'flammable' out of consideration for those who found some inconsistency between 'inflammable' and 'incombustible'; hence *non-flammable* and *non-combustible*, according to a letter in *The Times* (10 Mar 1964) when the Flammable Materials Bill was going through Parliament.

as mentioned above. Thus '... the Americans decided to de-emphasize their presence,' writes a professor contributing to *The Universities Review* of October 1958 (p. 11). There is nothing ultra-modern about this process in itself, for it has been in operation ever since the Middle Ages, but here again the users of the English language have suddenly become particularly prone to taking advantage of it in recent years, possibly because of the spread of the bureaucratic outlook in modern society and the handiness of this verbal trick when it is a question of creating administrative jargon, as in the following example. 'America in particular has declassified a great deal of information for the first time' (*Observer*, 7 Aug 1955). *Declassify* means 'to make public, to take off the secret list', and is the opposite of *classify* which in this technical sense is in the first instance an American expression. But it so happens that the root word in verbs made up with 'de-' need not itself be a verb and may well be a noun, as in one of the most famous expressions coming into this category, i.e. 'debunk' an original Americanism current in Britain from the late nineteen-twenties onward. Of the same period, but now somewhat neglected, is 'debag', meaning 'forcibly to remove the trousers from someone' (i.e. the so-called Oxford bags of the nineteen-twenties, trousers as wide as the present ones are narrow). The more recent *debriefing*, on the other hand, is not a punishment inflicted on female students but a technique used when an astronaut has come back from a space flight, so enabling all available information to be extracted from him in the shortest possible space of time. The expression is also applied to a mode of interrogation which checks the good faith of alleged defectors from foreign regimes who may in fact be espionage agents planted by a hostile secret service.

In recent times there has also been mention of *de-oathing* in connection with the remedial indoctrination of former members of the Mau Mau terrorist movement. 'A de-oathing ceremony took place,' wrote *The Times* (8 Oct 1959), but it is likely that this word will die out with the cessation of the events that gave rise to it. Perhaps the process of *de-flying* (clearing an area of tsetse flies) as mentioned in the *Times Educational Supplement* (17 Feb 1956) will last longer. The name is somewhat reminiscent of the de-lousing which was a well-known feature of the First World War. What is striking about the verb 'delouse' (though it antedates the period we are primarily discussing) is the fact that it was ever coined at all. Ever since the Middle Ages the verb for 'ridding of lice' had been 'to louse' and indeed the *S.E.D.* takes cognizance only of this form, totally ignoring 'delouse' (as it ignores 'debag'), though in reality the use of 'louse' as a verb is dialectal nowadays. The point is that the addition of the prefix to an old-established word is significant of how fashion in verbs was going even in the early part of the twentieth century, when the language was evidently already moving towards an increased reliance on this type of verbal pattern. In the House of Commons the then prime minister, Sir Anthony Eden, stated that it was not exact to say that Colonel Nasser had nationalized the Suez Canal – he had *de-internationalized* it. That is not a mere quibble or play on words, but a definite distinction made possible by this useful prefix, just as in 1964 it was said that the new Labour government did not intend to nationalize steel but to de-denationalize it. Just as during the economic crisis in the summer of 1966 Mr George Brown, having offered his resignation from the government to the Prime Minister and then changed his mind, was said to have *deresigned*.

'De-' may sometimes be the sign of a removal of part of the human body, as in the old-established 'decapitate', though here the semantic motivation is not apparent except to those who are aware of the relationship of this verb to the Latin *caput* 'head'. The same is true of 'depilate' meaning 'remove hair from', where the link is with Latin *pilus* 'hair' (as in the 'pile' of a carpet). In fact it is almost impossible to find any simple word based on the formula 'DĒ + part of human body', with the exception of the highly metaphorical 'deflower'. Yet modern usage is not afraid to coin words of this structure in respect of animals or insects, and so a description of 'broilers' explains that '... they have to be de-beaked to prevent them tearing one another to pieces in sheer boredom' (*Observer*, 8 Mar 1959), and it is likewise possible to hear of the *de-stinging* of wasps by small boys.

All told, this prefix is chiefly useful in the creation of bureaucratic jargon, and in this sphere there is virtually no limit to what can be achieved with it. Thus the president of the National Union of Boot and Shoe Operatives stated at the Duke of Edinburgh's conference on human problems in industry: 'A real craftsman may lose his opportunity to shine, but de-skilling gives opportunities to many' (11 Jul 1956). But in addition to verbal forms of this type there are also new nouns in *de-*, and thus a letter to *The Times* speaks of 'a process of de-education' (29 Jan 1960). The word looks barbarous at first sight but why should it be any less acceptable than 're-education'? Perhaps only because the social process thereby described is less pleasing. *De-mythology* is even less familiar in sound because there is no related *re-mythology*. 'We do not have to agree with everything that is written by continental advocates of de-mythology,' wrote the Rev. Mervyn Stockwood (now Bishop of Southwark) in the *National and English Review* (Dec 1957). Perhaps more will be heard of this word as a result of the discussion initiated by the Bishop of Woolwich's booklet *Honest to God* in which the theme is the need to remove the allegedly mythological aspect of Christianity.

'Dis-' has likewise entered a period of public favour. *Disincentive* – 'an act, a measure, etc., which tends to discourage production' – is dated 1951 by the *S.E.D.* though in fact it can be dated earlier by Professor Zandvoort (*Wartime English*, p. 84) when he quotes from the *Observer* (18 Apr 1948) 'Only a few months ago some ass first wrote "disincentive" when he meant "deterrent"'. But in fact it seems that 'deterrent' is increasingly associated with the 'nuclear deterrent' and regarded as a technical term of modern diplomacy and warfare, and its more general sense is in some danger of withering away. At all events 'deterrent' is in much wider use nowadays than ever before, after being a comparatively infrequent word. In the economic sphere we have *disinflation*, which is not exactly deflation pure and simple but rather the return to a state of equilibrium from an inflationary state. Such is the theory, though perhaps in reality this supposed difference is merely a cloak for a verbal taboo, 'deflation' itself being regarded as something of an unpleasant term (a 'dirty word' as modern idiom has it) ever since the depression of the nineteen-thirties. 'Disinflation' has a curative ring about it, sounding as it does like the cessation of an unhealthy state. The *S.E.D.* also lists *dis-saving* and *dis-spending* but not *disinvestment* which is much commoner and was used by the late Morgan Phillips in an unscripted statement on the B.B.C. when he spoke of 'a long period of disinvestment' (28 Oct 1955). More recently there has appeared *diseconomies*, as in '. . . this should not involve diseconomies to the British Motor Corporation' as a television speaker said (22 Jan 1960).

One of the most striking changes in present-day English is the one affecting 'disinterest' and the corresponding adjective 'disinterested'. Of the latter the *S.E.D.* states that the sense of 'uninterested' attached to it 'has latterly become frequent in illiterate usage', while the 1938 edition of *The development of modern English* by the American scholar Stuart Robertson mentioned that 'a present tendency even in fairly careful use, seems to disregard this useful distinction in meaning' (p. 376).[1] Examples abound in modern texts. Suffice it to quote the *Times Educational Supplement* of 25 March 1954. 'Women came out of the enquiry extremely well. Often teased for being politically disinterested, they here show themselves the reverse.' The noun is used similarly, as in a review in *Encounter* of the work of Françoise Sagan in October 1956: 'Utter incomprehension, utter disinterest, utterly unconcealed'. This use, or misuse, of 'disinterest' and 'disinterested' has not failed to meet with a great deal of resistance, though in this connection it is salutary to consider the opinion of

[1] The tendency was already at work in the early nineteen-twenties as pointed out by Emlyn Williams in his autobiography *George* (p. 167), and his teacher Miss Cooke warned him at that time not to say 'disinterested' when he meant 'uninterested' (Hamish Hamilton, 1961).

Professor Thomas Pyles as to what would be the effect on the English language of the triumph of the new fashion. 'There will have been no great loss to language *qua* communication. We shall merely have lost a synonym for *impartial* and acquired on all levels another way of saying "uninterested". Educated readers of the future will be no more annoyed by the change than they are by similar changes that have given some of the words used in, say, the plays of Shakespeare and in the King James Bible different meanings for us from those which they had in early Modern English.'[1]

Mini- is a new prefix easily recognizable as implying miniature proportions, and seems virtually to have been brought into the language by the British Motor Corporation's Mini Minor, the car produced in 1960. It was this vehicle, more exactly, that popularized *mini* on a large scale, though in 1953 there was a motor-cycle known as the Mini-Motor and much earlier, in 1935, there had been the Eavestaff Minipiano whose name was registered as a trademark but made no impact on the language. Because of the Mini Minor's popularity the next development was the *minicab*, a diminutive taxicab. 1963 was a great year for the further extension of this prefix which suddenly became available for general plundering. 'The inculcation of mini-morals, mini-maxims and mini-history stands no chance once children sense that they are being angled for . . .' wrote the *Observer* (1 Dec 1963) making typical use of the new device. In June of the next year chemist's shops were advertising 'A satisfying slimmer's mini-meal' and before long the prefix had predictably been taken over by feminine fashion, whose vocabulary is always avid for words implying smallness and daintiness, hence *mini-bra* and *mini-belt*. By December 1964 there was a headline in the *Daily Express* referring to a number of bye-elections to be held in the New Year: JANUARY – THE MINI ELECTION. *Mini-budget* has also usefully been applied to small interim budgets, separate from the traditional Spring budget. In 1966 came the *mini-skirt*, for

---

[1] *The Origins and Development of the English Language* (Harcourt, Brace and World Inc. 1964), p. 304.

the invention of which Mary Quant was deservedly decorated by a grateful country. There seems to be no doubt that 'mini' is all set for a splendid career in commerce, politics and the press.

At the other end of the scale of magnitude is *mega-*, known to the public chiefly because of *megaton*, used for evaluating the power of nuclear explosions and equalling in force the strength of a million tons of 'conventional' high explosives. 'Bomber Command is now in process of being equipped with bombs in the megaton range,' announced the *Observer* (8 Dec 1957). An even grimmer designation is that of *megadeath*, 'a million deaths' (in nuclear war) and there has even been some use of *megabirth* in relation to the 'population explosion'. But it does not seem likely that 'mega-' will have the same success as 'mini-' because it is somehow less self-explanatory and is not attached to any well-known word, subjectively speaking, since 'megaphone' (literally 'big voice') and the less frequent 'megalith' ('big stone') are not generally realized to be compound words, though radio enthusiasts may know the exact sense of 'megacycle', i.e. a thousand kilocycles (a million cycles) and similarly a megawatt is equal to a thousand kilowatts (a million watts). The source of all these terms is the Greek *megas* 'great', reduced to *mega-* in compounds and widely used in technical and medical terminology, e.g. 'megacephalic' (large-headed).

According to its Greek etymology a helicopter is a machine having a 'screw wing' (*helikos + pteron*) so the logical division of the word should be 'helico/pter'. These two Greek elements are in fact respectively to be found in the 'helical spring' (a spring having the form of a screw) and the prehistoric flying creature known to science as a 'pterodactyl' (wing-fingered). But in the popular mind 'helicopter' has been considered as being divisible into the elements 'heli' + 'copter', so much so that *'copter* is an abbreviation found in journalistic writing. The rather useful outcome is that the resulting prefix *heli-* is henceforth available for the creation of any number of neologisms having to do with helicopters; *helibus, helidrome, heliport* and even, according to *The*

Times (29 Oct 1960), *helipod,* apparently a portable operating theatre for front-line combat areas. It may be noted that 'helicopter' is not itself a particularly recent word, since it began to appear regularly from 1906 (*Modern Language Review,* 1962, p. 79).

Such an old-established prefix as 'ex-' has shown some signs of extending its functions in present-day English, particularly in the word *ex-directory.* 'Mr Chambers's telephone number . . . is ex-directory' (*Observer,* 18 Mar 1962). The meaning of this is 'not in the telephone directory', which would more logically have been expressed by '*extra-directory' with 'extra' in the sense of 'outside', as in 'extra-mural' or 'extraordinary'. Another neologism including 'ex-' is *ex-works,* apparently meaning 'direct from the factory', whereas *ex-G.P.O.* means 'separate from the G.P.O.' in 'The telephone here [Hull] is ex-G.P.O.' (*Daily Express,* 20 Jan 1966) since in Hull the telephone system is privately run and so is quite outside the normal G.P.O. system. This type of prefix seems to be spreading and gaining general acceptance in at any rate journalistic style, so that a *Catholic Herald* book reviewer speaks of little birds 'flung ex-nest by siblings or careless parents' (4 Dec 1964).

A few well-established expressions begin with the prefix 'off-', e.g. 'off-colour', 'off-side', 'offhand', 'offprint' and so on, together with the more recent *off-white,* 'not quite white'. A new addition brought to this series from America is *off-key* for the older 'out of tune'. During the 'fifties this transatlantic expression rapidly gained ground in Britain and now threatens to challenge the very existence of the evidently less expressive 'out of tune'. It is noticeable that sometimes a speaker who is obviously striving to be up to date will get a little confused and produce the hybrid form 'off-tune'. The prefix in question is potentially a very productive one – thus a reviewer in the *London Magazine* invented the word *off-English* to describe a foreign-sounding type of English (October 1957, p. 58) but it remains to be seen whether this pattern will find favour with a wider circle. *Off-beat* has of course been borrowed from the United States and was highly popular by 1958, being applied to anything unusual or novel, and is an obvious musical metaphor.

Sometimes a word leaps back into prominence after many years or even centuries of disuse. In the *Guardian* of 31 May 1956 various readers carried on a correspondence about what was referred to as an 'editorial' or else a 'leading article' dealing with the British government's treatment of Cyprus, and which had evidently been entitled BLOODYMINDED, echoing the word applied by Aneurin Bevan to the Tory mentality of that time. One correspondent implied that the adjective had been coined by Mr Bevan, but in fact it is an old word, though admittedly it had never been much in evidence in the twentieth century until the nineteen-fifties. Shakespeare uses it in *Henry VI*, part 2. 'Yet let not this make thee bloody-minded.' Here the meaning is quite simply the literal one, more or less equivalent to 'blood-thirsty', and the same is true of the word as introduced by Fielding in *Tom Jones* where a landlady is made to say that she would like all her country's enemies to be killed.

'O fie! Madam,' said the lieutenant smiling, '*All* is rather too bloody-minded a wish.' 'Not at all, sir,' answered she, 'I am not bloody-minded, only to our enemies, and there is no harm in that.'[1]

In Victorian England the inhibiting influence of 'bloody' would seem to have caused 'bloody-minded' to be neglected, though George Eliot did not hesitate to make it part of her literary vocabulary. Nor had it quite died out in American literature, since it is to be seen in *Tom Sawyer*. In the second world war 'bloody-minded' was sometimes applied by British officers to their men, though in the sense of 'resentful, angrily brooding' rather than with reference to any eagerness to engage the enemy more closely. In fact this is the dominant meaning in contemporary English. 'There is as much bloodymindedness, bitterness and resentment as ever,' says the Reverend N. Stacey of his parishioners at Woolwich (*Observer* supplement, 6 Dec 1964). There is no denying that this term is a very telling and expressive

---

[1] Collins ed. of 1955, p. 308.

one which is likely to remain in currency for a long time to come.

Compounds such as 'air-minded' and 'security-minded' have a modern ring, but this type of adjective was being formed in the seventeenth century, though even such a seemingly indispensable word as 'narrow-minded' goes back only as far as 1828, to Wordsworth. Yet in the second quarter of the present century this sort of compound came into particular prominence as a result of the constant emergence of new attitudes, and also official exhortations to be 'air-minded' and so forth. These creations are not quite the same as those made with '-conscious', in that they tend to imply a slightly more active attitude. 'Security-conscious,' for example, seems a more passive awareness than the frame of mind indicated by 'security-minded'.

The political policy of *brinkmanship* (the readiness to advance to the very brink of war in order to impose the will of one's government) is associated in the public mind with the late John Foster Dulles, but there are grounds for believing that Adlai Stevenson was the first to make use of the word itself, in 1956. By now it can be applied to any policy which consists of daring one's opponents to take matters to the point of catastrophe. 'Are we not all diminished by last week's miserable spectacle of decent but neglected men driven to industrial brinkmanship?' asked a letter to *The Times* after an averted railway strike (17 Feb 1960). The suffix itself is not of course a new one, witness such old words as 'seamanship, craftsmanship' and 'penmanship' but it has lately shown a tendency to be more than usually productive of new words, particularly perhaps as a sequel to the works of Stephen Potter on *gamesmanship, lifemanship* and *oneupmanship* which have opened the door to any number of similar compounds, often nonce-words, such as *committeemanship, Franksmanship* (i.e. the tactics of Lord Franks when chairman of an inquiry at Oxford in November 1964), *Taxmanship* (title of a booklet on taxation in 1964), *motorbikemanship, grantsmanship* (the art of obtaining educational grants from the government), *Investment Upmanship* (heading of a unit trust advertisement), GROWTHMANSHIP

(title of an editorial in the *Observer*, 27 Sep 1964). In R. M.
Brown's *Observer in Rome* we find 'The delicate art of Observer-
manship' as a chapter heading,[1] while in the *Daily Express* an
article is boldly headed A CASE OF DOUBLECROSSMANSHIP
(23 Dec 1964).

The English language is not on the whole very fond of diminutive forms, unlike Italian and Spanish or – to a slighter
extent – French, though the '-y' or '-ie' ending of 'hankie',
'Kitty' and so forth is still vigorous and very much available for
new creations. A favourite diminutive ending is still '-ette', an
early borrowing from French which can of course be attached
to words of non-French origin, as in *kitchenette*, a creation of the
nineteen-twenties, probably coined in order to avoid the notions
of labour and drudgery associated with the existing 'scullery'.
Usherette, which has had a great success, happens to be made up
from a term of French ancestry, since 'usher' is from the medieval
French word for 'doorkeeper' in spite of its impeccably English
appearance. In the case of *maisonette* it is more likely a case of a
French word which has been borrowed whole in recent years,
though in fact in French it is far from being a neologism, having
existed in that language since the twelfth century. (As a matter
of spelling, the French form has double 'n' and this is also permissible in English. In *launderette* we have once again the application of the prefix to a word which happens to be of French
ancestry, producing a neologism meaning 'establishment with
automatic washing machines available for public use'. Rather
curiously, the most notorious of recent creations based on the
diminutive in '-ette' is in fact spelt by its author with final '-et',
namely *nymphet*, due to Vladimir Nabokov in *Lolita*. Unlike
'trumpet' or 'limpet' this is pronounced as though written
nymphette (a form which has indeed been created in French in
imitation of the English word). It must be remembered that
Nabokov wrote in the United States, where 'cigaret' is a variant
spelling of 'cigarette', hence 'nymphet' where 'nymphette' might
be expected. A lone voice in this connection is that of Lionel

Trilling, who considers the stressed ending '-ette' to be a heavy sound and cites *drum-majorette* as a somewhat unconvincing proof of his contention (in *Encounter*, Oct 1958).

Curiously enough, 'nymphette' was an established word in Britain at a time (1958) when *Lolita* still lay under a ban in Britain, presumably in order to protect the morals of middle-aged men. But as the book was already a best-seller in the United States we have here a perfect illustration of American influence on British English.[1]

The ending '-dom' was at one time thought to be 'dead' in the sense that it could no longer be used to create new words. Although it is a very old feature of our language this suffix is by no means moribund, however. Here again the impetus seems to have come from the United States, where as early as the nineteenth century it was possible to coin the word 'newspaperdom', for example.[2] This is something of a nonce-word perhaps, but British English has readily accepted *gangsterdom* and *Nazidom* and while not a great many words in '-dom' have found their way into the dictionaries ('boredom' and 'officialdom' are from the middle of the last century) the great strength of this ending lies in its ability to form words created on the spur of the moment. The main meaning attached to such creations appears to be 'province or sphere of something', as in the case of all the examples given above, except for 'boredom'. The possibility of forming humorous creations in '-dom' has in fact long been available to English writers. In *The Water-babies* (1865) Charles Kingsley was able to speak of 'lobsterdom' during the incident concerning a lobster who 'had live barnacles on his claws, which is a great mark of distinction in lobsterdom ...' (chap. IV). In 1942 Jespersen noted that '*filmdom* and *stardom* may ... be on the threshold of being accepted into Standard English', and instanced such nonce-words as *butlerdom*, *snobdom*, *Christmasdom* and so on.[3] 'Stardom' is attested in fact as early as 1865, and is certainly a

---

[1] For some examples in British usage, see *Notes and Queries*, 1959, p. 161.
[2] *American Speech*, 1964, p. 182.
[3] *A Modern English Grammar*, vol. vi, p. 462.

perfectly respectable member of the vocabulary nowadays. Finally, WAIFDOM has been the telegraphic address of the head office of Barnardo's Homes since February 1966.

'The English -*ster* of *spinster* and *Webster* is an old agentive suffix, but as far as the feeling of the present English-speaking generation is concerned, it cannot be said to really exist at all; *spinster* and *Webster* have been completely disconnected from the etymological group of *spin* and *weave* (*web*).' So Edward Sapir wrote in 1921 in his *Language*.[1] However that may be, there is no doubt that the suffix itself has remained a living one, especially in Sapir's own country, which has given the world *mobster*, *gangster*, *roadster* and *speedster*. 'Oldster', which has all the appearance of a word recently invented by *Time* magazine, goes back in reality to the early nineteenth century, while 'teamster' – which always baffles most Englishmen reading about American labour disputes – is in essence an eighteenth-century creation, though of course it has since undergone some semantic development in the United States so that it is usually translated by British journalists as 'lorry-driver'. (The point is that 'team' can in American parlance be applied to a vehicle, as Horwill points out.)[2] Perhaps the most remarkable creation to embody the suffix '-ster' in recent times is *hipster*, though it may well be that this expression will never become part of the standard language, either remaining only in slang or rapidly dying out even there. The root is the adjective *hip* (earlier *hep*) meaning 'in the know, well-informed as to latest trends'.

'Cavalcade', etymologically a procession of horsemen, has given rise in American English to a series of new words in which the -*cade* element denotes the idea of 'spectacular display', e.g. *aquacade*, *musicade* and *motorcade*. Of these, only 'motorcade' has as yet penetrated into British use, chiefly in connection with the procession of cars taking part in visits by royalty, foreign statesmen

[1] p. 141 in the Harvest Book reprint (Hart-Davis).
[2] As formerly in the North of England. John Trotter Brockett's *Glossary of North Country Words* (1824) defines COUP-CART as 'a short team, closed with boards'.

and so forth. It remains to be seen how productive this ending will be in Britain, though there seems every likelihood that the world of entertainment will develop such a useful suffix.

Another productive ending which has been created quite unexpectedly, as it were, is '-burger'. Again the story begins in America, where the starting point was the 'hamburger steak', i.e. a steak prepared in the Hamburg manner (as in Frankfurter sausage). The '-er' ending is simply the sign that the adjective is German in origin. Although a 'hamburger' contains no ham, the word must have been analysed as 'ham + burger', in view of the large number of expressions next formed with '-burger'; *cheeseburger, beefburger, fishburger* and many others in the U.S.A. In England the best-known are probably *steakburger, beefburger* and *baconburger*, though in the course of 1964 the more flamboyant *Big Boy Burger*, with the suffix launching forth as a separate word, was encountered. It is clear that an endless series of creations in this direction is possible in Britain, just as in America.

In the sphere of advertising there is no doubt that one of the happiest of recent inventions is the slogan DRINKA PINTA MILKA DAY, admirable in the sense that it exactly reproduces the pronunciation of millions of people. (Though apparently it breaks the golden rule of modern advertising which frowns upon instructing the victim to do something.) It now remains to be seen whether *pinta* will emerge as an independent word in its own right, like *cuppa* (duly recognized by inclusion in the *S.E.D.* though derived therein from the phrase 'cuppa cha' rather than the straightforward 'cuppa tea'). There is also some possibility that whole new phrases will be modelled on it, and HALFA CROWNA LUNCHA DAY has already been seen on the window of a snack-bar.

Nouns ending in '-ee' have long been a feature of the English vocabulary, and such a modern-looking formation as 'payee' goes back to the eighteenth century, while 'recognizee' (the person to whom one is bound in a recognizance) is dated 1544 by the *S.E.D.* These particular examples show the fairly characteristic passive meaning implied by this suffix, which is continued

in modern times by such forms as *expellee* or *interviewee*. Such
indeed is the usefulness of this device that an endless succession
of nonce-words based on it is made possible, like the one made
up by Gilbert Harding when he wrote in his *Book of Manners* that
'. . . a hug from the Russian bear might well crush the huggee to
death' (p. 118).[1] This semi-humorous procedure is not a new
one, for in *Mr Sponge's Sporting Tour*, published in 1853, R. S.
Surtees refers to a person being toasted as the 'toastee'.[2] But in
spite of the strong passive idea evoked by the ending it is nonetheless capable of being used in a non-passive sense. Admittedly
the distinction is not always easy to establish with any great
precision, since a *retiree* (*Observer*, 13 Jan 1957) may be described
actively as a man 'who has retired' or else passively as one 'who
has been retired'. Yet a *resignee* (*Universities Review*, Feb 1959) is
an active and not a passive word. But once again the possibility
of using this suffix in an active sense is old-established, because
'absentee' goes back to 1537 and 'refugee' came into the language
in 1685, the year of the revocation of the Edict of Nantes by
Louis XIV when many French Huguenots fled their country to
escape persecution. *Escapee* is attested in 1865. Examples from
more recent years are *dilutee* (i.e. an unskilled worker placed in a
group of skilled personnel), *biographee*[3] (subject of a biography),
and *evacuee*, dating from 1939. An unusual case is that of
bummaree, regarded by the general public as a neologism but
having a history going back to 1786. It refers to a porter of the
Smithfield meat-market and was more or less confined to the
jargon of the London markets until a legal decision recently
brought the word to the public attention. Here the '-ee' ending is
similar in function to that of the older 'bargee', denoting a particular occupation, but unfortunately the picturesque 'bummaree'
is of unknown origin.

Nouns in '-eer' are likewise of long standing in English, but
their purpose is less ambiguous than that of '-ee' since they

---

[1] Putnam, 1956.   [2] p. 305, World Classics edition.
[3] Monsignor Ronald Knox, p. 83 of *Literary Distractions* (Sheed and Ward,
1958).

invariably indicate the agent of some action. Sometimes a rather pejorative air clings to them, as in the case of the 'profiteer' of the 1914-1918 War, and the modern 'racketeer' of American origin, or even the much older 'buccaneer', but this has not been a general movement, so that centuries-old words such as 'auction-eer' and 'scrutineer' are quite unaffected in this way. A striking feature of contemporary English is the way in which 'engineer' has undergone a broadening of sense in everyday parlance, so that a plumber may describe himself as a *sanitary engineer* and if he deals with central heating he will be a *heating engineer* in addition. That is merely a particular example of a well-known sociological phenomenon, and the use of the word is intended to enhance the standing of the trade concerned, just as the barber is now a 'gent's hairdresser and stylist'. Newer coinages in '-eer' are *puppeteer* and *gadgeteer*. The *black marketeer* was a familiar figure during the years of rationing occasioned by the 1939–45 War and has receded into the past with the arrival of happier days, but *marketeer* has emerged in the middle nineteen-sixties as the name of any person advocating Britain's entry into the European Economic Community, the so-called 'common market'. Whether this is a pejorative usage is doubtless a matter of personal opinion.

In the domain of the verb it is the suffix in '-ize' that has enjoyed greatest favour during the last twenty years or so, and although an old verbal ending it seems to have entered a period of renewed vigour. It is seen in *liquidize*, i.e. to make liquid; especially of fruit and vegetables put into a *liquidizer*. Clearly the existing 'liquidate' could not be used in this connection because of its strong associations in other directions. Among new verbs in '-ize' are *vitaminize, homogenize, pressurize, hospitalize, Africanize, sanforize* (together with any number of verbs describing patent processes preventing shrinkage, etc.) and *finalize*. This latter has aroused much opposition on the grounds that it is an unnecessary creation adding nothing to 'finish' or 'terminate'. It is evidently an Americanism in origin, and Sir Norman Birkett (as he was then) noted in his diary during the Nuremberg trials of the German war-criminals in April 1946 that he was wearied by the constant repetition of this word.[1] But it soon became a favourite with British administrators, though it was not until the middle 'fifties that it became well-known to the general public. When Harold Wilson visited the United States as Prime Minister in 1964 he introduced the expression into a speech, perhaps in deference to his host, since two American presidents had already done likewise.

In the ending '-ish' the English language possesses a tool of amazing flexibility and usefulness. It is of long standing, but a striking feature of recent colloquial English has been the extension of this suffix to numerals in order to indicate an approximate time of day. *Sixish* equals 'at about six o'clock' in 'See you sixish'. (Since the nineteen-thirties, there has also been a tendency to omit the preposition 'on' with days of the week, as in 'See you Monday'. This is almost certainly in imitation of the similar American custom.) Likewise *fortyish* means 'about forty years of age'. Such was the vogue for '-ish' by 1958 that Pendennis of the *Observer* included abstention from its use as one of his New Year resolutions (along with '-manship'). Perhaps the fashion for this ending is to be ascribed to an unconscious fear of appearing too precise or dogmatic in expression, or to a careful refusal to say more than is warranted by the facts. As one example, '. . . authority turns a blindish eye to a vast illegal network of undercover dealings' (*Observer*, 3 Nov 1963). The next extension is likely to be that of '-ishly', long extant in such words as 'foolishly, sheepishly' where the '-ish' element does not at all express approximation but is simply an adjectival ending (compare also 'garishly' or 'freakishly'). But there are signs – again in colloquial speech – that an adverbial ending '-ishly' is in the making, as in a B.B.C. interview where it was said that 'We had a lot of stuff in warehouses which we got out very smartishly' (1 Nov 1964). This development is in its early stages at the moment, but the meaning is plain, i.e. 'rather smartly'.

A few words that have in British English traditionally ended in

[1] H. Montgomery Hyde, *Norman Birtket* (Hamish Hamilton, 1964), p. 515.

'-ing' now show signs of exchanging this for '-ed' under American influence. The most noticeable of them has been 'heading' in the expression 'heading for', now very much on the defensive against *headed for*. IS THE US HEADED FOR A SLUMP? enquired a headline in the *New Statesman* (9 Jul 1954) while a year later the *News Chronicle* asked MARKETS HEADED FOR A SLUMP? The next year a speaker in the Home Service of the B.B.C. judged that 'It looks very much as though we are headed back to the Cold War', as recorded in the *Listener* (22 Nov 1956). The likelihood at the moment is that 'heading' in this sense is doomed to extinction. (When did 'headed' become general in American English? What about that cowboy song of the 'thirties? Wasn't it 'I'm a-headin' for the last round-up'?) A similar fate is also tending to overtake 'sprawling', 'stooping', 'slouching' and 'crouching' (though *crouched* is found as early as Kenneth Grahame's well-known *The Wind in the Willows*). In these words the change is taking place at a much slower rate than has been the case for *headed*, if only because they are not used so constantly in journalistic vocabulary. Horwill notes that 'In American the verb *stoop* seems to be transitive as well as intransitive. At any rate, it has a past participle, *stooped*=Eng. stooping. "A tall, gaunt, stooped man"' (p. 308). Again, Horwill notes the American use of *headed for*, being so struck by this turn of phrase that he gives four quotations containing it.

The replacement of 'heading' by 'headed' is only one example of a process that has been going on in English for centuries, and while we are now obliged to say that we are 'inclined' to be something or other it was perfectly feasible in earlier times to use 'inclining' in this case, as can be seen in one of the Knyvett letters. 'My brother . . . is inclining to be a most excellent coxcombe.'[1]

The process of regularizing strong verbs, which has likewise been going on for centuries, continues to replace 'irregular' forms by more 'normal' ones. The most striking illustration of this is to be seen in the verb 'thrive'. On consulting the *Concise Oxford*

[1] Letter no. 65 of 1644 (Constable, 1949).

Dictionary, even in its 1964 edition, we find the past tense given as *'throve* rarely *thrived'* and the past participle as *'thriven* rarely *thrived'*. In reality this is outdated, and was outdated in 1964 when already the opposite was the case, whether in the spoken or written language. As a typical example of present-day treatment of this verb we may quote from Joseph Dean's introduction to his *Hatred, ridicule and contempt*. 'This technique was devised by Labouchère, the great editor of *Truth,* who thrived on libel actions . . .'.[1] At the present rate 'throve' will soon be as archaic as the 'shrove' that was the past tense of 'shrive' and is now commemorated only in the name of Shrove Tuesday. The verb 'swell' is showing a similar tendency, though not quite so strong, to appear as 'swelled' in the past participle, instead of 'swollen' in spite of the *Concise Oxford Dictionary*'s note to the effect that this rarely happens. 'To be sure,' wrote Monsignor Ronald Knox in 1952, 'there is no lack of *récits de conversion*; you and I have both swelled the lists of them.'[2] More recently, in the *Daily Telegraph*, '. . . the volume of protest . . . has swelled daily' (26 Jun 1958). At the same time, it should be noted that the form 'swelled' has existed since the seventeenth century, but was mostly restricted to the sense of 'morbidly enlarged', hence the humorous creation 'swelled head', dating back to the nineteenth century. 'Bet' is also often regularized, with 'betted' more and more used for the past tense and past participle, whereas in earlier decades the normal form was 'bet' in each case. An interesting experiment consists of consulting three different dictionaries for the forms of this verb.

(i) *The Concise Oxford Dictionary* (1950 edition) gives only 'bet' as past tense and past participle.

(ii) *The Shorter Oxford English Dictionary* (1955) gives '*bet*; also *betted*'.

(iii) *The Concise Oxford English Dictionary* (1964 edition) gives only '*bet, betted*' for the two forms respectively.

[1] First published 1953, Constable.
[2] *Difficulties* (Eyre and Spottiswoode), p. 261.

It is clear that on this point the language is at present in a state of uncertainty. As an example of the newer trend let us cite a sentence from the *Sunday Times*. 'He once betted that he would carry Barrymore so many times round the Steine at Brighton ...' (19 Jan 1958). In addition it is true to say that in a very much earlier tradition 'betted' was a good Shakespearean form.

By one of those inexplicable contradictions of language there is a movement to replace the past participle 'proved' by 'proven'. In Scotland, of course, the verdict 'Not proven' has long been part of the legal vocabulary as an alternative to the stark choice between 'Guilty' and 'Not guilty', and it is theoretically possible that the present tendency to favour 'proven' in British English (or English English in this instance) comes from Scotland. But it is more likely that once again it is a question of transatlantic example, for as Horwill pointed out as late as 1952 'The past participle *proven* is archaic in English but current in American'.[1] Yet in the case of the phrase 'Not proven', often used nowadays in non-legal contexts, the motivation very probably comes originally from knowledge of the Scottish phrase. This is occasionally confirmed by the use of the Scottish pronunciation of 'proven' in which the vowel rhymes with 'doe' rather than 'do'.

To return to affixes, we may now note a few prefixed forms currently enjoying popularity. An obvious example is that of 'super-', which probably came into fashion by way of scientific terminology, e.g. 'supersaturated solution, superheated steam' and so on, though of course the prefix has existed in the language since Middle English. The *S.E.D.* also points out the importance of 'superman' as a model for further coinages, though here it is perhaps necessary to point out that what is meant is the term invented by Shaw for his play *Man and Superman* (1903) and based upon the word *übermensch* which described the ideal, superior man dreamed of by Nietzsche. In the words of Brewer's *Dictionary of Phrase and Fable* 'The wide popularity of the term gave rise

---

[1] The chief factor behind the appearance of *proven* is probably the large number of American films shown on British television, especially as at least one long-lived serial of this kind had a court of law as its setting.

to many compounds, such as *superwoman, super-critic, super-tramp, super-Dreadnought,* and *super-tax'.* We now have many others of this type; *supersecrecy, supermarket, supersonic* and inevitably an endless number of additions to the lingo of advertising – *super-special, super-soft, super-digestible* and so on ad lib. It is even possible to use it, at any rate in slang, as a separate word *super* expressing the ultimate degree of approval.[1]

Since the Second World War the English language has steadily been developing the use of the combination form 'para-' denoting a connection with parachuting. The starting point was the wartime word *paratroops* – with the ensuing singular *paratrooper* – followed by such neologisms as *paraflare, paramine, para div* (parachute division) and so on. Clearly it is now possible to form any number of nonce-words in this way, e.g. we find in the *New Statesman* 'Something more than para-diplomacy is needed' (27 Nov 1964). This was a reference to the large-scale Belgian parachute operation in the Congo towards the end of 1964, and this coinage goes to prove the versatility of the form. But of course there is some possibility of confusion with the other 'para-' which is a prefix of Greek origin meaning 'beside, beyond' or 'wrong', as in 'paramilitary' or 'parachronism' (error in chronology). The prefix in 'parachute' is of different origin, being the Italian *para,* from the verb *parare* 'to ward off, shelter from', so that a parachute is etymologically a device for sheltering someone from the bad effects of a fall, just as a parasol shelters its bearer from the sun.

It is sometimes said that 'anti-' is much more frequent in American usage than in British and while this is perhaps the case from a statistical point of view there is no denying that it has long been regarded as a good British prefix, and the history books make mention of the Anti-combination laws, the Anti-Corn-Law League, the Anti-vaccination league and others, while the political struggles of the nineteen-thirties gave great impetus to its polemical use, as in *anti-Fascist, anti-Bolshevik, anti-Nazi,* etc.

[1] A car is said to be 'souped up' when it is fitted with a supercharger (pronounce 'soopercharger').

More striking are those words in which the root is formed by a common noun, the whole then being endowed with the properties of an adjective. 'One does not have to be anti-progress to deplore the poor example set in this matter of custom and decorum . . .' declares a letter to *The Times* (1 Jan 1964).

In English as in European languages in general there is a proliferation of acronyms, that is to say forms made up of the initial letters of a series of words or names. This is particularly noticeable in the province of politics and economics, if only because these subjects are widely reported in the press and so become known to a vast public – U.N.O. (United Nations Organization), N.A.T.O. (North Atlantic Treaty Organization), S.E.A.T.O. (South East Asia Treaty Organization), G.A.T.T. (General Agreement on Trade and Tariffs). These are pronounced as words in their own right, and can readily be spelt without full stops.[1] Sometimes more than the initial letters is involved, as in *Benelux*, an ingenious name for the customs union of *Bel*gium, the *Net*herlands and *Lux*emburg. The use of acronyms is not confined to our period, since it was in full swing during the First World War (the Anzacs – from *A*ustralian and *N*ew *Z*ealand *A*rmy *C*orps) and initials were very widely used for purposes of abbreviation in general, e.g. V.A.D. (Voluntary Aid Detachment) and the R.F.C. (Royal Flying Corps). But there is no doubt that in recent times there has been an epidemic of such forms as a result of the great increase in official posts and organizations. The happiest creations are no doubt those where the process of abbreviation is in fact soon forgotten, as in *Benelux*, or better still, *Pakistan* (*P*unjab, *A*fghan Frontier, *K*ashmir, *S*ind, Bal-uchi*stan* – the earlier form being *Pakstan*). At all events a fully comprehensive list of modern abbreviations requires a volume to itself and is doomed always to be behind the times and incomplete, many abbreviations being known only to a small specialized circle of initiates. Knowledge of the meaning of certain ones will

[1] When it is the actual initials that are pronounced it can happen that there is no saving of time at all – P.A.Y.E. takes just as long to say as 'Pay as you earn', since each contains four syllables!

in itself be a species of shibboleth indicating superior familiarity with the subject under discussion, so it may well be, for example, that the members of the A.U.T. (Association of University Teachers) and of N.A.L.G.O. (pronounced 'nalgo', National and Local Government Officers) would be hard put to it to recognize the meaning of each other's initials. One interesting point which emerges is that the unexplained use of initials in the press is a good indication of general interest in a particular subject, and it is significant that even the 'quality' newspapers long found it necessary to gloss E.F.T.A. in brackets (European Free Trade Association, on the analogy of the full title of the 'Common Market', i.e. the European Economic Community, or E.E.C. which none but experts seem to use). Only when the Government (or 'the Labour government' as its opponents call it, as though some mysterious illegitimacy were thereby being hinted at) offended Britain's partners in 1964 by imposing a 15 per cent trade tariff did the general public awaken to the existence of E.F.T.A. at all, and the unexplained abbreviated form then became much more frequent.

A rather widespread and far-reaching tendency in recent English is the one affecting what grammarians call 'the plural attributive noun'.[1] Hitherto, for instance, such a type as 'wage award' has been regarded as the norm, but now we often come across *wages award*. It is true that in some kinds of phrase the attributive noun has always taken the plural, but these were so few as to be relegated by text-books to the status of exceptions to a general rule; dice-play, goods-train and scissors-grinder, and in long compounds of loose construction, e.g. Contagious Diseases Act (indeed there is a suggestion in the article mentioned below that modern legislation has provided a large number of models for the usage). Certainly it is clear that contemporary English has become much fonder of this type, though the move in this direction appears to have been under way at the very

---

[1] The present remarks are inspired by an article entitled 'The Plural Attributive in Contemporary English' by N. E. Osselton and C. J. Osselton-Bleeker, in *English Studies*, XLIII, 1962.

beginning of the twentieth century, for it was commented on as early as 1914 by the Danish scholar Jespersen. The situation now is that in very many cases the speaker has in effect a free choice between such forms as 'greeting card' and 'greetings card', 'no-claim bonus' and 'no-claims bonus', 'expense account' and 'expenses account'.

5

Sentence Structure

ENGLISH is remarkable among the well-known European languages for the looseness of its sentence-structure and consequently for the stylistic scope it offers to the individual writer ('style' being understood here as the *way* a thought or feeling is expressed, or the *choice* made by the writer from all the possibilities open to him or which he can create for himself). Writing about a new reference-book a reviewer recently said that 'It is a volume which should form part of the library of all hope-to-be-novelists'. 'Aspiring novelists' would have been a more usual specimen of English from the point of view of the grammar-books, but 'hope-to-be-novelists' is in fact a fairly typical piece of English by modern standards, especially by the standards of journalism and advertising, where the aim is to make a sudden impression on the reader rather than to create prose of lasting beauty. Our civilization sets great store on change for the sake of change, and the assumption is that a man who has a new way of saying things will have a new thought or product to offer. This sort of style has existed since the beginning of our century, according to Professor Whatmough, but is greatly on the increase.[1] An illustration given by him is 'better-than-leather-miracle-covering', taken from a popular magazine in 1950. The hyphens are not absolutely necessary since the phrase would be quite understandable without them and a similar kind of syntax is familiar to readers of newspaper headlines such as BID FOR BETTER THAN EVER BRITAIN. Headlines in any case like to put nouns in the place of adjectives, if only because they save space. MOROCCO KING'S AIM IS ALGERIA PEACE says the *Sunday*

---

[1] *Language – a modern synthesis* (Secker and Warburg, 1956), p. 249.

Times (31 May 1959). Newspaper headlines are admittedly a highly specialized type of English, and as an editor of the *Yorkshire Post* has put it 'You never hear a man say, "Have you heard of the surprise Portugal diplomacy shock? A mystery man has caused a sensation and a Whitehall probe is not ruled out. ...."'[1] Yet the average man is quite prepared to talk about a 'mystery man' or even a 'Whitehall probe' on occasion and the whole tendency of the modern language is towards doing away with adjectives, or at least, using nouns as epithets. The 'sexual maniac' of the nineteen-thirties is the *sex-maniac* of our time. Under a similar American influence the sparking plug is often the *spark plug*. In 1936 Horwill instanced such examples of typically American usage as *pupil activities, child guidance* and *teacher guidance*, this last one being ambiguous, in his view.[2] He would have been even more surprised by the ambiguity of the title of *The Idiot Teacher* published in Britain in 1952. This construction is undoubtedly on the increase. Thus the *Observer* speaks of certain arrangements which 'could be convincingly justified on efficiency grounds' (13 Mar 1955). Traditionally this would have been 'on grounds of efficiency'. According to a recent advertisement ladies have 'figure control problems' and some of them have been known to protest against 'job opportunity discrimination' (meaning that they were at a disadvantage in competition with men). To parse 'job opportunity discrimination' into the time-honoured parts of speech would not be an easy task, and the phrase is a fine example of the fading distinction between nouns and adjectives. Again, the tendency is not a new one in English but is merely more daring and productive than ever, especially in official or professional jargon. Perhaps as a compensation for this we have a proliferation of adjectives in the spoken advertisements of television publicity. 'Wash your precious lily-white hands in lovely swan-soft SPLURGE. ...'

[1] *Newspaper English; its vices and virtues* (p. 14), a presidential address to the Bradford English Society, 1956, by Sir Linton Andrews, LL.D.
[2] S.P.E. Tract No. 45, p. 192.

Over half a century ago Bradley commented in his well-known work *The Making of English* on the peculiarity of such American sentences as 'Does she have blue eyes?', his point being that in British usage the construction with 'do' was reserved for restricted or temporary possession, e.g. 'Do you have a book?' But even at that time Bradley noted that certain British writers were following the American habit, and nowadays this has become very widespread in British writing and speech. So a letter to the editor of *The Times* says 'I do have a cockney accent' (29 Jan 1958). Similarly in the negative, as when A. J. Ayer writes of Pekin that 'It does not have the direct appeal of Paris or New York', in the *Listener* (2 Dec 1954). Yet even in the middle 'fifties it was possible to find Englishmen who were totally unacquainted with this type of syntax, as recounted by the American playwright, the late John van Druten, in *The Widening Circle*.[1] An English friend whom he took round California was 'fascinated' by the waitress's reply when she was asked if the establishment could provide buttermilk. '"Yes," she said, "We do have buttermilk." The insertion of the word "do", unnoticed by me, had a new significance for an English ear' (p. 136). And it is interesting to see that a review by Muriel Spark criticizes a novelist for causing a British character in his work to say 'I don't have . . .' instead of 'I haven't got . . .' (*Observer*, 6 Oct 1957). In addition to this particular use of 'do' along with 'have' there is a new fashion for replacing the second 'have' (or 'has') in a sentence by 'do'. So a British speaker explaining the structure of a Haydn symphony declares 'After all this we think he can have nothing more up his sleeve – and of course he *does*' (B.B.C., 17 Feb 1958). This phenomenon is American in origin, though in essence it is a mere extension of the replacement of verbs other than 'have' by 'do' when an idea is repeated in the sentence, as in 'I like it more than you do'. What is new in British idiom is the replacement of the verb 'have'. A simple example of the new fashion is seen in the case of a B.B.C. speaker who said 'Some have money, some don't' (7 Oct 1956), which can be contrasted with the more usual

[1] Heinemann, 1957.

'Some have money, some haven't'. A month later a professor of London University speaking on the Third Programme of the B.B.C. said that '. . . the Greeks had less feeling than we do for . . .' (27 Nov 1956). But as always happens in matters of linguistic change some speakers are evidently in a state of uncertainty and try to cling to the old way of doing things while instinctively being drawn towards the new, for in the following year a lady speaking extempore on the B.B.C. 'corrected' herself as follows. 'I think I had stronger feelings than she did – she had' (29 Oct 1957).

To express obligation the American variety of English does not make much use of 'must' but shows a preference for the 'have to' construction, which in any case is also extremely frequent and old-established in Britain, except that the American 'Do you have to do that?' had not hitherto been current, being represented by 'Must you do that?' or more colloquially, 'Have you got to do that?' Here again, however, transatlantic influence is very strong, so that the American form is more and more used in this question. The same is true of the negative statement, where 'You don't have to do that' is now as common as 'You needn't do that'. In her novel *Mother and Son* Miss Compton-Burnett puts the question 'Do we have to be ashamed of it?' into the mouth of a child living in 1890, but in the British setting this gives rather an anachronistic flavour.[1]

Over and above all this there is a great extension at the present day of the emphatic function of the verb 'do', in the sense that this usage is invading written English whereas until now there was a general tendency to restrict it to the spoken language. Here, first of all, is an extreme instance. 'We do know collapse of the lung does occur not only post-operatively but in other conditions as well' (Newcastle *Evening Chronicle*, 7 Apr 1956). In this sentence the emphatic usage actually appears twice. Lest this be thought a peculiarity of the provincial press, here is an example from the *Observer* with similar repetition. 'When you do buy these once-in-a-lifetime contraptions do see that you get value for

[1] Gollancz, 1955.

money' (30 Oct 1958). A golden rule in these cases is that emphatic 'do' ('does', 'did') is invariably stressed though this is no longer indicated nowadays by the use of italics. (This is not of course true of the totally different Biblical construction of the type 'And they did eat and were filled' where there is no stress and no emphasis involved. What is curious is that the two types, ancient and modern, look identical on paper and only the voice shows the difference.) It is not by any means suggested that the emphatic type never appeared in print before the twentieth century – Anthony Trollope has a fine example in *The Way We Live Now* (1875); 'That his heart was all the other way he was quite sure; but as yet it did seem to him that there was no escape from his troubles open to him'.[1] But what is striking in contemporary English is the great frequency of the construction. Here is a rather earlier example than those quoted above from the press. From Hilaire Belloc's *An Essay on the Nature of Contemporary England* (1937); 'The number of Catholics in England, lacking any Irish connection, does not appreciably increase; on the other hand their social tone and colour do take on the tone and colour of the Protestant world around them' (p. 76).[2] It may be that the increased incidence of this construction in written English stems from the less formal character of present-day writing, greatly influenced by colloquial style, but one regrettable and accidental inconvenience of this development is that it camouflages misprints, for a moment's inattention of the compositor, transforming 'does not' into 'does', can ruin the whole sense of the sentence in an insidious manner. A case in point is to be seen in A. C. Gimson's *Introduction to the Pronunciation of English* (1962) where – as a reviewer has pointed out – 'does show' appears in the text for 'does not show'. At one time, and not so long ago, the appearance of 'does show' would have alerted the proof-reader, but nowadays it is a plausible form so that only a knowledge of the subject-matter of the sentence can reveal the error.

[1] World's Classics edition, p. 255.
[2] Constable.

While the average man is vaguely aware of the introduction of new words into his language (and 'vaguely' is used advisedly here), he tends to consider grammar as something eternal and immutable. Even so, the constructions accompanying certain verbs quietly change over the years without causing any great outcry. Some notable changes of this sort are once again products of American idiom, a typical example being seen in the omission of the preposition 'to' after 'help'. Now this phenomenon was not unknown in poetical and somewhat archaic language, as in Matthew Arnold's 'I would fain stay and help thee tend him', but an early instance of it in more prosaic style is seen in Kipling's story *With the Night Mail* (1909). 'Magniac invented his rudder to help war-boats ram each other....'.[1] But only in the late nineteen-thirties and early 'forties did the construction really make headway in Britain. Its acceptance into the standard language was very rapid and J. Hubert Jagger, writing his *English in the Future* (1940), commented on 'the speed with which the American habit of omitting *to* after *help* has invaded Britain' (p. 55).[2] But in spite of this speedy acceptance of the new form the old one is still well entrenched and the two rivals seem destined to battle it out for some time to come. Some other new constructions based on American idiom also involve the omission of part of the traditional expression. Thus 'to adjust oneself to something' becomes 'to adjust to something', while 'to identify oneself with' increasingly gives way to the shorter form without the pronoun, i.e. 'to identify with'. So, writing in the *Sunday Times*, George Schwartz declares 'If more and more people take their board and lodgings round with them the catering trades and the resorts will have to adjust to the new situation' (26 May 1956). And in the *Observer*, 'No doubt it is a pity that car owners choose to identify so closely with their cars' (25 Oct 1959).

In the earlier part of this century the English language distinguished between the simple verb 'approve', without any following preposition, and 'approve of'. The former implied a

---

[1] *Actions and Reactions* (Macmillan).   [2] Nelson.

formal or official act of approval, as when someone approves the act of a subordinate by denoting his agreement, whereas the latter carried a more emotional connotation, and implied liking or admiration on a personal basis. It would therefore be quite possible for an official to 'approve' something (in his administrative role) which he did not 'approve of' (in a private capacity). It is true to say that the distinction has never been a hard and fast one in the works of British writers, and even in the nineteenth century we find it disregarded by such authors as Hazlitt and Robert Louis Stevenson. Closer to our own time, A. J. Cronin has an example of omission of the preposition in *The Citadel* (1937) where he writes 'He told her of his desire for success. She approved it.' It would have been more usual at that date to say 'She approved of it', since here there is evidence only of an emotional and not an official approval, but at all events such an omission is now becoming extremely frequent, having begun to spread in the middle nineteen-fifties in Britain. Should the use of the preposition in this case ultimately die out altogether there will be no great harm done to the language, and indeed we shall merely be returning to the situation as it existed in the time of Shakespeare, since the distinction betwen 'approve' and 'approve of' is first found only in the later seventeenth century.

In the first part of the twentieth century *cope* was invariably followed by 'with' and a predicate, but towards the middle of the century a new fashion began to appear and it became possible to leave this verb suspended in the air, as it were, without a preposition or anything else following it. In Raleigh Trevelyan's *The Fortress*, an account of wartime experiences at Anzio, we find in the entry for 10 May 1944, 'Imagine Six Platoon even trying to cope'.[1] By the nineteen-fifties this had passed into the general vocabulary to such good purpose that it was possible for a book by Michael Cronin to bear the title *I Can Cope*.[2] This idiom has in fact taken over some of the functions of 'manage'. It is dated 1932 by the *S.E.D.*

Most speakers now omit the 'to' in such a phrase as 'If I knew

[1] Penguin Books.   [2] Museum Press.

how to', e.g. 'I wouldn't do it even if I knew how'. This was at one time regarded as an Americanism, but by the middle 'fifties it was on the increase in Britain. In 1955 twelve out of a group of university students putting a foreign text into English chose to use '... If I knew how', while the remaining two, including the best stylist and translator, opted for '... if I knew how to'. Very significantly, none thought of writing '... if I knew how to do so'.

A special case arises in connection with the interrogative form created by the use of 'how?', 'what?', 'where?' or 'when?' with an infinitive. The traditional formula was such a sentence as 'How are we to do this?' but the modern one shortens that to 'How to do this?', on the American model, and for example we read in *The Times* 'But how to find authors of good screen plays?' (27 Jan 1960). This syntactic pattern established itself very rapidly in Britain in the early nineteen-fifties. In his *Author by Profession* (1952) James Leasor uses it several times.[1] This new type must not of course be confused with an old sentence construction which at first sight looks rather similar, and whose simplest form is seen in such a sentence as 'How to do this I do not know', though it may well be that inverted sentences of this sort were a contributory factor in the creation of the new pattern. Here is a more compli- cated example from an article in *Encounter* by T. R. Fyvel. 'How to satisfy this mass demand and at the same time maintain cultural standards is a difficult problem' (Nov 1955). A question mark after 'standards' and the suppression of the last four words would give a satisfactory illustration of the new construction, which in essence would mean the same thing as the thought expressed here. But in addition there exists a rarer but even shorter con- struction, as in *You Have a Point There* (1953) where Eric Partridge asks 'How distinguish between ...' (p. 163).[2] This would seem to be an older type, separate from the above new construction. In the general run of European languages there is of course ample precedent for them and similar ones are found in Germanic, Romance and Slavonic tongues.

[1] Cleaver-Hume Press.   [2] Hamilton.

Another case of shortening and remodelling (albeit of a construction other than a verbal one) is seen in the type 'of whatever kind' as contrasted with the longer 'of any kind whatever' or else 'of whatsoever kind'. This is not in itself a newly created form, for it was familiar to Dr Johnson in the eighteenth century. 'Money, in whatever hands, will confer power' (*S.E.D.*). The construction continued throughout the following century in such writers as Herbert Spencer (*On Education*), Swinburne (in his critical essay on William Blake), and Stevenson, who in *Will o' the Mill* (1878) wrote that '. . . he determined, at whatever cost, to bring it to an end'. In 1895 G. H. Haswell spoke in the preface to *The Maister* of 'an abiding conviction that no child, of whatever class, could by any possibility be over-educated . . .'.[1] Yet it is not easy to find further examples in the British writing of the first half of the twentieth century and the construction seems to have become more or less obsolete on the British side of the Atlantic. In the United States it remained fully alive and was re-imported into Britain in the nineteen-fifties, soon becoming a feature of fashionable writing and speech. '. . . Most people, of whatever social class, are simply not, at any time, going to be interested in general ideas' says Richard Hoggart in *The Uses of Literacy* (p. 86) in 1957.[2] Speaking with some emphasis in the House of Commons Mr Harold Macmillan – then the Prime Minister – declared that a certain commission 'would be free in practice to hear all points of view from whatever quarter on whatever subject' (3 Dec 1959). Here, once again, American usage has kept alive an idiomatic construction which could otherwise have been lost to the English language. This is not to say that it ever disappeared completely from the scene, even in British writing. Thus Chesterton writes in *St Francis of Assisi*, published in 1923, 'There is something dangerous and disproportionate in its place in human nature, for whatever reason' (chapter 2). Yet it must be remembered that by that date Chesterton was nearly sixty years of age, and that he was using a type of phrase no longer current among younger speakers and writers. The situation is very

[1] Scott, London. [2] Chatto and Windus.

different at the present day, when it is precisely the younger set who are more likely to make use of it.

The problem of whether to place a singular or plural verb after 'none' has never been finally solved in modern English, and the O.E.D. simply notes 'In later use commonly with plural verb'. Purists usually seem to insist on the singular verb, and it is likely that the present widespread idea that it is 'correct' to observe this rule was driven home by the B.B.C. wartime phrase 'None of our aircraft is missing'. In this connection it is often argued that 'none' means 'not one', but this is to twist the facts to suit a theory, and indeed the opposite conclusion could be reached just as easily by this mathematical approach, since one could claim that the sentence means 'All of our aircraft are safe' and therefore use the plural with 'none'. These are not matters of logic but of usage. Logically there is nothing to choose between the singular or plural verb with 'none' but perhaps a plural is more satisfying when the verb immediately follows a plural noun,[1] as in the following example taken from The Times Law Report. 'On the issue of diminished responsibility, none of the facts were disputed by the appellant' (2 Apr 1958). Elsewhere the dogma that 'none' equals 'not one' leads to some curious practical results, as in a sentence from the New Statesman where the outcome is self-contradictory. 'As yet none of my characters has been industrialists, economists, trade union leaders' (17 Jul 1954).

Singular and plural are also involved in the use of 'less'. In his 1940 edition of Modern English Usage Fowler noted that 'Plurals . . . will naturally not take less; less tonnage but fewer ships'. With respect to the use of 'less' with the plural the O.E.D. had also said 'Now regarded as incorrect'. It was in fact a most venerable construction at one time, going back to Old English. The last example quoted by the O.E.D. is for 1579, though in reality there happens to be a slightly later instance quoted incidentally under fee (II, 7) and which is of 1583: 'The lawyers I would wish to take lesse fees of their clients'. But one of the most striking features of

---

[1] A plural noun ending in '-s', that is, unlike 'aircraft' which is invariable.

good English usage since about 1950 has been the sudden reinstatement of what was considered a vulgarism in the inter-war
period, and so 'less' is treated as a synonym of 'fewer' by being
coupled with plural nouns. '. . . the same amount of money will
buy less goods,' says the *Observer* (6 Oct 1957). This development
– or reinstatement – is a normal one from the point of view of a
simple analogy whereby speakers unconsciously reason that since
it is possible to say 'More haste, less speed' then one can also say
'More money, less goods'. In other words, since 'more' can be
used with both singular and plural it is only to be expected that
the same treatment will be accorded to 'less'.

Should 'everyone' (or 'everybody') be followed by a singular
or a plural? 'Everybody has got to play their part,' said Mr Harold
Macmillan in a Budget speech. The advantage of the plural is of
course that it avoids the clumsy 'his or her' which is the logical
alternative. The same applies to 'someone'. Speaking on the
B.B.C. about a recent novel, W. H. Auden said 'If someone dislikes it I shall never trust their literary judgment again' (quoted
in the *Spectator*, 2 Dec 1955). But it would be wrong to think of
these plurals as constituting a new development in our language,
for the struggle between singular and plural in these cases has
been going on for centuries. Indeed as Professor Thomas Pyles
points out in his article entitled *The English of VIPs*[1] the *everyone . . . they* construction is probably of far more frequent
occurrence since the seventeenth century than *everyone . . . he*.
This plural construction is in fact of surprisingly early origin, and
the *O.E.D.* instances for about 1530 the sentence 'Everye bodye
was in theyr lodgynges' (under *everybody*). To this might be added
an example taken from the well-known play of *Everyman*,
assigned to the early sixteenth century. 'Here begynneth a treatyse
how the hye Fader of heuen sendeth Dethe to somon euery
creature to come and gyue a-counte of theyr lyues in this worlde.'
The plural usage in connection with 'anyone, someone, everyone'
and 'everybody' is frequently denounced but the most that can
be said at present is that it does not look as though there is any

[1] *College English* (March 1955).

likelihood of educated users of the English language coming down firmly in favour of either singular or plural.

On another negative note, it is interesting to see that British is so far firmly opposed to the American habit of bringing a simple past tense into play when a very recent action is indicated. For example the American scholar and translator E. A. Nida states in *Learning a Foreign Language* that it is quite possible to say 'I finished the book' after just putting it down.[1] This is perfectly true in the American variety of English but – at the moment – is quite foreign to British idiom. In Britain I have only once ever seen a case of it, and this was in the middle nineteen-fifties when the London Casino of Old Compton Street, London, issued a souvenir card concerning the new Cinerama technique. This card, of American inspiration, bore the legend I WAS IN CINE-RAMA. To the British eye this sentence appears incomplete and prompts such queries as 'When? Where?' The normal British expression would have given some specific information with this past tense, e.g. 'I was in Cinerama to-day'. Alternatively, with the perfect tense, 'I have been in Cinerama'. It should perhaps be added that such syntax is known to Englishmen via the famous 'Kilroy was here', let alone such Hollywood film phrases as 'I just ate' and the ever-recurring 'So you finally got here'.[2] But they show no tendency to copy it.

A weakness often observable in modern style is the liking for a negative form of expression when really a positive question is intended. In conversational English this first became widespread during the wartime shortages that caused bashful customers to ask fierce shopkeepers 'You haven't any cigarettes, have you?' This betrays a pessimistic fear of receiving the answer 'No' or else is to be attributed to a desire to avoid giving offence. Presumably the former motive was uppermost when in May 1957 an M.P. speaking in the House of Commons said 'The Chancellor

[1] New York, 2nd edition, 1950.
[2] The word 'finally', which has long been a favourite in spoken American use, has now taken firm root in England where it was hitherto something of a bookish term.

should consider whether he cannot do something to get couples to marry for love instead of for income tax purposes'. Replace 'cannot' in this sentence by 'can' and the logical sense is the same. (It is also a fine example of what I have elsewhere termed *contravalence*, i.e. the situation arising when it is possible to replace a word by its own opposite without changing the general meaning of the sentence.) And in his appropriately titled book *The Mind at the End of Its Tether* (1945) H. G. Wells uses one of those elaborately negative sentences which almost defy analysis. 'But my own temperament makes it unavoidable for me to doubt that there will not be that small minority who will see life out to its inevitable end' (p. 34).[1] What does this mean? To be at all sure of the answer to this question we should have to deduce meaning from context, for even a careful process of cancelling out of negatives would not give us any certain conclusion, for after all when people say 'I shouldn't be surprised if it wasn't right' this logically ought to mean that 'I should be surprised if it was right', but in fact the very opposite is intended by such speakers, who would doubtless be shocked to hear anyone use a 'double negative' of the type 'I haven't got none', in which the general principle (of emphasis) is the same.

The subjunctive mood of the verb is certainly a rather feeble and restricted device in modern English as compared with the fine flowering of the subjunctive in various European languages, and clearly its recent history has led some commentators to believe that before long even its few remaining vestiges would quietly disappear from the scene. There is no longer any necessity, for example, to say – or even write – 'If this be the case' rather than 'If this is the case' and doubtless many people would consider the latter form to be the more natural. As between 'If I were you' and 'If I was you' the odds are perhaps evenly balanced in conversational English. Numerous stock phrases embody the subjunctive mood, but these are simply automatic expressions demanding no choice from the speaker – 'Thy kingdom come', 'perish the thought', 'God save the Queen', 'heaven forbid', 'pull

[1] Heinemann, 1945.

devil, pull baker', 'be that as it may' and so on. Certainly there exists in many quarters the tendency to disregard the existence of a subjunctive; so 'It is essential that nuclear weapons are not banned' (*Sunday Times*, 13 Feb 1955) states a letter to the editor from a reader who is on internal evidence a rather young man. Taken out of context, this sentence would not make it clear whether a ban on nuclear weapons is in operation or not, whereas the use of the subjunctive would have made the position clear: 'It is essential that nuclear weapons should not be banned'. In this particular case it can readily be argued that the objection is a theoretical one since all readers will be well enough informed about this point of international law, yet on occasion the lack of the subjunctive 'should' gives rise to a real danger of ambiguity, as when a letter to a popular newspaper stated 'They insist that I pay them ten pounds a year'.

Yet when it has been conceded that there has been in some respects a movement away from the subjunctive there must be added the reminder that the situation is at present complicated by a current of influence flowing once again from the United States where it so happens that this verbal mood is held in high esteem. Furthermore there is a strong liking in American usage for the use of a shortened form of it, and the practical result is that among the younger generation of British writers there is a move in the same direction. 'He agreed on condition that I bombard the enemy house,' writes Maurice Rowdon in *Of Sins and Winter* (p. 43).[1] In a more usual style this might have been 'that I should bombard' or even 'that I bombarded'. The upshot of all this is that usage is in a somewhat fluid state. Let us take for example a sentence spoken by the actor Albert Finney in a B.B.C. *Face to Face* programme in 1962: 'The headmaster suggested I went to drama school'. He might alternatively have said 'The headmaster suggested I go to drama school' or else '. . . suggested I should go to drama school'. There also arises the question of the negative subjunctive which also shows signs – admittedly very sporadically as yet – of copying an American pattern, as in a

[1] Chatto and Windus, 1955.

sentence heard in a committee meeting in 1963, 'What we are asking is that they be *not* examined in French'. This type not only omits 'should' from the subjunctive form but also alters the word-order by making 'not' follow 'be', thereby providing a rather neat and economical phrase.

The adverb is 'currently' (to use a case in point) fashionable in British English, so that one does not so much 'make a valuable comment' as 'comment valuably', and 'more importantly' sounds smarter than 'more important'. This preference for the adverb as against the adjective has long been a feature of American English, at least of the genteel variety as opposed to the un-varnished idiom of the people. Indeed there must have been an element of reaction among 'correct' American speakers against the quite opposite vulgar tendency to make adjectives do the work of adverbs ('I just can't take him serious') which is by no means unknown in the British Isles. The American classic *What Katy Did* by Susan Coolidge (died 1905) may be cited for a typical example of use of the adverb where British idiom would favour the adjective. 'It was so interesting to do this, that Katy felt dreadfully when they carried the man off to the state prison.' Earlier still, we find from Professor Eliason's *Tarheel Talk* that the use of *-ly* forms in such cases was increasingly common among better educated writers, at any rate in North Carolina, in the 1850s, e.g. 'I expected to find her looking badly . . .' (p. 240). It should incidentally be noted that this type may conceivably be due to the survival of ancient usage rather than to the hyper-correctness which is usually held to account for it, since examples are found in Shakespeare's 'The skies look grimly', and in the Bible in Genesis, chapter 40, when Joseph asks Pharaoh's officers 'Wherefore look ye so sadly today?'

The sentence 'I felt very badly' is now to be heard in the British Isles where it was first noticed by me in 1957 in a university common room, though by 1964 it had become so familiar that a television adaptation of one of Kipling's stories did not hesitate to make a British officer use it in the nineteenth century. A special case is that of 'I feel poorly' whose form is obligatory since 'I feel poor' would mean something quite different.

In these adverbial usages such as 'I felt badly' there has obviously been a shift of psychological emphasis from the descriptive word to the verbal sense, that is, from the subject to the action. This comes out clearly in a quotation from an article in the *Listener* by Angus Wilson. 'I rate Zola and George Eliot more highly than he does' (3 Mar 1960). This would formerly have been rather 'I rate . . . higher', i.e. higher on an imaginary list, but now the word is linked with the action of rating. Such at least is the implication of the adverb.

'The hearth burns more redly . . .' said Robert Louis Stevenson in *The Scot Abroad* and an adverb of colour is nothing new in English, but it would seem that such adverbs are being given something of a surrealistic twist in the latest style. 'The river Ouse flows yellowly alongside the gardens,' says *Time and Tide* (p. 84, 1961). Logically this is inexplicable. How can the manner of a river's flowing be said to be yellow? The river itself is yellow but what has this to do with the mode of flow, since presumably the Ouse would appear just as yellow if stationary? In fact the yellowness and the flow are merely co-existent and the adverb of colour implies nothing more than that. The position is quite different in such an expression as 'gleaming whitely', to be found in John Wain's *Hurry On Down*, for here the colour is intimately connected with the action of gleaming.

Overly existed in earlier English in a number of meanings but all of these are marked as obsolete in the *S.E.D.* for the usage of England, as against Scotland and the U.S.A. However the word is slowly being reintroduced from America into at any rate the London press, thus 'Perhaps one is overly sensitive [i.e. oversensitive] to the supposed rigours of other people's regimes' (*Sunday Times*, 1 March 1964). In the same year the *Catholic Herald* wrote that '. . . girls seemed to feel the Sisters overly confined' (4 Dec 1964). It is difficult to see what is to be gained by the use of this form apart from the ever-present novelty so esteemed nowadays. The coinage of unusual adverbs has indeed become quite easy (witness 'matter-of-factly'). So much so, indeed, that the structure of well-established expressions can be upset by the preference for the form in -*ly*. Thus, while traditionally there is the phrase 'to open wide' one can now hear 'widely' in this connection, as in a B.B.C. television programme; '. . . the snake's mouth is not hinged, thus allowing it to be opened widely' (24 March 1964). Perhaps by the year 2000 dentists may be saying 'Open widely!' to their patients, if this tendency continues.

In 1899 Henry Sweet mentioned in his book *The Practical Study of Languages* that at Edinburgh 'presently' meant 'at present' – as distinct from the usual sense of 'in a moment'. This meaning of 'at present' is noted in the *S.E.D.* as obsolete or dialectal, but it is one which once again has been reintroduced from across the Atlantic where it had also lingered on, with the result that it is now in good use in England. 'Warm air is presently moving north-east' reported a B.B.C. weather bulletin (20 May 1963). Here we have a fine example of the relative instability of meaning affecting expressions of time, as also seen, by the way, in the three different meanings of 'just now' in different parts of the English-speaking world, alluding respectively to past, present and future.

Only continues in modern English to be relatively untrammelled by rules governing its position in the sentence, so that excellent stylists are accustomed to placing it in what might be considered inelegant places. In less capable hands the results can be positively misleading, as in an article appearing in the *Daily Telegraph* which stated 'The law obliges a motorist to have only one windscreen wiper' (10 Sep 1955). This implies on the face of it that possession of two wipers is illegal, but presumably what was intended was that only one is obligatory, while a second wiper is optional. Commonsense allows us to resolve what would otherwise be a difficult problem of interpretation. It may incidentally be observed that the *S.E.D.* is not altogether correct in saying that the placing of *only* away from the word or words limited by it 'is now avoided in careful writing' for it would not be difficult to collect a list of examples to the contrary. Nor was the situation any different in the nineteen-twenties, when in *A Room of One's Own* Virginia Woolf said that '. . . ladies are only admitted to the library if accompanied by a Fellow of the College or furnished with a letter of introduction'. Indeed the subject of the position of *only* is a very controversial one among writers on contemporary English and this state of affairs promises to continue for some time to come. Eric Partridge vigorously attacks 'misplaced *only*' in his *Usage and Abusage* and carefully points out that 'Shakespeare makes this "mistake" in

> *The summer's flower is to the summer sweet*
> *Though to itself it only live and die.'*

A contrary view is to be found in *The Origins and Development of the English Language* (p. 240) where Professor Pyles quotes Sir Ernest Gowers' coinage of '*only*-snoopers' to denote those who indulge in the 'sport of pillorying misplaced *onlys*' (*Plain Words*, p. 185), and ironically indicates that in the United States the positioning of this troublesome word readily becomes a matter of tremendous importance.

'Only' is on occasion equivalent to 'but', though the *S.E.D.* does not comment at length on this and merely characterizes the usage as 'modern'. But how modern? Certainly it is to be found in the early part of the twentieth century, for Sir Walter Raleigh of Oxford affords us an example in a letter of 30 March 1906. 'But it is really there, only Blake was not an educated man.'[1] In fact this can be antedated by some sixty years by an instance likewise taken from a letter, this time from the pen of Cecilia Ridley, February 1845. 'The shawls are beautiful, only too delicate for this dirty place.'[2]

Schoolboys used to be taught that *due to* could not be used as a synonym of 'owing to'. It was therefore correct – so the explanation went – to say 'His absence was due to illness' but not 'Due to illness he was absent'. Yet very rapidly, and in accordance with a tendency beginning in the United States, this

---

[1] p. 296 of vol. ii of his correspondence.
[2] *Cecilia*, ed. by Viscountess Ridley (Hart-Davis, 1958).

distinction has been weakened even in good style. The tide seemed to turn around the year 1956. On June 10 of that year we could read in the *Observer* 'The Countess of Harewood opened THE OBSERVER Film Exhibition in a reconstructed building on [*sic*] Trafalgar-square last Thursday with workmen still on the premises – due to a series of difficulties in the final days . . .'. On October 30 of the same year the editorial of the *News Chronicle* stated that 'Due to the American elections and the Hungarian revolution we cannot expect much initiative from the United States and the Soviet Union in the immediate future'. It cannot be said that much has been lost in this change whereby *due to* has – like 'owing to' – become equivalent to a preposition. Another construction stigmatized as a vulgarism until quite recently is the replacement of 'as' by 'like' in the sense of 'in the same way'. Once again even this has at last found favour with even careful exponents of the language. So 'O'Casey wrote like Nijinsky danced', in the literary review of *Time and Tide* (5 Mar 1956). By 1959 this syntax had reached the House of Lords and even the Woolsack itself when the Lord Chancellor declared 'If someone attacks a colleague of mine like he did, he is going to get the answer from me' (16 Dec). In linguistic matters as elsewhere it sometimes happens that rivalry between two possibilities is settled by the triumph of a newly-arrived third party and this may ultimately be the case for the dilemma involving 'It looks as if . . .' and 'It looks as though . . .', for the future victor might well be 'It looks like . . .'. The sphere of action of *like* is certainly enjoying an extension in present-day English.

It is difficult to predict linguistic change, but it would seem that a certain type of drift is occurring in English which may ultimately bring to completion an ancient tendency, namely the gradual abolition of formal distinctions of grammatical case. The complexities of Old English noun declension have long since been simplified, with the result that the form of a singular noun varies only in the genitive, indicated by the ending '-s', and takes no account of the accusative and dative cases still retained in German and Russian. Hence such an English sentence as 'He gave the man the book', where no difference of form shows the dissimilar functions of 'man' and 'book'. Only the pronouns retain an accusative form; I – me; he – him; she – her; we – us; they – them. Even here there are only two forms for each pronoun as against the three extant in German, for example, *ich* 'I'; *mich* 'me'; and *mir* 'to me', while English 'you' and 'it' are quite invariable. 'You' is an all-purpose pronoun in English as compared with the usage of some other languages, because it includes the plural (expressed in English only in the vulgar 'youse') as well as the singular ('thou' formerly fulfilled this latter function, as it still does in dialect and liturgy). The practical result is that the one word 'you' covers in English all the concepts which German would express as *du, dich, dir, Sie, Ihnen, ihr, euch*. Yet when we say 'You see me' and 'I see you' there is not the slightest ambiguity, and the same applies to 'It struck him' and 'He struck it'. Will it be possible some day to carry the process a stage further and say – as in Chinese – 'You see I' as well as 'I see you'? Such is the strength of linguistic habit that such a development seems at the present day almost against nature (though Somerset men have been known to say 'I love she'). Yet already we can detect forms such as 'She – like they – cannot get out' (25 Apr 1954), which violate a cherished canon of the grammar books whereby a preposition cannot be followed by the subject case of the pronoun. 'Like them' is required here. The quotation is taken from the *Sunday Pictorial*, a weekly which cannot perhaps be claimed as an arbiter of English usage. Let us therefore look at a leading article from the *Sunday Times*. 'They, like he, ask how we are to use the coming years while the present phase of deterrence lasts' (6 Mar 1955). But these examples are striking only because the pronoun immediately follows the preposition which supposedly governs it. A more frequent case arises when the preposition is followed in the first instance by 'you' or by a personal name and only then by 'I', 'he', 'she' or 'they'. The commonest example springing to mind is that of the ever-present 'between you and I' instead of 'between you and me', though of course the former existed long before the twentieth century.

Or to take a case from the pen of an experienced journalist, Kenneth Allsop, writing in *Picture Post* and alluding to 'pressmen who like Chillingworth and I are put to pursuing her' (13 Nov 1954). The subject case of the pronoun can likewise appear when governed by other prepositions, and particularly by 'to'. Taken from a letter written by the headmaster of an English school – 'I do hope the weather was kinder to you than it was to we here in England' (8 Aug 1953). Similarly 'the *Manchester Guardian* has said some nice things about we in the North-East', from *The Northern Life* (April 1957). But in the strictest sense all this must be considered as the Queen's English in view of the next example, pronounced by Her Majesty on her return from the Commonwealth tour of 1954. 'It is a wonderful moment for my husband and I.'

It cannot be doubted that such developments are partly due to an unconscious analogy with the invariable 'you', and on some rare occasions this analogy actually becomes explicit in the mind of a person trained in the observation of his own linguistic lapses. Professor Charles F. Hockett recounts in his *Course in Modern Linguistics* that twice when answering the telephone he has exclaimed 'It's for she'. On analysing his own unconscious reasoning he discovers that this solecism arises from a simple analogy. It is possible to say 'You are wanted on the 'phone' and 'It's for you'. Therefore on this basis his unthinking assumption was that since he can say 'She is wanted on the 'phone' it is consequently permissible to state 'It's for she'. All this is of course made feasible by the invariability of 'you'.

If one sees a similar type of analogy at the root of the disfavouring of 'whom' as against 'who' then it can also be argued that the analogy with 'you' is strengthened fortuitously by the similarity of the final vowel of 'who' and 'you'. In traditional use we have:

Subject case	*Object case*
YOU	YOU
WHO	WHOM

But in this scheme 'whom' is the odd man out with its final consonant, so in' much modern writing the unevenness of the pattern is 'rectified' by the abolition of the offending word.

Subject case	Object case
YOU	YOU
WHO	WHO

Needless to say, the process is an unconscious one. WHO DO YOU WANT TO SAVE? asks the *Observer* in letters an inch high (6 Apr 1958), thereby helping to bring about the situation forecast as follows by Edward Sapir half-a-century ago. 'It is safe to prophesy that within a couple of hundred years from now not even the most learned jurist will be saying 'Whom did you see?' (*Language*, chap. 7). At present the position is that the average writer has a vague idea that it is correct to use 'whom' on certain occasions, but the feeling for grammatical case in English is now so weak that he is not always very sure what these occasions are, and so is led by excessive zeal into producing such a sentence as 'The teacher asked whom was ready' where the neighbouring verb makes it appear that an object case is required. Such mistakes are not confined to beginners, and here we have a more sophisticated example from a university lecturer in English, writing to the *Times Literary Supplement*. 'And whom among our poets . . . could be called one of the interior decorators of the 1950s?' (3 Feb 1961). The object case 'whom' is not correct in this instance, and 'who' should be used as the subject of the sentence. This sort of uncertainty in the handling of a particular linguistic form by even highly-educated practitioners of the language is an infallible sign that the form in question is doomed to fade away after a more or less protracted period of artificial stimulation. So far as the intuitive feeling of the speakers of English is concerned it may be said that 'whom' is in fact already dead for the majority.

But if 'whom' is past recovery there are only very rare signs of any breakdown in the distinction between 'he' and 'him' or 'she' and 'her' when a verb (though not a preposition) is involved, and in a period of some fifteen years only a couple of examples have been found for the present study. The first one, however, is a specimen of some value, being taken from the *Times Educational Supplement*. Speaking of the French philosopher Descartes, the article runs as follows. 'Later in his life he was persuaded to attend another royal lady, Queen Christina. She he instructed in philosophy three times a week at five o'clock in the morning' (10 Feb 1950). 'She he instructed . . .' is indeed a curious case, brought about by the inverted construction of the sentence. Logically it should be 'Her he instructed . . .', but most people would doubtless find this somewhat heavy and awkward. This being so, why did the writer not simply take advantage of the normal word-order? 'He instructed her . . .' Evidently because he wished to stress the feminine pronoun, contrasting it with the other royal lady alluded to, and the emphasis was effectively obtained by removing the pronoun to the head of the sentence. But it must have seemed to the writer that it constituted the subject of the sentence by the very fact of standing in initial position, and so it was that 'She' was used rather than the grammatical 'Her'. An interesting problem arises if we consider the sentence in isolation, without any knowledge of the context allowing us to know whether the man or the woman was being instructed. 'She he instructed in philosophy . . .' Mathematically speaking it might be thought that the problem is insoluble, granted that we have here two subject-pronouns each fighting for recognition as subject. Yet surely everyone would unfailingly identify 'he' as the true subject of such a construction. Why is this? Presumably because one does not ever find the sequence SUBJECT + OBJECT + VERB, i.e. in the English tongue as at present constituted we say 'I like him' or even 'Him I like', but never 'I him like'. So by an unconscious process of elimination based on these patterns of syntax we realize that 'She he instructed in philosophy . . .' must represent OBJECT + SUBJECT + VERB and so it was the man who did the instructing.

The same principle would hold good even if the sentence used proper names and not pronouns, for it might have run 'Queen

Christina Descartes instructed in philosophy'. In a sense this is a more straightforward sentence if only because there are no grammatical cases in the forms to confuse the issue. Once again we can readily conclude that the subject is in fact Descartes and not the queen, on the same grounds that a subject cannot be separated from its verb by an object. Of course if only the sentence were read aloud the intonation and stress of the voice would 'pick out' Queen Christina as the object in a way unavailable on the printed page, and the same is true of our original sentence 'She he instructed in philosophy'. Aspiring writers are often told that they should read their texts aloud so as to judge the effect, but this advice can be a little misleading, since what is very clear when uttered aloud can be ambiguous when in print. So, for example, 'I hope you can manage this time' will be either 'I hope you can manage this TIME' or – something quite different – 'I hope you can manage THIS time'. Here English differs from French, where the sense of the written phrase is less dependent on the gloss put upon it by the voice.

It so happens that my second example combines a subject-pronoun with a name. 'He Alan Whicker met in London,' said Derek Hart in the B.B.C. programme *Tonight* (21 Jun 1960). Again we see the extraordinary case of a subject-pronoun functioning as an object, and again there is no ambiguity, even in the absence of a context. No doubt the huge majority of listeners did not notice anything unusual, especially as they were 'helped' by vocal intonation.

There remains the question of the first person. Here the situation is a little more complicated, since it would appear that in the English of both Britain and the North American continent there has slowly arisen the feeling that there is something vaguely improper or ill-mannered about the use of the pronoun 'me'. This probably accounts in part for the popularity of such constructions as 'between you and I', already noted. Nevertheless, no speaker of English has hitherto shown any signs of evolving such a sequence as 'I like you and you like I', and in this domain the all-purpose pronoun is now 'myself'.

One cannot escape the impression that over the last couple of decades or so there has been a marked increase in the use of 'myself' for 'me'. 'I am sure that business people like myself will leave' (23 Feb 1956) states the writer of a letter to the *Daily Telegraph* in a typical example of this usage. A factor favouring it seems to be the idea that it is somehow less personal and thrusting than 'me', so much so that it can head a list of names. 'The *Daily Express* immediately asked myself, Hastings and Osborne to contribute to a series of articles called "Angry Young Men",' wrote Colin Wilson in *Encounter* (Nov 1959). In enumerations of this type 'myself' is almost becoming the rule rather than the exception. 'Now you see myself and the diver,' explained a naval officer in an unscripted television programme in 1959, and a few seconds earlier he had said 'Now here you see myself on this occasion'. The meaning was simply 'me', without any strong contrast with any other person. A fine example of this was also heard in another T.V. programme where a potholer was explaining why he would always attempt to rescue people in difficulties. 'It might well be that an accident could befall myself and I would like somebody to rescue me' (1963). What was striking here was that the strong stress fell on the final word of the sentence, and not at all on 'myself'.

Another obvious use of this pronoun arises when it acts as a sort of solution to the dilemma occurring when the speaker does not want to choose between 'I' and 'me'. 'She was three years older than myself,' wrote Samuel Chamberlain as long ago as the nineteenth century in his *Recollections of a Rogue*[1] (p. 15), and this construction is now on the increase because it avoids both the pedantic 'I' and the prosaic 'me'. On the other hand, a nineteenth-century example which has not been imitated much is Edward Fitzgerald's

> *Myself when young did eagerly frequent*
> *Doctor and Saint and heard great Argument...*

This is held to be a reduction of 'I myself', and one would be

[1] Museum Press, 1957.

hard put to it to unearth another fairly recent example. What is noticeable, however, is a growing tendency to place 'myself' before 'I'. 'Is the task hopeless? Myself I think not' (11 May 1956), from the *Times Educational Supplement*. The origin of the construction is not clear. Is it a mere inversion of 'I myself', or – more probably – a shortening for 'As for myself'? Is its present popularity due to the fact that it is possibly being used as a genteel equivalent to the colloquial 'Me' in the initial position, as in 'Me, I like it'? Perhaps future writers to the learned periodicals will be stating, by a continued process of abbreviation, 'Myself think not', and Romeos and Juliets of some distant century will murmur 'Do you like myself like myself like you?'

The choice of preposition in a number of constructions is at present subject to influences tending to upset traditional practice and once again it is America that sets the pace. For example, a growing preference for 'on' as a prepositional maid-of-all-work is one of the most striking features of modern style, and as an Americanism was already noticed by Horwill (under ON): '*on* is frequently used in American where other prepositions would be used in English'. To speak of being 'on a train' rather than 'in a train' is quite universal among the younger generation in Britain. As mentioned above, railway terminology is somewhat dissimilar east and west of the Atlantic, for the self-evident reason that – like the motor-car industry, whose technical terms are likewise divergent – steam railways were not in existence when the United States became a separate political entity. As a result of the vigorous development of fluvial transport in America there was a tendency to apply to trains the vocabulary of the river-boats, hence the American custom of calling out 'All aboard!' when the train is ready to depart, whereas in Britain the corresponding signal is merely the blowing of a whistle. It is possible, therefore, that the American preference for 'on a train' was the result of an analogy with 'on a boat'.[1] It is now possible in British English to

---

[1] But note a mention in 1848 of 'The new-fangled and lubberly abomination of saying 'on a steamboat' or 'on a ship' (O.E.D. supp. under 'on'). 'Aboard' was evidently called for.

find an occasional use of 'on' with the name of a railway station, as in a B.B.C. play inspired by a work of Agatha Christie: 'You can't say things like that on Paddington Station'. But British speakers seem to be resisting the American habit of prefacing this preposition to the names of streets, especially as the phrase 'on the street' has a sexual meaning in Britain. American 'on the street' is perhaps due to the influence of immigrants accustomed to the corresponding idiom in other Germanic languages, e.g. German *auf der Strasse*.

There is no knowing in what sense 'on' will turn up in contemporary English. To return to Horwill, he cites an early American example (taken from James Fenimore Cooper) of the idiosyncratic treatment it could receive. Cooper had written 'The distinction is arbitrary, though an innovation on the language'. But this type of function is constantly seen nowadays in the headlines of British newspapers, where its shortness makes it preferable to 'about, concerning, in connection with', etc. The following were all seen in 1956.

FEARS ON TECHNICAL EDUCATION
MRS LUCE'S ILLNESS: DOUBTS ON CAUSE
PUBLIC MUST GET FAIR DEAL ON EGGS
ARMY'S EXTRA COSTS ON SUEZ

The *Daily Telegraph* of 24 July of that year yielded no fewer than three examples on a single page.

FALSE HOPES ON BLIND CHILDREN
NO DOUBT ON DETERRENT
WARNING ON CALL-UP

Apart from headlines, there are constant instances in the main text of newspapers. 'Bourguiba's preoccupation with French politics, on which he is a great connoisseur, is hardly surprising' (*The Observer*, 1 May 1955), is a typical case. But this liking for 'on' is not confined to journalists. Michael Young's imaginative glimpse into the future, *The Rise of the Meritocracy* (1958), states 'I shall illustrate my essay with reference to the period, between 1914 and 1963, on which I specialized . . .' (p. 13).[1] In a weightier tome, *Language and History in Early Britain*, by Professor Kenneth Jackson (1953), we find 'Our information on Brittonic begins with the first contacts of the Greeks and Romans with this island' (p. 4).[2]

Though the case of 'on' is striking, it is true that the use of a number of prepositions is in a state of some uncertainty. In 1936 Horwill pointed out in a pamphlet written for *The Society for Pure English* that the use of 'into' was an Americanism in the phrase 'An investigation into the status of . . .', and what is noteworthy here is that he did not trouble to give the usual British form (presumably 'of'), so self-evident did it seem to him then. Yet nowadays 'into' is the usual preposition following 'investigation', even in British English. Another example of American syntax quoted by Horwill in the same article is 'The writer wishes to express his appreciation *for* the aid received'. Again he did not show the normal British idiom in such a case; presumably it would be 'appreciation of', but both are possible at the present day. 'For' is indeed rather a favourite preposition in American syntax, and traces of this influence are to be detected in Britain, as when it is gratuitously added to the verb in the sentence 'I could not bear for him to stay elsewhere' (*Daily Mail*, 21 Nov 1955). It replaces 'of' in '. . . the patient loses all memory for recent events' (*Lilliput*, Mar 1955). The writings of Robert Graves, who has lived abroad for many years and meets numbers of American visitors, swarm with transatlantic expressions and syntax. So it is that an article of his reports that an earthquake '. . . made several telephone operators faint for terror' (*Encounter*, Jul 1955). A very typically American turn of phrase that is showing signs of headway in Britain is the replacing of 'named after' by 'named for'. My first specimen of this is in the magazine *The Northern Life* for June 1957 though there are surely earlier

[1] Penguin Books, 1961. First published by Thames and Hudson, 1958.
[2] Edinburgh University Press.

attestations: 'Saville Row was named for Col. Sir Geo. Saville' (that is, in Newcastle upon Tyne).

American authors seem invariably to dedicate their books with the formula 'For' so-and-so as against the British 'To . . .'. When in 1952 Eric Partridge addressed his *From Sanskrit to Brazil* to his friend in the formula 'For John W. Clark' the choice of preposition was perhaps a conscious act of courtesy towards an American scholar, but since that time the fashion has spread and is perhaps no longer to be regarded as an Americanism.

Though in some ways the handling of prepositions by modern writers may strike the observer as lacking in system, in one respect at least there is a tendency for them to use some prepositions in an increasingly analytical manner. There appears to be a growing belief that prepositions should when possible have a logical link with the adjective they follow, so that the argument goes that it is better to say 'averse from' rather than 'averse to' since the adjective itself implies a turning away *from* something. The saying of the Latin poet Terence that 'Nothing that is human is alien to me' is well-known in that translated form, but the following sentence shows 'alien' with a construction modified by the modern outlook: 'I still find that the whole is alien from me; alien come to that from the best work of William Blake'. So says Dilys Powell in the *Observer* (20 Dec 1959). It may of course be that in this particular case Miss Powell is using a Latinism based on the phrase *alienus a me*, or taking her model from John Milton, himself a writer much dominated by Latin models and who makes use of the 'alien from' construction. At all events 'alien from' fits in very well with the modern liking for logical harmony between adjective and preposition. Yet no language is consistent in these matters and speakers of English do not yet say 'opposed from' or 'hostile against'.

Schoolboys were long taught that 'different from' is superior to 'different to' on the grounds that 'from' underlines the idea of difference, unlike 'similar to' where the preposition stresses the likeness. The question remains a vexed one, but is further complicated by the arrival of a third party, 'different than'. This comes from America in the short run, but historically speaking is no stranger to England, having been used by Goldsmith and other writers, so once again it would seem to be a question of an idiom surviving in the United States after it had virtually died out in the literary language of Britain. As an instance of a recent appearance of the phrase in British writing here is a sentence from the pen of a reviewer in *Books of the Month* for September 1956. 'Mr Kerr is writing of the American theatre, which is clearly suffering from a different malaise than ours'. 'From ours' or even 'to ours' might have been written in this case, but there is no denying the handiness of 'different than' in sentences where either of the other two would be clumsy or impossible. An American writer, Charlton Laird, states that '. . . the world itself looks different to Christians than to Mohammedans'. The double occurrence of 'to' in this sentence is merely caused by the construction with 'looks' and has no connection with 'different'. The use of 'different than' is neater and more incisive than 'to' or 'from' in this instance. In cases where 'different' refers not to a noun but to a phrase the neatness of the effect is even greater; indeed it is likely that this type never quite died out in Britain in the course of the centuries. Certainly it is pressed into service by Trollope in *Barchester Towers* (1857), where we read that '. . . things were constructed very differently now than in former times' (chap. XLVIII).

A distinct trend in modern syntax is the omission of the definite and indefinite articles in various ways familiar to students of the main European languages, though this phenomenon is not brand-new in at least one of its manifestations, since Thomas Carlyle's *Heroes and Hero-worship*, published as long ago as 1841, contains such chapter headings as 'The Hero as Divinity' and 'The Hero as Prophet' (and not 'The Hero as a Divinity', etc.). But it is significant that Carlyle was an accomplished German scholar and it is likely that in this omission of the article we can detect the influence of the corresponding German construction. Certainly it was usual at that period to include the indefinite article before the second of two nouns linked by 'as'; so it was in the title of an article in *The National Review* of 1856, 'Defoe as a novelist', and so it was generally. Towards the end of the century Oscar Wilde was writing of 'The critic as artist' (1890), but as we have seen his travels in America had left some mark on his vocabulary and there is no doubt that this type of syntax was fashionable in the United States early in the nineteenth century, possibly because of German scholarly influence. On the other hand James Joyce in *Portrait of the Artist as a Young Man* clings to the old construction, though it is true to say that in this phrase the semantic value of 'as' is not quite the same as that hitherto considered but approximates rather to 'when' or 'while' in meaning. At all events Dylan Thomas's *Portrait of the Artist as a Young Dog* preserves the pattern.

Though the detailed history of the elliptic construction with 'as' is at present insufficiently investigated there is no doubt that it has suddenly spread rapidly in Britain in the last twenty years or so after hanging fire for over a century. It is a well-known feature in the titles of academic books and articles, e.g. 'The town as symbol in some German novels' (*Modern Languages*, Dec 1957). But latest fashion has taken this sort of idiom one step further, since 'as' need not be preceded by a noun but may follow other parts of speech or even head the sentence. 'As manipulator of words, the author reminded me of William Etty as manipulator of pigments' (*Observer*, 25 May 1958). Or in another sentence which likewise illustrates two contexts for the omission of the article; 'As sea-captain, poet, translator and lover, Sir Kenelm Digby was Renaissance man' (*Observer*, date not noted, but post-1955). And again with reference to an occupation; 'His clowning is founded on extreme skill as juggler and acrobat' (B.B.C., 13 Jan 1961). But even a word denoting an object can lose its article in this way, as in a caption from *Picture Post*. 'Noel Coward's bust remains as relic of his tenancy on the windowsill of the detective's bedroom' (3 Dec 1956). Furthermore it is perfectly possible nowadays for an adjective to be interposed between 'as' and the following noun. 'The view that the Soviet system . . . could no longer be regarded as sole model for Communism everywhere . . .' (*The Twentieth Century*, Dec 1956, p. 484).

But language development does not proceed by neat, all-embracing stages, and the old construction with 'as' is by no means totally outmoded even in America. In 1957 it appeared in the titles of two books published there; Max Lerner's *America as a Civilization* and Richard M. Chadbourne's *Ernest Renan as a Thinker*, which may be contrasted with Eric Bentley's *The Playwright as Thinker*, published in New York in 1946.

Students of French are familiar with the idea that in that language a noun in apposition is not accompanied by an article, and there are strong signs that a similar state of affairs is rapidly coming about in English. Again, though this tendency has become very noticeable only since about 1950, it is perfectly possible to cite isolated examples from an earlier period, e.g. from Meredith's *The Egoist* (1879). 'His cook, M. Dehors, pupil of the great Godefroy . . .' (first page of chapter 10). It is indeed quite possible that in this context the omission of any article before 'pupil' is a conscious or unconscious Gallicism induced by the mention of a French character in the novel.

It is true that the use of the noun in apposition without any article has been established for some considerable time in the case of particular posts or offices. So, . . .'Mr Thomas Martin, General Secretary of the Royal Institution' (*Times Literary Supplement*, 25 Sep 1930), which is typical of a usage known throughout the present century. The omission is especially characteristic – and long-standing – in the designation of academic posts. But more recent usage has extended the construction so as to include names of occupations in general. 'Clarissa, American business woman, comes to England' (*Radio Times*, 27 Oct 1960). In fact the omission of the article is common enough with any noun, provided that it is in apposition. 'Nansen, hero and humanitarian, moves among them a little apart' (*The Times*, 30 Jan 1958). So far as occupations are involved there is in fact a tendency to use no article even where the noun is not in apposition. A curious example appears in the *Radio Times*, a publication more than normally addicted to the omission of the article. 'Spud Lewis is mechanic in a motor car factory' (17 Jan 1958). But it is also clear that these constructions are confined to the written language, or at all events do not penetrate the normal conversational style of spoken language.

It is typical of the linguistic situation that is created when a new construction is making its way into the language that it is sometimes quite possible to find examples of old and new in the same sentence, as in a review in *The Times*. 'They deal with East-man, a book-keeper, revolutionizing photography; with the inventor of the ball-point pen who was sculptor, painter and journalist' (30 Jan 1958). On closer inspection, however, it is clear that the grammatical context of 'book-keeper' is not quite the same as that of the final series of occupations mentioned in the sentence, since it is further qualified and they are not. A more telling case which actually makes use of the presence or absence of the article to evoke a difference of meaning is to be seen in the next example. '. . . the Duke of Northumberland was duke of Northumberland as the Duke of Devonshire was not duke of Devonshire' (*Spectator*, 9 May 1958). This is a most ingenious sentence altogether in view of the difference of meaning implied not only by manipulation of the definite article but the reinforce-ment of that difference by spelling, i.e. 'duke' and 'Duke'. The tenor of this article was in fact that the Duke of Northumberland was more intimately attached to and concerned with the county named in his title than was the Duke of Devonshire with his. This confirms that in the sentence quoted the idea of the writer was that 'the Duke of Northumberland' is, as it were, the name of an individual whereas 'duke of Northumberland' with the small 'd' and with loss of the article implies more of a function or occupa-tion.

These examples of the omission of the article concern persons rather than objects or concepts but these latter – at any rate in journalese – can undergo the same treatment. In a contribution to the *New Statesman* John Braine writes '[he] lit a Gauloise – souvenir, like his espadrilles, of his holiday in France' (5 Oct 1957). More curiously, from the *Sunday Times*, 'They shouted "Isabel, Isabel", Portuguese version of Elizabeth . . .' (17 Feb 1957).

But in addition to these various syntactic patterns which can be applied to any number of sentences there is also the loss of the definite article which has affected certain specific idioms. Thus when a writer in the *Atlantic Monthly* lays it down as a rule that 'We go to school and college, but we go to the university' (Mar 1960, p. 81) it must be realized that today this is no longer true of British usage in the main. The change has been quite a rapid one, but the huge majority of people now speak of going 'to university'. Even at the time when the above claim was made in the *Atlantic Monthly* the change was already on its way, as 'At the end of the war he went to university' (*Radio Times*, 25 May 1956). A cynic might explain the older phrase 'to go to the university' by appealing to the belief of the Englishman of the old school that there is really only one university worth mentioning – Oxon.; Cantab.; Dunelm. or whatever it may be. Following this not too serious line of argument one could then point out that the recent proliferation of university foundations has made even the most fervent Oxonian (and others) realize that universities have become a category, and hence the loss of the article. Possibly there is a grain of truth in this, but what is more likely is that it is a mere case of analogy with the series 'to go to school, college', etc. 'Public school' also belongs to this type without the article. 'Of his four sons, two have left public school ...' (*Sunday Times*, 19 Jan 1958).

Another extremely rapid change in fashion, following American idiom, has replaced the type 'all the morning, all the winter', etc., by 'all morning, all winter'. The prevalence of the shorter phrase in the United States was pointed out by Horwill in his *Dictionary of Modern American Usage* (2nd ed. 1944) but even in Britain the short form without article had long existed in 'all day' and 'all night' though not in 'all the morning', 'all the week', 'all the summer', etc. It is difficult to pinpoint the moment when British speakers suddenly copied the thoroughgoing American usage but certainly by 1958 the change was in full swing. 'You can be driven round Lisbon all afternoon ...' (*Manchester Guardian*, 13 Feb 1958). And from a B.B.C. news bulletin; 'Talks have been going on about the bus strike all afternoon' (18 Jun 1958). 'All week' was also to be found that year. 'Britain and America who exploded nuclear devices feverishly all week . . .' (*Observer*, 2 Nov 1958).

There is a case in British English where 'the' is tending to be replaced by 'a', once again in imitation of transatlantic idiom, namely in the phrase 'a majority of . . .' replacing 'the majority of . . .'. 'A majority of even cultured Frenchmen seem to have lost their feeling for Racine,' says Dr J. G. Weightman in the *Observer* (24 Jan 1960). It is difficult to see anything to be gained by the change so far as distinction of meaning is concerned, since the old and new forms appear to be synonymous.

6

Pronunciation

PRONUNCIATION is one of the most fleeting aspects of linguistic development, though this is often masked for the modern reader who reads Shakespeare in the modern spelling convention and hears the plays pronounced by modern standards, apart from an occasional old-fashioned stress made necessary to preserve the scansion of the line, as in 'perséverance' or 'aspéct'. Yet the pronunciation of the sixteenth century was very different indeed from that of Olivier, Redgrave and Gielgud, incorporating as it did many features which now survive either provincially or not at all. Could we miraculously overhear the first night of *Hamlet* our first reaction might well be one of amazement at the rusticity of it all. And as to the intonation of the sentence we are totally in the dark so far as the practice of past generations is concerned, for only with the invention of the gramophone in the late nineteenth century did it become possible to keep a record of the sounds of spoken language, thus registering the voices of Gladstone and Tennyson, for example, though of course early recording techniques leave much to be desired in quality of reproduction. Then recordings of the early days, like the photographs of the time, were highly stylized, so that the spoken word appeared only in the declamatory style of poetry or oratory. Future generations of students of English are greatly to be envied in that they will have at their disposal an endlessly rich series of recordings and spoken archives stretching over many styles and accents and spanning centuries of linguistic development.

It is self-evident that the changes affecting the sounds of English in recent centuries must have been relatively rapid, since Shakespeare's England is less than four centuries removed from us.

Such changes have not suddenly ceased to operate in the twentieth century, yet elderly people scarcely ever seem conscious of changes in the actual quality of sounds used by the younger generation, possibly because this type of change seems gradual in a given lifetime and so is not very striking. However we shall not be concerned with this general and far-reaching type of sound-shift – especially as our viewpoint does not go much beyond a single generation – but only with the changing *distribution* of existing sounds in particular words.

Once again it is impossible to survey the scene without taking some account of the influence of American English, for just as the British vocabulary has been infiltrated on a grand scale, so the American mode of pronunciation is making some impression on British speech. In one sense this is the result of the sheer power and prestige of American civilization; it is hard to ignore a colossus, especially when you understand his language. Still, American *speech* would have quite literally remained a dead letter in the British Isles – at least for the great majority of the population – had it not been for (*a*) the invention of the talking film, (*b*) the tremendous preponderance of the American 'entertainment industry'.

Some surprise may be occasioned here by the omission of television from this reckoning. But it is intended to be included implicitly, since the greater part of the American material shown on the T.V. screen is filmed, and 'personal' appearance of American artists is relatively rare. It may also be wondered why no reference has been made to the gramophone or to radio. But the fact is that transatlantic voices were not often heard either on records or on the B.B.C. until the early 'thirties, which is precisely when the all-conquering American talkie film was getting into its stride in Britain and so dwarfing all other sources of American speech there. (Round about 1930 it was indeed widely believed that the gramophone record had no commercial future because of the invention of the wireless loudspeaker which did away with the clumsy and annoying headphones associated with the older type of receiver.) It was above all films which caused the American type of pronunciation to be associated with ideas of romance, adventure and big money and the association is driven home by constant exposure of the British television and cinema audiences to this type of accent day after day and year after year so that in the end resistance has been broken down. Linguistic influence is rather like advertising in this respect that it is greatly helped to become operative by sheer endless repetition. Sooner or later some impression is bound to be made. We have come a long way since the actor Emlyn Williams first heard the American accent when he went to Oxford in 1923 as he tells us in his autobiography.

Contrary to popular belief it is difficult to draw a hard and fast line between American and British pronunciations of specific words, apart from glaring examples like 'schedule' or 'pyjamas' (U.S. 'pajamas' though the difference in spelling gives no hint as to the difference of pronunciation), 'bananas' and so forth. 'American' and 'British' in this context refer to the whole of the pronunciation systems to be found in each country, in all areas and classes. In other words, a southern Englishman regards the usual American pronunciation of 'last' with a close vowel as idiosyncratic and typically American, whereas a northerner will consider it right and proper. President Kennedy, on the other hand, could be heard to pronounce 'lahst' with the best of them. In mentioning this type of difference, one can also remember that standard British pronunciation usually gives to 'plastic' and 'plastics' the American value, as against the traditional sound of 'plaster' with the broad vowel.

An obvious way in which American usage has been directly copied (not necessarily in a conscious manner) is that affecting the tonic stress of individual words, especially in cases where the stress is brought forward to the first syllable by younger speakers in the American fashion – hence the frequent 'mágazine, résearch, cígarette' and so on. The phrase 'after all' is similarly pronounced more and more with the stress on the first word – 'áfter all' as against the indigenous 'after áll'. On the contrary there is a strong tendency in American practice to shift stress to the final syllable of certain personal names which customarily have first-syllable stress in Britain (e.g. Maurice). This has not so far taken hold in British English but the same cannot be said of the stress given to the final '-ell' of family names, which in Britain as in the United States is now somehow felt to be more esthetically pleasing than stress earlier in the name, though contrariwise it may be noted that the B.B.C. resolutely clings to 'Púrcell' with the stress on the first syllable, while specific names such as Mitchell, Russell and others appear to be resisting the change to final stress.

One major way in which British pronunciation is following in the wake of American (whether because of direct imitation or on account of the reverence accorded to the printed word that accompanies mass literacy) concerns the importance attached to harmony between spelling and sound. Lacking a trustworthy traditional standard of pronunciation, the huge mass of people cannot but be influenced by the written word. One result of this is that the old American complaint that Englishmen pronounce 'manufacturer' as 'mana-facturer' is speedily being attended to, and it is extremely common nowadays to hear 'man-yoo-facturer' in Britain. Similarly 'often' very frequently is pronounced with the 't' sounded (unlike 'soften'), as in America, so that it looks as though this will be the universal practice by the end of the century. At one time considered as an Americanism, this pronouncing of the 't' seems now to be carried out in response to the exigencies of decorum, as pointed out by Sir Ernest Gowers in a presidential address to the English Association in 1957. '. . . the conviction seems now to be almost universal that when one is before a microphone or on a platform the dignity of one's position demands the articulation of the "t" in "often"'. Since it is usually the case that frequently recurring words cling to their traditionally aberrant (in the sense of not according with spelling) pronunciation more readily than rare words, it is not easy to account for this exception. Perhaps the reluctance to go on pronouncing 'often' as 'offen' arises from a confusion, possible in some contexts, with 'off and' colloquially rendered as 'offen'. Thus it would be theoretically feasible for 'He's often on' to be momentarily confused with 'He's off and on' if the 't' were not sounded.

One spelling pronunciation certainly springs from special semantic circumstances. To 'salve one's conscience' was originally to apply metaphorical salve (that is, balm) to it and the 'l' was silent ('sahv'), as it still is in the speech of the older generation of speakers. But most young speakers seem to imagine that the reference is to a salvage operation, a sort of dragging up of the conscience from the depths into which it had sunk, so logically they give the letter 'l' its full value. Presumably the reason for all this is a matter of statistical frequency, the medical sense of the word 'salve' being somewhat rare in contemporary English and the verbal sense being virtually unknown apart from this particular idiom.

Some youthful speakers in England like to use the American pronunciation of 'record' as a mark of their modernity (say, 'reckered'), if indeed they are not in the habit of saying 'disc'. Here for once the American version is more 'clipped', to use an adjective that Americans regularly apply to British speech. What is interesting is that there are grounds for thinking that it is the American pronunciation which is the older, quite apart from the useful rule that the pronunciation which is closest to the spelling is most likely to be the new-fangled one, since precisely it is a mere spelling pronunciation. Charles Dickens, no mean observer of idiosyncrasies of speech, made a point of spelling the word as 'rec-ord' in *Oliver Twist* as part of a context making it likely that a vulgar pronunciation was thereby indicated.[1] The hyphen can only be meant to represent a pronunciation imposing two evenly spaced syllables, as in modern usage in England (not necessarily in Scotland and Wales). We must conclude that at the time of publication of *Oliver Twist* the accepted pronunciation of the word was the short and snappy one now considered typically American and that our present version of it began life as a vulgarism.

In the fourth edition of his *English Pronouncing Dictionary* issued

[1] *Oliver Twist* was published as a serial, 1837–9.

in 1937 Daniel Jones recorded the pronunciation '"accomplish" rarely "accumplish"'. By virtue of the principle put forward in the previous paragraph one might imagine that 'accumplish' was the traditional pronunciation, but here we have the exception that proves the rule since in reality it is the newcomer, and on p. 50 of *The Queen's English*[1] Arnold Wall reckons that it must have edged its way into the language around 1930, though in reality this is probably a little late. True, the *S.E.D.* did not give it as an alternative in 1933, and in 1929 Vizetelly's *Desk-book of Words Commonly Mispronounced* made no mention at all of it. Yet this pronunciation is possibly that of the majority of the British population nowadays. How is it to be accounted for? Perhaps after all it is a spelling pronunciation in disguise, based on an illogical unconscious association with 'come', whose phonetic value has therefore been copied. Similarly for 'accomplice'.

In these matters of pronunciation it is often none too easy to establish the facts of even twenty or thirty years ago, and in his article *Contemporary Trends in English* (in *Essays and Studies*, 1960, published by John Murray for the English Assoc.) D. M. Low writes that 'In the last ten or twenty years the word *housewife* has been brought into general use, largely, it may be thought, by the journalists'. This in itself seems to be a remarkable chronological underestimate, but the article proceeds to speak of the pronunciation. 'It seems to be pronounced invariably as spelt. This breaks with a long tradition of *hussif* or *housif*'. To say the least, only a few elderly speakers were still pronouncing *hussif* in 1940 (i.e. 1960 minus 20 years). True, the spelling *hussif* was officially used in the Army at that time in the special sense of a small cloth container for the soldier's needles and thread, but even this was always pronounced as 'housewife'. However, those who regret the loss of the traditional short form can rejoice that an even shorter version survives in 'hussy', applied to a woman of light or worthless character.

To return to the question of American influence, it is in some cases admittedly difficult to know whether a given change in

[1] Pegasus Press, 1958.

pronunciation would not have come about in any case even if America had never existed (or if, as might have happened, Americans spoke French or Spanish). For instance, 'transparent' is often rhymed with 'arrant' in present-day Britain, rather than with 'parent'. This new pronunciation coincides with the usual (but not quite universal) American one, but is the latter the source of it? After all, 'apparent' met with a similar fate well over a generation ago, when there was little likelihood of any influence from spoken American. Possibly, then, 'transparent' was fated in the long run to follow this same evolution, though it can scarcely be doubted that American example may have accelerated and reinforced the tendency. In a similar way, it is common to hear 'secretary' pronounced with four syllables in the American fashion, rather than in the traditional British manner, that is 'secretr'y' with three syllables only. The new pronunciation, more or less rhyming with 'wary' is now heard frequently and from excellent speakers so that it seems likely to drive out its rival in the space of another generation or so. But again, is this evolution due to spelling or to imitation?

In certain words there is a fluctuation between long and short 'o', the chief of these being 'progress'. The short vowel, standard in this word in the U.S.A., has made great headway in Britain since the Second World War and in fact the pronunciation of 'progress' in this way can rightly be described as the Queen's English now that it has been used by Her Majesty in a television address to the nation. As a rare variant it had in reality existed since the nineteenth century in British pronunciation, though it is recounted that Tennyson expressed great surprise when someone spoke of 'prŏgress', saying 'Oh, why do you pronounce the word like that? Pray give the ō long'. It will be interesting to see what will happen in future to the pronunciation of The Pilgrim's Progress which hitherto always seems to retain the traditional long vowel. A short vowel in 'process' is still rare in Britain and is probably considered by most people to be an Americanism, though the S.E.D. allows both long and short vowels here. 'Polka' is known to the younger generation in the phrase 'polka dot' for what was known before as 'bird's eye pattern' on clothing material, and this Americanism is appropriately pronounced for the most part with the long 'o' by these speakers, though the short sound was usual earlier this century (again the *S.E.D.* allows both) i.e. when it was the name of a dance. The phrase 'polka dot' is incidentally included in the 1955 addenda of the *S.E.D.* and dated 1883. The fact that it took a couple of generations and more to be noticed is sufficient proof of its former rarity in Britain.

There is currently a strong tendency in England among young southern speakers to shift -ŏ*lve* to -ō*lve*, particularly in 'solve, involve, revolve' and, less frequently, 'revolver'. This movement has attracted some vigorous opposition, as in a letter to the *Sunday Times* calling this pronunciation of 'solve' and 'involve' 'a revolting affectation' and declaring that 'perhaps worst of all is "golf" pronounced "goalf" which I have heard lately' (17 Feb 1963). In fact 'goalf' was to be heard at least ten years before that letter was penned, though very curiously the *C.O.D.* of 1964 gives only the alternative pronunciations 'gŏlf' and 'gŏf', which latter most people outside of Scotland have never heard at all. Nor does that dictionary take any notice of 'sōlve, revōlve, invōlve' etc. What is the starting point of the new fashion? Possibly it is to be traced to 'revolt', always given the long vowel.

In some cases hesitation in the pronunciation to be given to 'o' springs from pedantic considerations of classical learning. For many years the official B.B.C. pronunciation of the musical term 'opus' was given the long 'o' but towards 1960 it was laid down that the short vowel must henceforth be used because of the short quantity of that syllable in Latin. And at the beginning of 1963 all B.B.C. television and radio announcers were instructed by the Corporation's pronunciation unit that in future the word 'homosexual' must be spoken as 'hommo-sexual'. This instruction came in a memorandum explaining that the word is derived from a Greek root meaning 'same' and that in consequence the B.B.C. should use the more etymologically correct short 'o', lest the public should be betrayed into thinking that the derivation was from the Latin 'homo' meaning 'man'. 'This will bring to the knowledge of the listener the fact that we are aware that the word applies to either sex', explained the Director-General, commenting on the change of policy. Basing English pronunciation on considerations of how their languages were spoken by Greeks and Romans usually leads to contradictions, and this case is no exception for unfortunately the Director-General proceeded to add that 'In other words our pronunciation should be "hommo" (the first "o" as in "homage")'. But of course 'hŏmage' is itself ultimately based on Latin 'homo', which weakens the B.B.C.'s case for 'hŏmosexual'.

In 1935 the late Professor A. Lloyd James, himself an arbiter of B.B.C. pronunciation, claimed in *The Broadcast Word* (p. 50) that there was a growing tendency to keep the original stress of the root word in all the derivatives of that word, so that 'indispútable' was gaining ground from 'indísputable' because of the analogy with the root form 'dispúte'. It can now be said that 'indísputable' is virtually unknown and in fact it was rare even in 1935. Certainly the tendency to unchanging stress is a reality of English development, or at any rate of one aspect of that development. But it must be said that English has a long way to go before the principle of unshifting stress as between root word and derivative is an accepted feature of the language. To the educated speaker there is something satisfying – however perverse this feeling may be – in the fluctuating stresses of such a pair as 'contríbute' and 'contribútion', and it will be many a day before 'démocrat', 'demócracy' and 'democrátic' all have the same stress. Indeed in some cases the tide is flowing in the opposite direction, so that while traditional usage keeps to initial stress in both 'primary' and 'primarily' there is a strong movement towards the adoption of the stress current in America in the pronunciation of the adverb, i.e. 'primárily' (cf. temporárily, etc.). This is unnoticed by the 1964 *C.O.D.* but if it becomes general, as seems likely, then some pairs of words which each had initial stress will henceforth show a discrepancy of stress as between adjective and adverb, with *-ary* unstressed and *-árily* stressed. The truth of the matter appears to be that speakers of English have not yet succeeded in making up their collective mind about how words should be stressed and what principles should be applied in this connection. In his *Modern Linguistics* (1957) Professor Simeon Potter agrees implicitly with Lloyd James that the general movement is towards initial stress (which would incidentally bring English into line with Czech and Finnish in this respect if ever it became a general rule, and would be a great simplification for children and foreigners) but points out that nothing is yet finally decided. 'As for Modern English, the drift of stress to the initial syllable is still a living issue. I myself say *démonstrable, déspicable, dísciplinary, lámentable* and *réputable,* but, I cannot yet bring myself to say *íllustrative*' (p. 65).[1] On the whole then, we can cautiously say that the movement of stress is in the main towards the first syllable (seen at its most picturesque in some American rural pronunciations such as 'réward' and 'Únited States') but that it will not do to be too dogmatic on this point. One of the more disconcerting variants of this kind is 'recluse' which can now be heard on occasion as 'wreck loose', that is, with stress on the first syllable. The older generation does not always take kindly to the change to the initial stress, as when Sir Compton Mackenzie protested during the Oxford Union Debate of 1956 against this type of pronunciation of 'quandary', 'sonorous' and 'decorous'. From the other point of view, I remember my own astonishment as a boy round about 1935 on hearing one of my schoolmasters pronounce 'sonórous'.

Recently there has been a marked tendency, on the other hand, to give 'complex' a final stress when used adjectivally, and the same is true, though not quite to the same degree, of 'concrete'. It is difficult to see any reason for the first of these tendencies, though the new 'concréte' is perhaps unconsciously influenced by the final stress of 'discreet', of similar ending.

A special and rather regrettable case arises with respect to the adjective 'coronary' which used at the beginning of the present century to be a rare word. During the nineteen-fifties it became

[1] André Deutsch.

known to the general public because of the vastly increased incidence of coronary thrombosis, and there was at first a tendency to
pronounce it with stress on the second syllable, on the analogy
of 'corona', but the initial stressing had all along been preserved
in the medical profession and this has now won the day. On the
other hand, the doctors have not succeeded in imposing their own
pronunciation of 'abdómen', mostly stressed by the public on the
first syllable. Do these contrasting cases perhaps hint once again
at a general drift towards initial stressing?

But prophecy about future linguistic developments is a
hazardous matter, and maybe the really significant trend in stress
will prove to be one which is unnoticed and scarcely under way
yet, namely the beginnings of a movement towards more even or
balanced stressing of syllables. For example, 'bamboo' has until
now been pronounced as a short syllable followed by a long, but
some speakers, including B.B.C. announcers, are beginning to
copy the more even American division of stress and say 'bamboo', where the syllables have more or less equal stress and the
'm' is lengthened. Likewise for other words where the final 'm'
of the first syllable is followed by another consonant; 'campaign'
(cam pane) and 'champagne' (sham pane). This is also noticeable
when 'l' ends the first syllable in similar circumstances, thus
Telstar becomes 'tell star' (Jul 1962) and so forth. Americans are
wont to comment on the 'clipped' sound that British English
seems to them to possess, and one reason for this impression is
certainly the stronger tonic stress used by British speakers (at
least by southern speakers. Northern Englishmen and Scotsmen
are less addicted to powerful accentuation of the stressed syllable).
If the above tendency, which is at present minute, should spread
to other types of word then British English will be embarked on
a major change which could bring it in line with the transatlantic
variety. Another factor tending in the same direction is the
movement to give a fuller phonetic value to unstressed vowels
than was previously the case in standard British English. This
process is of course well advanced in the United States and there
is no doubt that it has now begun in Britain. As early as 1935

Lloyd James was beginning to feel that something of the kind was afoot but could not at that time perceive the direction of the change. 'The unstressed vowels in English are working out their own destiny, and it is impossible to predict what the future has in store' (p. 51 of *The Broadcast Word*). A generation later we are in a better position to see which way the wind is blowing. As Professor Potter puts it in *Modern Linguistics*, after speaking of the corresponding situation in America, 'Even in Britain itself a growing inclination may be discovered among "affected modern" speakers to assign fuller qualitative and quantitative values to unstressed syllables in accordance with that notable drift towards "spelling pronunciation" which is proceeding today with increased momentum' (p. 69). No actual examples are given to illustrate this trend but one might cite the full value frequently given to the ending '-on' in such words as 'nylon, pylon, skylon, rayon, coupon, crayon, caisson' etc. The situation is a shifting and inconsistent one, and we can at least see that the traditional weak ending is kept in old-established words like 'lion, salmon, gammon, lemon, Zion, lesson, mammon', and 'Lebanon', which preserve the traditional pronunciation. It is amusing to see how Ronald Knox dealt with this type of pronunciation in a letter of 1950 (postscript to *Difficulties*, p. 258), where he wrote of 'the Vaticann (I spell the word with two N's to indicate the modern pronunciation).'[1] Like Monsignor Knox, Rose Macaulay was born in the eighteen-eighties and it must have been to this type of spelling pronunciation that she was alluding in a letter of 22 June 1951, published in *Letters to a Friend*.[2] 'I think it's true that English speech has changed a good deal. It has become more *mincing*.' Noteworthy spelling pronunciations are those affecting 'appreciate' (this one has spread amazingly rapidly); 'racial' (race-ial), which was in existence by the late nineteen-thirties; 'social' (so-sial) and 'sociable' (so-siable) which are still fairly infrequent, but have been heard from the nineteen-fifties; 'ensure' (ensewer); and, annually, 'Ascot' (ass cot).

Before leaving the subject of stress one must make some

[1] Eyre and Spottiswoode, 1952. [2] Atheneum, New York, 1962.

mention of a sudden and remarkable development affecting the stressing of prepositions, namely the tendency to give to prepositions a strong emphatic stress even though the meaning is not particularly emphasized. In origin this was a mannerism of B.B.C. commentators, especially used when they were speaking of movement or position in geographical space. The pattern is roughly like this. 'So for the last half-hour we've been *at* Oxford but now we're taking you *from* Oxford and *over to* Monte Carlo. Yes, and here we are *at* Monte Carlo and *in* the casino, etc.' This is quite illogical by the traditional standards of the language but one can sense behind this technique the attempt to capture precision and graphic presentation at the same time. Certainly this type of stressing pervades all broadcasting at the present time and has done so for some years. To take some actual examples: 'Do you think there has been a change in the theme OF the audience in the last few years?' (T.V. discussion); 'How long has this formed part OF your act?' (T.V. interview); 'Actually I was rather surprised that you asked me TO lunch' (B.B.C. satirical programme). These three quotations are all from 1965. The next step has been, as might be expected, a rapid imitation (doubtless unconscious) of this broadcast English and it now remains to be seen how far this type of stress will spread from the academic and mannered circles which affect it at present to British society in general. If the tendency takes an extreme turn we may yet live to see the day when 'a cuppa tea' becomes 'a cup OF tea'.

At all events this extremely rapid development denotes a complete break with existing linguistic custom, and something of a linguistic mutation. Up till now prepositions have been stressed in accordance with the general principle governing exceptional stressing in English, that is, for the sake of special emphasis, and it would now appear that this system is to some extent being abandoned. If we take one of the above quotations, 'Actually I was rather surprised that you asked me TO lunch', it is clear that this could have been expressed traditionally as 'Actually I was rather surprised that you ASKED me to lunch' or even 'Actually I was rather SURPRISED that you asked me to lunch'. Now the guiding rule in English emphatic stress until now has been that the word whose meaning is to be underlined receives reinforced stress. Yet in this sentence 'to' has very little real meaning in the first place, being a species of linguistic counter required for the purposes of the outward construction (whether we parse 'lunch' as a noun or even a verb). So the word actually stressed by the voice is not really the one whose importance is being underlined. Similarly for the other two sentences quoted above, where in the first one the real logical stress is associated with 'audience' or 'theme' rather than 'of', and where in the remaining sentence the concept to be emphasized is not 'of' but 'part' or 'act'. Only one previous pattern of prepositional stress was remotely like this, and that is the type 'What shall we do? – There's nothing TO do'. This stress, found on both sides of the Atlantic, has a semantic function in that it expresses with great emphasis the total lack of choice available, though of course this pattern is not obligatory, and can be replaced by 'There's NOTHING to do'. But this does not serve at all as a starting point for the generalized stressing of prepositions which clearly corresponds to some new need vaguely felt by a great many speakers, and remains to be explained.[1]

Just as a knowledge of reading and writing added to a feeling of educational inadequacy has tended to break down the traditional pronunciation of certain words in favour of 'safer' spelling pronunciations, so too has a greater knowledge and awareness of foreign languages taken its toll of traditional pronunciations of continental names. Consequently Don Quixote is often given a would-be Spanish flavour and emerges as Don Kee-hoh-tay, though in fact in the time of Cervantes the Spanish phonetic system had not yet reached that stage and he himself would have said something more like 'Kee-shoh-tay' (which is confirmed by the French version, Don Quichotte). Mercifully

---

[1] See also *English Studies* (1962) pp. 66–102, 'On the stressing of prepositions', by A. C. Doodkorte and R. W. Zandvoort, and pp. 492–5, 'Further comment on the stressing of prepositions', by J. Posthumus.

there are no signs of people wanting to say 'keehohtic' instead of 'quixotic'. A similar fate has overtaken the fine old name of Maria. There are still a few old ladies of this name who pronounce it to rhyme with Obadiah, but in productions of Sheridan's *The School for Scandal* one of the characters is often called 'Mareea' as though she were an Italian film star. Conversely the old pronunciation is faithfully retained in the name of the Black Maria, or police van, in Britain.

In the nineteen-twenties it was good form to pronounce 'ski' in the Norwegian manner as 'shee'. Contrary to the usual tendency this has now come to be pronounced in an anglicized version 'skee', doubtless because of the obvious puns to which the first version gave rise, and possibly the shifting of the centre of gravity of British interest in this sport from Norway to France and Switzerland helped the change, since the French, in whose language the Norwegian pronunciation would have been positively improper (or hilarious, according to the point of view adopted), had firmly pronounced the word on the model of its spelling.

Since French is the best-known foreign language it can happen that unfamiliar names are given a frenchified pronunciation, so the hound known as a borzoi is sometimes called a 'baw-zwah' and the obvious pronunciation is applied only by those who know no French or realize that the name is Slavonic. A curious convention of a similar type is that the drink called Advokaat loses its final consonant in pronunciation as though it were French (like Muscat) instead of Dutch.

Even the pronunciation of the humble definite and indefinite articles is not immune from the changing whims of fashion. In 1957 a speaker on a B.B.C. programme objected to T. S. Eliot's rendering of the definite article, 'the song' evidently having been changed by the poet into 'thee song'. Mr Eliot was by birth an American but this does not in itself suffice to explain this usage which is shared by very many true-born Englishmen today. Of course the transformation of 'the' into 'thee' has long been a feature of English in two clearcut cases.

(*a*) When the ensuing word begins with a vowel, as 'the apple'.

(This seems to be something which has deliberately to be instilled into schoolchildren, who left to themselves will happily pronounce 'th'apple' in Shakespearean fashion.) (b) When an element of emphasis is involved. 'It's definitely *the* thing.'

What is new in Britain is the extension of this pronunciation to almost any definite article at all, as required by individual fantasy and particularly when the speaker is not quite sure what he is going to say next. An odd belief of many naive speakers is that 'thee' is somehow more easily understood than 'the', so that it is especially favoured when carefully enunciating a name or address, thus producing 'Thee Pines' or 'Thee Mount', to the bewilderment of at least one listener.

The indefinite article calls for less comment, though over the nineteen-fifties there was established in Britain the American habit of giving it the fuller pronunciation rhyming with 'hay' in contexts which show hesitation rather than emphasis, or even, like the definite article, in cases where there is no apparent reason for its use except as a sort of stylistic variant. An added complication, however, is that the indefinite article also has the variant form 'an'. This is obligatory before a vowel or a mute 'h' (optional before a sounded 'h'; a historian, an historian) so that in at least one instance the question arises as to whether the 'h' is sounded or not, namely in 'hotel'. In June 1956 the House of Lords spent much time discussing the weighty question as to whether 'a' or 'an' is the article required before this noun. Actually the pronunciation of 'hotel' without the aspirate is one of the few things calculated to shock modern adolescents, who consider this ancient custom as 'slangy'. In the end their lordships decided on 'an hotel', the amendment being moved by Lord Faringdom, who said he wished to avoid preciosity but 'it was a mistake to throw the baby of elegance out with the dirty water of the precious'.

In linguistic textbooks it is frequently said that certain phonetic changes take place 'in order to avoid difficult pronunciations', but this is really begging the question because difficulty of pronunciation is a highly subjective factor varying in time and space. The legendary 'braw bricht moonlicht nicht' is easy to pronounce in Scotland and rather more difficult in England, though the ancestors of the English were perfectly capable of getting their tongues round this elusive 'ch' consonant. Similarly a good many speakers are currently beginning to experience difficulty with the final consonantal group -*cts* which they tend to reduce to -*cs* by dropping the middle element. So from good standard speakers we hear 'axe' for 'acts', 'tracks' for 'tracts' and so forth. In May 1963 a speaker on B.B.C. television, demonstrating a machine during a scientific programme, explained '. . . then the hot air passes through a series of ducks' (=ducts!). Actual examples of this comic type prove beyond doubt that the adjustment is an unconscious one, since the speakers would be horrified if they realized what they were saying.

The so-called intrusive 'r' has been a feature of southern English since the nineteenth century, for in *The Practical Study of Languages* Henry Sweet drew attention to such pronunciations as 'the India(r) Office' and 'the idea(r) of it', which he was even then (1899) content to describe as a colloquialism that was widely spread in educated speech.[1] Incidentally, his point in mentioning it was to emphasize that since it was not universal and in any case occurred only in rapid speech it would merely be incongruous for a foreigner to imitate the habit in his own slow speech. In the present period of heightened consciousness of the written word it might well have been expected that the intrusive 'r' would rapidly die out but on the contrary it has gained ground. References from the pulpit to 'the law of love' become 'the lore of love', while members of the staff of the B.B.C. often pronounce 'awe-inspiring' as 'ore-inspiring'. In the 1945 edition of *The Phonetics of English* Dr Ida C. Ward pointed out that in Cockney speech the phrase 'I saw it' was often pronounced with the intrusive 'r'.[2] Since that time the habit has spread to the educated

---

[1] As a vulgarism the intrusion of 'r' has been found in England since at least the late eighteenth century, when the early phonetician and lexicographer Thomas Spence condemned *'Idear'* and *'Noar'* (Noah). See David Abercrombie, *Studies in Phonetics and Linguistics*, p. 73.

[2] Heffer.

classes, so that during the B.B.C. programme 'Lift Up Your Hearts' of 1 July 1955 it was possible to hear in the Gospel account of the Resurrection that 'they saw(r) a young man' and this same 'saw(r) a' form was used in the B.B.C. news bulletin for 9 a.m. on 20 February 1960. In view of these examples there must be some very compelling motive which obliges highly-educated speakers to introduce this sound into their speech, and the motive is evidently analogy. As is well-known, it is perfectly possible in standard English to pronounce or omit the 'r' in such a phrase as 'for a man', or 'a sore eye'. Likewise then for 'the lore of love'. But it so happens that in this variety of English 'lore' and 'law' are spoken identically when in isolation, as indeed are various other pairs 'ore/awe', 'sore/saw', with the unexpected but logical result that the 'r' of one member of the couple easily transfers to the other member when the next word begins with a vowel. The case of 'drawing' pronounced as 'droring' is not so readily explained, because of the absence of any word '*drore' in the vocabulary. It possibly depends on association with some other pair such as 'pawing/pouring' or 'sawing/soaring'.

'Few speakers of Southern English make any distinction between *which* and *witch* or between *when* and *wen* . . .' says Professor Brook in his *History of the English Language* (p. 204) published in 1958.[1] In the same year a New Zealander, Arnold Wall, went further than this in his book on *The Queen's English*. 'We have *wh* for the sharp sound of *w*, formerly spelt *hw*. In standard English this has really vanished; authorities agree that the old sharp sound is dead and gone, it was discontinued gradually during the nineteenth century' (p. 22). But this is too categorical a statement for England and any impartial observer is bound to agree that at least some of the best speakers use the full value indicated by 'wh' and differentiating it from 'w'. Professor H. C. Wyld, writing in 1927, said 'Many English people, even in the south, now use this sound, but it is certainly not natural in English speech from the Midlands downwards and has been introduced comparatively recently – within the last thirty and

[1] Deutsch.

forty years – apparently through Scotch and Irish influences, backed up by the spelling' (*A Short History of English*, p. 33).[1] And he goes on to say, quite correctly, 'Many excellent speakers of standard English never use the sound at all'. Wyld therefore sees the distinction – when it is made in standard southern English – as an artificial one (inasmuch as one can speak of any linguistic phenomenon as being artificial. However, the sense is clear). Dobson comes to a similar conclusion in the second volume of his *English Pronunciation 1500–1700*.[2] He says of the pronunciation that '. . . probably in most cases it is an artificial pronunciation due to the spelling and the influence of non-Southern speakers . . .' (para. 413). Certainly it is not so long ago that standard speakers, or indeed many people not possessing the 'sharp sound' of 'wh' regarded it as somewhat unpleasant, and in the words of Jespersen 'a great many good speakers always pronounce [w] and look upon [hw] as harsh or dialectal' (*Modern English Grammar*, part I, 13, 51).[3] There are signs, indeed, that the lack of distinction between 'w' and 'wh' goes back nearly four centuries, witness a pun made in Sir John Davies' *Orchestra*, written in 1596 and quoted in Robert Southey's *Commonplace Book*, p. 431:[4]

> *Behold the world, how it is whirled round.*
> *And for it is so whirled, is named so.*

Scotland and Ireland preserved the older distinction between the sounds and various scholars indicate that it also existed in northern England up to the nineteenth century. Ellis's survey of dialects, published in 1889, reported that at Newcastle these sounds were kept distinct (p. 650), but this is somewhat surprising since [hw] was most certainly not present there within living memory and one suspects that Ellis was in error.

In the case of those southern speakers who have consciously re-adopted a distinctive 'wh' sound it must be that since there is a difference in spelling between 'wh' and 'w' then that difference

[1] John Murray.   [2] Clarendon Press, 1957.
[3] Heidelberg, 1909.   [4] London, 1851.

must surely correspond to some distinction in pronunciation. They possibly experience some feeling of rectitude in so doing. The distinction is rather favoured by B.B.C. announcers – very conscious of the written text – but there does not at the moment appear to be any likelihood that it will soon be adopted by the public in general. It is perhaps worth pointing out that in early 1956 attention was drawn to the fact that Harold Macmillan (of Scottish extraction!) was the only Cabinet minister to pronounce 'wh' as 'hw'.

Although spelling is merely the outward form of a language, and relatively unimportant from the strictly linguistic point of view (for Russian would still be Russian even if it discarded the Cyrillic alphabet for the Roman) there can be no doubt that on the practical level the average speaker can be powerfully affected in his pronunciation by considerations of spelling, as we have seen. This is particularly the case in a language like English where there is often great discrepancy between sound and symbol for historical reasons. So great are the peculiarities of English spelling that it is natural that many attempts should have been made to improve or even entirely revolutionize the system. The most spectacular one made in recent times is unquestionably that due to George Bernard Shaw who left a great part of his fortune for that purpose. The distinguished author had long been a sharp critic of the orthodox alphabet, let alone the spelling system, and was accustomed to write his works in a shorthand of his own devising. After his death some legal difficulties arose and indeed at one time it seemed that because of huge death duties on his estate there would be little money available for the project of alphabetical reform. By a curious irony it was the enormous profits arising from the transformation of *Pygmalion* into the musical show *My Fair Lady* which enabled the executors to come to terms with the Inland Revenue authorities and so clear the way for the interpretation of the will, for as Mr Justice Harman observed in Chancery, Shaw would have detested *My Fair Lady*. A revealing light was thrown on the British interest in spelling reform when it was seen that the public gallery was empty as the learned judge began a sixty-minute explanation of his ruling in the case. It was favourable and in the end Penguin Books printed a copy of Shaw's *Androcles and the Lion* in the patent alphabet which proved to be totally different from the normal Roman one. This book made not the slightest impression.

Though the chances of Shaw's alphabet being adopted are absolutely non-existent it is fair to say that this is based on the force of inertia rather than a denial of Shaw's case that his own system is based on rational principles and affords a saving of time to those using it. Of course Shaw was a typical nineteenth-century man in that he thought that the public would adopt his suggestion through sheer weight of logic and did not make due allowance for conservatism and inertia. Yet it must be allowed that even when Shaw's script is considered without prejudice it is hard to see how its inconvenience would not out-weigh its admitted advantages of simplicity and speed. In the first place the English language would be placed in a special position as regards its script just at a time when it bids fair to become a world language, and when on the other hand there is an increased interest by English-speaking peoples in other European languages. All children learning French, German, Latin and so forth would in any case have to learn the Roman alphabet. If there are to be major spelling reforms it seems at least advisable to retain at any rate the actual letters already familiar to us and in which a huge mass of books are already printed. But an even more serious difficulty arises from Shaw's script. It is all very well to talk of the phonetic notation of English sounds but the question is never asked: What sounds? Advocates of spelling reform are apt to think of English pronunciation as being one and indivisible, but would there be agreement about various points of phonetic spelling amongst educated Englishmen, let alone with Scotsmen, Irishmen, Americans, Australians, Canadians and so on? Would they all agree to write 'stalk' and 'stork' identically? On the other hand if we are to build up our spelling conventions piecemeal by the counting of heads we are likely to produce a spelling diction-ary corresponding to no variety of English ever spoken in this world. As it is, the illogicality of our traditional spelling is in one sense a boon, since it serves all English speakers equally well, being tailored to the requirements of none.

'Instead of changing the spelling of English to conform to the pronunciation why not the other way round – change the pronunciation to conform to the spelling?' Such was the pertinent suggestion made by a reader of *The Economist* (29 Dec 1962), and as has been seen in the present chapter this is to some extent exactly what is being done at present, albeit unconsciously and piecemeal. Spelling pronunciations are in fact a kind of spelling reform, though this is masked by the fact that the appearance of the word on the printed page is left unchanged. The reform is nevertheless quite real, since the cumulative result of several generations of this type of treatment is the closer correspondence of sound and symbol. 'Solder' was once pronounced·'sodder' and 'laundry' was 'lahndry'. 'Qualm' (quawm) is in process of becoming (quahm) to bring it into line with 'balm, calm', etc.

Reform of English spelling in this relatively painless way is proceeding apace, but certainly it must be agreed that specific anomalies could be cleared up and particular spellings simplified by a deliberate act of policy (though by whom? We have no national body which guides the English language). Since the ending '-or' already exists in British English (tailor, actor), there is no reason why it should not generally replace '-our' in words such as 'colour, honour' in the manner already customary in American spelling. (This suggestion would perhaps not have been to the liking of the late Nevil Shute, who used this national difference in spelling for his own artistic ends, and American characters in his novels were provided by him with the -or ending in their dialogue.) This minor reform would incidentally benefit the conscientious Englishman trying to decide whether he should write 'Pearl Harbour' to please himself or 'Pearl Harbor' as a compliment to the American spelling convention.

Double consonants are a curious and troublesome part of the British spelling system, as when from 'travel' we form 'travelling' and 'travelled'. Again these forms are already regularized in the

United States, giving 'traveling' and 'traveled'. Such a general reform in British English would spare us such difficulties as those presented by the various parts of the verb 'to parallel'.

But even without instituting any widespread and upsetting reforms some of the more curious individual spellings could be quietly improved over the years. Once again America has shown the way with 'plow' and 'ax'. Perhaps we could all imitate *The Times* and make up our minds in favour of 'jewelry' as against 'jewellery' since in either case the pronunciation is the same, with three syllables. The minor inconsistency between 'into' and 'on to' has been resolved in the U.S.A. by the creation of 'onto' and since about 1955 this has been appearing in the British press with some regularity, being adopted officially by the publishing house of Secker and Warburg in 1957. But such is the force of habit that Sir Compton Mackenzie rebuked Ivor Brown for using 'onto' which he denounced as 'that horrid little Siamese twin of a preposition' (*Observer*, 24 Mar 1957). This sort of opposition is sometimes aimed at any attempt to introduce '-or' instead of '-our'. A book critic in the London *Evening News* wrote an enthusiastic review of *All Honorable Men*, by David Karp, but then went on to disagree over a question of orthography. 'My one spark of dislike is directed against the spelling of the second word in the title. I hope Mr Karp does not one day write a book with "center" in its title' (30 Jun 1956).

Such dislikes as these are a matter of unfamiliarity. After all, adjustments to spelling have slowly been taking place throughout the history of the English language, though we tend to forget this because the classics of English literature are printed in modern guise. Yet only in the last century the spelling 'musick' still prevailed and perhaps even now there are scattered individuals who still write 'shew' rather than 'show'. Clearly the process of change will continue. Yet it seems that writing is less of an automatic activity than speech and that spelling is more of a conscious choice, so that change is more vigorously resisted in this domain than elsewhere in the language.

Index of Words
and Phrases